Allan Whigham Price has had a varied career. From 1931–1935 he was a shipping clerk with NYK Line in London and he then went on to be a Presbyterian minister in Reading and Low Fell, Gateshead. In 1958 he left the ministry to become a schoolmaster in Yorkshire and three years later was appointed a lecturer at Bede College, Durham. He taught there until his retirement in 1979.

Allan Whigham Price is the author of

The Man at the Bell (1954)
The Hidden Signature (1967)

The Ladies of Castlebrae

A. Whigham Price

HEADLINE

TO MY WIFE
Marvellously tolerant
of my obsessive love affair
with these two women
which has lasted for many years

Copyright © 1985 A. Whigham Price

First published in hardcover in Great Britain in 1985
by Alan Sutton Publishing Limited

First published in paperback in Great Britain in 1987
by HEADLINE BOOK PUBLISHING PLC

ISBN 0-7472-3079-X

Printed and bound in Great Britain by
Collins, Glasgow

HEADLINE BOOK PUBLISHING PLC
Headline House
79 Great Titchfield Street
London W1P 7FN

FOREWORD

The Ladies of Castlebrae is an unusual and fascinating book, the result of long and arduous detective work by its author, Allan Whigham Price.

Reading its early pages which deal with the formative years of Agnes Lewis and her sister Maggie Gibson (nee Smith), women eccentric even by Victorian standards, one might be pardoned for wondering whether the pair of them will ever get up a sufficient head of steam to make one want to know what subsequently happened to them and what they accomplished in the course of what were to be two very long lives; lives up to now principally remembered by academics and possibly by the odd castaway on a desert island fortunate enough to have been thrown up on its shores with a set of *The Dictionary of National Biography*.

Born in 1843, a year in which the most memorable Scottish happening appears to have been the Disruption of the Church of Scotland and the emergence of the Free Church, and in Asia the discovery of the site of Nineveh, they were the twin daughters of an Ayrshire solicitor with more cash than dash which had descended on him rather like the manna on the wilderness of Sinai in which they were to spend the most rewarding periods of their lives. Their mother died when they were three weeks old.

Totally unglamorous, frumpish to a degree (even when, as they later were, they were dressed by the couturier Worth), bluestockings who habitually wore white stockings, their appearance was enough to confirm the worst, chauvinistic fears of the male academicians with whom they came in contact. It is not difficult to imagine the decent, humdrum domestic security in which they would probably have lived out their lives in the Lowlands if their father had not died suddenly in 1866 when they were twenty-three years old; already getting a bit old for marriage.

His death gave them independence and a very considerable fortune. They were fortunate, too, in having a mentor, their sole mentor, a Scottish divine with a sense of humour who encouraged them to follow their own inclinations. And they did. Two years later, in 1868, they set off on the first of their journeys to the Near East which was to provide the *raison d'etre* of their lives for the next fifty years or so. In this instance they were a trio, the third still relatively young lady being one of their teachers from their Kensington finishing school.

They travelled unchaperoned through Hungary and Rumania to Constantinople and on to Cairo at a time when the institution of slavery still existed, at least covertly, throughout the Ottoman Empire. It was only some eight years previously that Sir Samuel White Baker, discoverer of Lake Albert Nyanza, following the same route to the Black Sea had acquired a practising odalisque whom he later married and introduced into London society, the beautiful, courageous Florence Finian von Fass. From Cairo, the Twins travelled up the Nile by boat to Wady Halfeh and the Second Cataract in the company of the crafty dragoman whom they were able to outsmart.

Two marriages, contracted when they were forty and forty-five years old respectively, two honeymoons (both of them spent as threesomes), and two husbands later, both of them savants and dying within four years of marrying the sisters (I call this jolly sinister – where is Poirot?), they set off on the journey that was to take them to the Monastery of St Catherine in the mountains of the Sinai Peninsula. To a place in which, as other visitors, however eccentric, have found, the occupants can teach them a thing or two about true eccentricity.

Already famous, largely due to the visit to it of Constantin Tischendorf, a name still anathema to the monks, it proved to be an unimaginably rich repository of Greek, Arabic, Syriac, Palestinian, Georgian, Armenian, Slavonic and

Ethiopic manuscripts, of which Tischendorf had succeeded in saving forty-three priceless leaves of the Septuagint (out of a total of one hundred and twenty-nine) from a monkish incineration. With these few sheets, his discovery of the Codex Sinaiticus had begun.

To discover what the twins themselves discovered there in freezing winter (no one who has not experienced winter at the Monastery can conceive how cold it can be) being used as dishes for great chunks of butter in the monks' refectory, you will have to read the book.

ERIC NEWBY
August 1985

CONTENTS

ACKNOWLEDGEMENTS

The author wishes to express his gratitude to The Friends of Westminster and Cheshunt Colleges for their generous financial support which made possible the inclusion of illustrations in this volume.

His thanks are also due to the following for permission to use copyright material: The Principal and Senatus of Westminster College, Cambridge, for the photographs of, and by, Mrs Lewis and Mrs Gibson, and of the College buildings.

INTRODUCTION

The reader need not feel in the least guilty if he has never heard of Mrs Lewis and Mrs Gibson, whose story follows in these pages, for the present writer shared his ignorance until (as the Prologue explains) his curiosity was aroused by the sight of their portraits in the Hall of a Cambridge College. These remarkable women, pioneers in an esoteric field hitherto entirely occupied by men, are by now forgotten except by the tiny band of Semitics scholars (still, I imagine, all male) who continue to pore over musty manuscripts in little-visited corners of museums and libraries, and by past and present students of Westminster College, Cambridge.

When I began my research I was able to talk with a few of their friends, though these were mostly in their eighties – Maynard Keynes' mother was well over ninety – but tracing material was less easy, and it sometimes seemed as though the biographical task was beginning to topple into an archaeological one: for when the twins died, childless and without relatives, in the 1920's, it is understandable that most of the material that would have been useful to a biographer was simply thrown away by their lawyers or their executor. Particularly difficult to round out were the details of their early life: some basic facts were known, but they inclined to be sketchy. For this period, I have drawn on Agnes' first novel, *Effie Maxwell*. First novels by minor writers are frequently autobiographical, and I have therefore ventured to treat as factual the account of their schooldays therein described. This is the only instance in which imaginative reconstruction has replaced 'primary sources'. The twins' journey to the Near East in Chapter II is fully documented in Agnes' travel book, *Eastern Pilgrims*. The dialogue given to the Castlebrae guests in Chapter VIII has been built up from actual letters and lectures which have been printed elsewhere.

On what grounds, it may be asked, are these two forgotten women worth bothering about? In the first place, they were interesting and adventurous 'characters', of the kind perhaps more frequently found in the Victorian age than today; in the second place, our age is keenly interested in women who made their mark in fields hitherto reserved for men. This the twins succeeded in doing, at a time when it was far from easy to do so, and in an environment – the closed, conservative world of Cambridge – that was hostile to intellectual aspirations by those whose bodies were of the unsanctioned shape. Little encouragement was given even to those who were members (as the twins were not) of the deplorable new-fangled institutions of Girton and Newnham, at that time recently accorded a grudging and very limited recognition by a sour Senate. Further, Mrs Lewis and Mrs Gibson worked in a field of study that was distinctly outré: Hebrew, Arabic and Syriac constitute a branch of knowledge in which, one ventures to think, women scholars are none too numerous, even today. And thirdly, they managed to win international respect for their scholarship without ever having attended a university, and with no more formal training than was afforded by a few lessons from kindly-disposed male scholars. But perhaps their greatest achievement was the liberating effect of their career upon those young girls who came to know them. In the words of the Chancellor of St Andrews University at the turn of the century, 'the spirit of enterprise which they showed produced for their age a higher idea of what woman can accomplish.'

Their story reads like a novel – which explains why I have chosen to give a chronological account of their lives: their home and background go a long way towards explaining why they were able to achieve what they did. The biographer of a well-known figure can presuppose, in his reader, a certain knowledge of his subject's achievements, which prompted the reader to pick up his book. But here, as in a novel, the reader starts from scratch, knowing nothing whatever about the principal characters; but will, I hope, be gradually beguiled into finding them interesting. And as the twins' lives fall into three distinct periods – each section arising directly out of the previous one – it seemed best to adhere to a chronological narrative. It is the hope of the present writer that this method will be found to justify itself.

A biography has certain affinities with those 'human pyramids' which were once an inevitable feature of gym displays at school Speech Days. Applause, on such occasions, was reserved for the small boy who, climbing into the apex position, waved a flag of triumph before the admiring spectators. It was easy, at such moments, to overlook the fact that that midget stood upon the shoulders of other people, and that, without their help and support, there would have been nothing to cheer. The present writer is very conscious that, in order to produce this book, he has stood upon the shoulders of many good friends. To these, he would now make grateful acknowledgement.

First must come his debt to the close personal friends of the twins, who showed remarkable patience with the endless queries of a complete stranger: Mr and Mrs Robert Ball, Mrs A.C. Graham (Aelfrieda Tillyard), Mrs J.N. Keynes, Mrs W.R. Sorley, Mrs P.A. Turner, Mrs Alex. Wood, Miss Anne Macalister, Miss Emily Free, and the Revd. Dr W.A.L. Elmslie. These friends should not be held responsible for any judgments on people or events which may appear in these pages. They kindly supplied me with the facts: the inferences and judgments are entirely my own.

Secondly, successive Principals and Librarians of Westminster College, Cambridge, gave me the utmost encouragement in the project, and allowed me free access to the many Lewis-Gibson papers and notebooks in their care, and to their stock of Mrs Gibson's photographs and Mrs Lewis' lantern slides.

Thirdly, my thanks to Revd. H.M. Angus, who generously lent me more than a hundred letters written by one or other of the twins from Sinai to his uncle, the late Professor J. Rendel Harris. This material added substantially to my knowledge of the years during which their most distinguished work was done.

Fourthly, others who helped greatly with source material: Mrs P.M. Leonard, Librarian of the Selly Oak Colleges, Birmingham, lent me three volumes of Mrs Lewis' press-cuttings; Miss Lillian Kelley, Librarian and Archivist of the Presbyterian Historical Society of England, allowed me access to the Society's fund of material; Mrs Laurie, and successive housekeepers of Castlebrae under Clare College, allowed me to ramble round the twins' old home and recapture something of its atmosphere; and the following gentlemen gave me much invaluable advice on matters of biblical scholarship, and saved me from many blunders: Revd. Dr J.Y. Campbell, Revd. Professor T.W. Manson, Revd. Principal A.G. Macleod, Revd. Professor J.Y. Sweetman, and Revd. E.W. Todd. Research in connection with their own locality was also kindly undertaken for me by Miss Penelope Turton of Boston, Mass., Revd. S.J. Knox of Dublin, Revd. D. Adam of Kingston-on-Thames and Dr I. Gordon Lennox of Edinburgh.

Finally, I wish to acknowledge the help of the following in various ways: Miss Peggie Armstrong; Miss Marjorie Anderson Scott; Mrs George Barclay; Miss Emily Blomfield; Mr Miles Burkitt; Mrs T. Bushe-Fox; Professor Kenneth W. Clark; Mrs M. Davis of the Royal Asiatic Society; Mr David Crane; Revd. Dr and Mrs H.H. Farmer; Mrs Silva Kirsopp Lake; Revd. E.C. Lane; Mr J. Lewis May; Mrs Marcus Spencer; Professor Julius Tillyard; Revd. Dr R.H. Strachan; Mr John Ramsay; Revd. Dr and Mrs R.D. Whitehorn; Miss Emily Willoughby. And not least, Mr Terry Harvey, whose technical skill conjured splendid illustrations out of old and often damaged negatives.

Durham   A.W.P.

PROLOGUE

The Giblews

'Tell me, who are the two old girls on the end wall?' It was more for the sake of something to say, than because I wanted to know, that I asked my neighbour this question: though admittedly it did seem rather odd to find full-length portraits of female 'doctors in scarlet' hanging in the Hall of an all-male theological college.

It was the evening of my first day as freshman. Dinner had almost ended and, our meagre stock of small talk having become exhausted, conversation had been reduced to the hopeful lobbing of an occasional pebble into the vast pool of silence: a situation which is liable to arise among people who have just met for the first time, are feeling shy and a little overawed, and have suddenly been thrust into the inescapable proximity of a College dining-table. I and my colleagues of the first year, feeling a curious responsibility for keeping the conversation going, had been looking round the Hall. We had already inspected the living, and had dismissed them with a very cursory glance – rarely had we seen as peculiar-looking a set of men as our seniors of the second and third year (no doubt they had come to a similar conclusion about us) – so we had turned to examine the dead, scrutinising the massive portraits which hung above the heavy oak panelling.

1

Several of these I had been able to recognise without needing to make any enquiry: John Oman, for instance, who occupied the place of honour over the mock-medieval fireplace. He had interviewed me a few weeks before he had retired from the Principalship, an occasion I recalled with some embarrassment. An unfortunate affliction of the throat made his utterances difficult to follow at the best of times, especially when mumbled through the filter of a thick beard – as they invariably were. On the day of our meeting, he had chanced to be recovering from a severe attack of 'flu, which had rendered him temporarily deaf. The result was that, in spite of the utmost goodwill on both sides, neither could hear a word the other said, and a complicated situation had arisen, in which it was difficult to discuss my future at all profitably. His portrait – by Hugh Rivière – was, as one of his colleagues remarked at the time, 'more like Oman than Oman himself.' He stood with his brooding philosopher's eyes half closed, his grey imperial beard thrust forward as though challenging all materialists and atheists to battle, and his hands thrust deep into his jacket pockets, with only the thumbs visible – his characteristic pose when lecturing. I was already familiar with the story connected with this portrait. As the canvas had stood, drying, in the studio, three of the artist's friends had entered in rapid succession, and had paused to inspect the finished work. 'That man looks like a fisherman,' the first had remarked; 'Is that chap a philosopher?' enquired the second; 'Well, there's the face of a saint!' said the third. The second and third of the visitors had been right – and even the first man had not been as far wide of the mark as one might imagine, for Oman's father had been Master of the little steamer which plied between the Orkneys and the Shetlands, and the sea had been in the son's blood.

My eyes shifted to the right, where Patrick Carnegie Simpson gazed down thoughtfully at us, the lace jabot of a Presbyterian Moderator beneath his chin – that chin which, perhaps anticipating the forthcoming control of bureaucracy over all our lives, was already in triplicate: Simpson was always ahead of his time. But the portrait somehow did not do him justice: perhaps no portrait could, for his massiveness of mind and personality matched his physical bulk. Church historian and ecclesiastical statesman, he had been a vast Chestertonian figure and endowed with a Chestertonian wit – his students filled the left-hand page of their notebooks with epigrams, as numerous as the facts which they jotted down on the right-hand page – though he was too good a scholar to be infected by what has aptly been described as 'G.K.'s boozy medievalism.' In 'conversations' with the Anglicans, he was a formidable debating opponent, and there was some truth in his quip, when he was being sounded as to his willingness to accept a Scottish Chair, that, if he went to Scotland, 'there would be no one left in England to tell the bishops what they mean.' 'Get the big books behind you, gentlemen!' Simpson was forever booming to his class; and successive occupants of Lambeth Palace had discovered to their cost that he had certainly followed his own precept, as he blandly demolished their arguments by quotations from the works of seventeenth-century Anglican divines. From his heavy gilt frame, 'Simbo' seemed to study us thoughtfully, and to feel disappointed with what he saw. We were small men, puny men, mere grasshoppers in his sight, on any estimate: even the most charitable.

From Carnegie Simpson, my gaze had travelled to the end wall, upon which hung the canvasses which had occasioned my question. The two women faced each other across the small stained-glass Venetian window. Within each frame stood an elderly woman, straight-backed as a poker, attired in a black dress with a long row of crimson buttons down the front, over which she wore a Geneva gown and a scarlet and white Doctor's hood. At first glance, both portraits seemed to be of the same woman, so alike were the features: a straight nose, a firm determined chin, keen deepset eyes, and iron-grey hair devoid of the slightest wave – hair so fine in texture and so uniform in colour that it looked almost as though it had been powdered. Even the two mortarboards (called 'squares' in Cambridge) were worn at the same faintly-tilted angle, and the neckband of each woman's hood was held in place by an exceptionally large cameo. The only difference between the subjects – apart from the fact that

3

they were facing each other – lay in the pose of the hands: one woman held a book at arm's length, against her gown, the other held a volume as though she had momentarily interrupted her reading to look up.

I repeated my question. My neighbour looked astonished and incredulous. 'Those two?' he exclaimed, with the maddening nonchalance of the knowledgeable, – 'why, that's the Giblews, of course!' (he pronounced the 'g' hard, as in 'give'). I tried hard to look intelligent. 'The Giblews?' I said, puzzled: it sounded like some peculiar animal, or an American jazz tune of the 'twenties. 'Mrs Gibson and Mrs Lewis, y'know,' my neighbour went on, observing my blank expression, – 'don't tell me you've never heard of 'em? Why, they're the tutelary deities of this place – almost what Gog and Magog are to London! They were Semitics scholars, old man – Hebrew and Arabic and Syriac an' all that; they discovered one of the earliest versions of the Gospels in some Middle East monastery. And they had pots of money – they gave the site for this place when the College moved here from London, and left it a lot of money.'

I studied the severe, elderly faces with a new interest. Women Hebrew scholars, eh? – that was something a bit out of the ordinary. I knew a number of women doctors, women lawyers were becoming more numerous, but women expert in such recondite tongues were (to me, at least) absolutely unheard of. 'Are they still alive?' 'Oh, no, – they died after the First World War, I think. But there are no end of legends about 'em,' my neighbour continued, warming to what was obviously a favourite theme, – 'they were twins, y'know – very eccentric – went everywhere together, even on each other's honeymoons. Haven't you heard any of the famous stories? Some of 'em are simply wizard. F'rinstance, there was the time when they . . .' He rattled on, telling one classic after another: each one (it seemed to my sceptical mind) more improbable than the last.

I had been introduced to Mrs Lewis and Mrs Gibson.

PART ONE

Miss Smith and Miss Maggie Smith (1843–1883)

I

Motherless Lassies

Delightful task, have poets sung,
To train and educate the young –
To teach the idea how to spring
And aid gay Hope to stretch her wing.

> – *The Nursery Offering, or Children's Gift Annual:*
> Edinburgh, 1835

'Is this the place, Papa? What a gloomy building for a school!'
The heavy-featured young girl in her early teens, her pigtail
bound with pale blue ribbon, jumped from the cab and gazed
steadily, with curiously grown-up eyes, at the dark square
villa which a brass plate proclaimed to be an 'Academy for
the daughters of Dissenters.'

'Well, Agnes, one cannot always judge by externals – after
all, one doesn't live on the *outside* of a house, eh Maggie?'
replied her father, his breath forming tiny bouquets of steam
on the frosty January air. Giving his hand to a second girl of
the same age, identically dressed but endowed with more
delicate features and a somewhat sweeter expression, he
continued: 'Come, girls, let us see whether the interior may
not prove to be rather more inviting.' He marched firmly up
the drive, a daughter clinging to each arm and the cabman

puffing and grunting in the rear under the weight of two extremely battered black boxes. It is obvious to this worthy that his young passengers are twins – youngish-like, in his opinion, to be the kids of a bearded gent who must be getting on for sixty.

The walk to the front door seemed interminable to the sisters: longer by far than any they had ever undertaken over the Ayrshire moors, more dismaying than twenty visits to the dentist. Experiencing all the emotions of Marie Antoinette on her way to the guillotine, their hearts sank further at every step into their buttoned boots. The tide of black misery rose higher and higher, engulfing them, cutting them off from all the security and happiness (yes, in retrospect it seemed like happiness at that moment) of the old life of home. To the normal apprehensions of children on their first day at boarding school were added, in the case of Agnes and Maggie, certain personal and private anxieties: for each was busy worrying about the other. At such an academy (Maggie was thinking), will Agnes find some companion who, by an identity of tastes or interests, will take her away from me? She is so clever! There are sure to be many clever girls in a place like this. It was a dismaying prospect, for, hitherto, she and her sister had been inseparable: each nature had complemented the other. Agnes' musings, however, had Maggie but known it, were taking a similar turn: hitherto, she had always been Maggie's leader, protector and guide – the initiator of games and entertainments, the organiser of all expeditions, the adviser in difficult situations, the blessed confidante in heartaches and disappointments; but, at boarding school, Maggie might well find someone else to turn to and to lean upon: someone who would bully her less and encourage her more, someone who would provide the same sustaining love, but at the cost of less domination. Behind Papa's back, the girls simultaneously stole a furtive look at one another, and exchanged encouraging smiles. The deep bond was reaffirmed without a word being spoken. 'Were your thoughts going that way? – how funny, so were mine!' the smiles said. 'Silly of me – I ought to have known! Of course things will be the same here as they have always

been!' With a slightly firmer tread, they followed Papa up the
steps to the front door.

The bell was answered by a uniformed maid, to whom the
bearded gentleman gave a card bearing the inscription: 'John
Smith, Writer to the Signet, Hamilfield, Irvine, Ayrshire,'
and asked to see the Headmistress, explaining that he had an
appointment with her. The three visitors were ushered into
the usual airless, overfurnished drawing-room which was to
be found in every middle-class villa in 1858, and invited to be
seated. Mr Smith had scarcely time to lay his silk hat upon
the table, give affectionate and encouraging glances at his
girls, and make a somewhat falsely-jaunty remark about the
handsome ormolu clock on the mantelpiece, when the
Headmistress entered.

'Good evening, Mr Smith. I trust you had a good journey
from Scotland?'

'Very comfortable, thank you, Miss Landor,' replied the
lawyer, rising.

'And these are your girls?'

'Yes, madam. This is Agnes' (he pushed forward the
plainer and more stocky of the two) 'and this is Maggie.'

The Headmistress, a tall lithe figure with a somewhat
severe expression, gave an astonished glance at the pigtails,
the dull grey merino dresses and the frumpy boots, and
hastily rearranged her features in a dignified smile. 'I am
delighted to have them in my school, Mr Smith; from all
accounts, they have the mental equipment to profit from a
stay here. I hope they will be very happy with us.'

'I am confident that they will, madam.' There was a
slightly awkward pause. 'Cold, is it not, this evening, Miss
Landor?' 'But seasonable,' retorted the Headmistress firmly,
dismissing the weather, like a refractory pupil, from her
awe-inspiring presence. 'Then I will leave the girls in your
care, madam,' said Mr Smith, reaching for his silk hat: he felt
more than a little intimidated by this commanding person in
the black silk dress. As a solicitor, he had interviewed many
clients, of very diverse types; but it was a new experience to
be interviewed himself, and by a clever woman. He
imprinted a hasty kiss on the cheek of each girl (who looked

at him with the imploring eyes of a drowning kitten), expressed the hope that he would hear good accounts of them, and disappeared in the direction of the waiting cab.

To the twins, still standing sheepishly and dismally by the table, the Headmistress said kindly, 'You must be tired with your journey. No doubt you will find it all a little strange at first, but I am sure you will soon feel quite at home here.' She rang the bell. 'Powell,' she said when the maid appeared, 'kindly give my compliments to Miss Walters, and say I should be obliged by her coming here for an instant.'

Miss Walters, it transpired, was the English teacher, a bright-looking little lady with blue eyes and long fair curls. She looks rather nice, Agnes said to herself, her low spirits momentarily rising at the comforting reflection that she was considered to be 'good at English'. But, when the Headmistress had disappeared, it seemed that Miss Walters was at the moment occupied with some younger pupils; and they were handed over to a senior girl, who was told to show them their dormitory and help them unpack. In her wake, they climbed the stairs to a spacious room containing six little iron beds with white counterpanes, and a single large wardrobe shared by all the occupants.

When their escort saw the twins' boxes, she pretended horror. 'Fancy coming to school, with a couple of Noah's arks like those! Wherever are you going to put them? They'll have to go downstairs in the cellar! You have far too many things!' Agnes and Maggie felt the tears rising suddenly to their eyes at her sneering tones. They were learning their first lesson about the curious world of boarding school, a world that requires of its inmates, as a first postulate, that all individuality be eliminated: that one's tastes, clothes, habits, opinions – even, it would seem, the very size and shape of one's luggage – must be exactly the same as that of one's neighbour. In a flash, all their apprehensions about their new life returned. They were not particularly worried about the lessons, for they knew that they both possessed a good grounding in all school subjects; but, for weeks past, they had feared that they would not be able to get on with the other girls. They had never before lived in a community of their peers. Motherless as they were, they had had little training in social relationships. Most of their fifteen years of life had been spent with adults, and with provincial adults at that. True, they were not without some experience of school life: they had attended Irvine Academy for several years, before their dear governess had taken over their education. But even at the local school, among the children of their father's friends and acquaintances, they had found it difficult to mix easily with others; for their interests were essentially adult interests, their conversational topics more appropriate to the drawing-room and the study rather than to the playground. Now, suddenly thrust into the midst of a strange and frightening world, they experienced something akin to panic; and, as always under such circumstances, they instinctively drew together. When the girl turned her back to clear a space for them in the wardrobe, Agnes felt for Maggie's hand, and gave it a quick, reassuring squeeze. It was all that was needed: courage began to flow back, the threatened tears did not materialise. They began to unpack.

It was as well that they had restored morale by this renewed affirmation of togetherness, for every garment, as it was lifted out by its owner, was subjected to a running fire of criticism before it was put away. Youth does not spare the feelings of its contemporaries, and the supercilious Emma was no exception to this rule. Exchanging forlorn glances, the twins bent over their boxes, confirmed in their conjecture that, from every point of view, Scots country girls would be bound to look very common and awkward in their new Merseyside surroundings. But perhaps (their patriotic hearts retorted) it was not their nationality, nor even their rural background, which was the cause of their trouble: it was their lack of a mother. For John Smith was a widower, who had lost his wife after only fourteen months of marriage. She had died three weeks after the girls were born. Disregarding the advice of his friends, he had never remarried, determined that the dead Margaret should have no rivals in his heart: a decision reinforced by his experience in legal practice, for too often he had seen widowers solve one problem merely to create others in its place. Stepmothers could often be as

11

harmful to children as no mother at all. Instead, he had
engaged extra domestics and a nurse and, a year previously,
an excellent governess.

It was this admirable woman whose shortcomings were
now becoming apparent to Agnes and Maggie as they knelt
before their boxes in their new fashionable Birkenhead
school. Whatever her personal qualities and her intellectual
gifts, her taste in clothes, it appeared, was not, after all
impeccable. She had all the preference of her kind for the
hardwearing and the serviceable – with the result that, when
set alongside their new schoolfellows, the twins looked more
like the products of an orphanage than the daughters of a
reasonably wealthy home. And when, their unpacking
completed, they followed their guide downstairs into the
common-room, it was only to encounter further humiliation;
for the other girls crowded round and pointed with glee and
derision to their wretched pigtails, to their drab merino
dresses with their linen collars, to their coarse stockings and
lumpy unfashionable boots. Jeering laughter filled the room,
and passing girls were urgently beckoned to come and inspect
the frumps. In the course of their lonely childhood, Agnes
and Maggie had spent many bleak, unhappy days; but never
had life been more utterly wretched than it was at that
moment . . . unless it was in the days that immediately
followed their first appearance. For even the staff joined in the
taunting and the laughter; and even the Headmistress herself,
far from coming to their defence, gave their pigtails a gentle
pull, remarking amid titters that they reminded her of a
couple of carthorses going to the fair. Humiliated by the
waspish remarks, and feeling that the whole world was
against them, they turned for comfort to each other, as they
had always done; so it might almost be said, paradoxically,
that the bad start was the best possible start for them. The
new situation had not, as they feared it might, driven them
apart: it had caused them to draw even closer together. It was
Agnes and Maggie against the world – little more than an
intensification of the normal state of affairs.

For their childhood, as has been hinted, had always been
lacking in companionship. Their father, though affectionate,

was busy and preoccupied, and they saw relatively little of him. Day after day had been spent in the company of nanny and maids, or, more recently, of governess and maids, or – between meals and lessons – simply with each other. The Scottish character is inwardly warm and affectionate, but outwardly austere – there are many Scots families whose members have never kissed one another, even after a long separation. Here and there, however, today as a hundred years ago, are to be found people to whom Nature has unkindly given quite the wrong temperament for such a social pattern: people whose feelings are warm, even passionate, demanding expression. Under this austere discipline they feel emotionally starved and are often desperately unhappy. The notorious Madeleine Smith was one such person, her Ayrshire namesakes a more respectable example. Everyone who had charge of them, through those fifteen years, had considered all overt emotionalism to be a weakness, certain to pamper, weaken, and 'spoil' a child. They had been kind, but firm; affectionate, but austere. The little girls had found themselves, from the outset, in a well-ordered but chilly world, lacking even in that subterranean warmth which was to be found in the homes of their schoolfellows. They longed not only to receive affection, but also to bestow it, and so were driven to find an outlet in the animal world. From time to time, a stray kitten would appear at the door of Hamilfield, and this they would hide in a cupboard or in the attic, smuggling food to it when Nanny's back was turned, and revelling in its cosy warmth and delighted purrs. But their joy was always short-lived: one of the maids would detect an unfamiliar smell in a place where no such smell should be, or would hear a gentle scratching or a timid miaouw . . . and, for all their bitter tears, their new friend, their only intimate and understanding friend, would be taken away and (they were told frankly) drowned.

So it had come about that, as the years passed, Agnes and Maggie had been compelled to look to each other for that love and comfort which there was no one else to bestow. Thus were laid the foundations of that intense emotional attachment to each other – excessive, even in twins – which was to persist, unabated, throughout their eighty-odd years of life: that devotion which prompted Agnes, in her last days, to make clear her wish to be buried, not beside the body of her husband, but in Maggie's grave ('because', she said, 'I would rather rise with Maggie than with Samuel' – a curious remark from one who was devoted to her husband). This emotional dependence, of course, was not given uninterrupted expression; it was not as though their nursery acquired, as it were, a Latin atmosphere, and became the scene of endless orgies of demonstrative affection. In actual fact, when the emotional temperature was raised, it was as likely to be a quarrel as an embrace that was staged – for the opposite of love, after all, is not hate but indifference; and what psychologists, in their unlovely jargon, term 'a love-hate ambivalence' was to characterise the relationship between the twins until death finally separated them. In their early formative years, as indeed throughout their lives, they quarrelled and were reconciled at regular intervals, and in between times were no more effusive towards each other than any other Scottish adults. But, deep down, they had found an inner security: each knew that the other, in a time of crisis, would bestow that healing warmth which alone can restore the numbed or fainting heart. The consciousness of being finally understood and loved, of having an ultimate emotional anchorage from which no blow of fate could dislodge one, eventually compensated fully for a preoccupied father and the lack of a mother, not to mention the drowned kittens. There is, indeed, a certain curious parallel between the twins' relationship and that between D.H. Lawrence and Frieda, who also needed one another, and whose fierce quarrels were – in spite of the very different aspect which these often presented to alarmed friends – mere surface ripples devoid of any significance, and in no wise affecting the fundamental unity where, deep down, each life flowed into the other and would always do so.

Fortunately for the twins, school malice is short-lived: some equally-odd new girl arrives a few days late for the beginning of term, or some fascinating teacup scandal is suddenly rumoured which provides the unkind tongues with fresh material, and the original victims are first ignored and then quietly accepted. Whatever their sartorial peculiarities, Agnes and Maggie were endowed with basically friendly natures, and in the course of a week or two they overcame their isolation and began to make friends. One of the first girls to whom they were drawn was a certain Jane Lewis, the daughter of a distinguished London surgeon of the Congregationalist persuasion. The friendship, however, did not ripen, for shortly afterwards Jane left the school; and it is only worth mentioning here because, thirty-five years later and long after the twins and Jane had lost touch with one another, Agnes was to make the acquaintance of her old schoolfellow's brother, and to marry him.

On the academic side, the girls quickly found themselves at home. They had marked ability, and a good grounding in all school subjects. Their governess had been a capable woman and, prior to her reign, George Paulin (the Rector of Irvine Academy) had expressed himself as very well satisfied with their progress – a tribute worth having, for his standards were exacting and his school highly thought of throughout the county. At Birkenhead, Agnes was found to excel at essay-writing, being constantly commended by her (male) teacher for her 'vigour of thought and chasteness of expression' which, he said, he had never seen equalled by any of his pupils, past or present. But the field in which they were outstanding was languages, for which they showed an unusual flair. The reason for this was that foreign languages had been something of a hobby with their father, and he had started them on Latin, French and German at an unusually early age. To encourage diligence, he had promised to take them to France and Germany the moment they had sufficiently mastered these languages to be able to make themselves understood there. It was his implementation of this promise which accounted for that battered condition of the twins' boxes which had so amused their dormitory guide on that first evening.

By the time term had ended, they had quite settled down; but they were glad to get back to Irvine and the familiar surroundings of home. When the train drew in to the railway station – a new acquisition to the town – it was welcoming to find everything unchanged, apart from a light rain of inkblots on the ticket-office counter. As the trap bore them towards Hamillfield and a high tea, they saw their town with fresh eyes – sleepy and restful and full of character after the cold impersonality and bustle of an expanding city like Birkenhead. Apart from the railway, which now linked Irvine with Glasgow and Paisley (then rapidly expanding under the impetus of their new industries), the place had changed little from the days when Rabbie Burns had worked there as a flax-dresser, and had had his shop burned down by over-exuberant citizens at Hogmanay. The broad main street possessed a kind of Dutch quaintness, reminding them of the coloured illustrations in one of their schoolbooks: a strange medley of gable ends, thatched cottages and eighteenth-century mansions with outside stairs, interspersed with recently-erected banks and shops and (while they had been away) still more new villas for the prosperous middle-class merchants. In the distance stood the centuries-old Tolbooth, standing in the middle of the street like a welcoming friend. Everything was unchanged – yes, there was even one of the imprisoned debtors craning out of its upper window, lowering a bottle on a rope and shouting hoarsely to some passer-by to take it to the Wheatsheaf Inn for refilling! And how slowly everyone walked, after Birkenhead! The few people still on the streets at that hour in the evening – not that there was ever much of a crowd, except on market days – strolled majestically about, as if they had all the time in the world; bowing gravely to one another, or joining one little group after another for a leisurely exchange of news. Dear Irvine! How good it was to be back again!

As they drove along, Papa hinted at a surprise for them at home, but absolutely declined to say what it was. The trap turned into the Kilwinning Road, where the lamplighter was already beginning his rounds; as he moved from one lamp to its distant neighbour (for the Town Council was stingy when it came to the expenditure of money on public utilities), each iron stalk suddenly flowered in the gathering dusk. Arrived at Hamilfield, a square, roomy detached villa, Papa hurried them inside – and behold, the surprise! The old house had been completely redecorated from top to bottom, and their bedroom was fresh with white paint and a charming wallpaper covered with rosebuds. 'Oh Papa – have you been able to do this because Holms o'Caaf has died?' exclaimed Agnes, revealing, already, the shrewd business head which was to stand her in good stead in after years. 'That's right, my dear – though why I should tell you, I have no idea: business matters are no concern of the young.' 'Well, Papa you *did* say that it was because he had left you some money that we were able to go to boarding school, you know!' 'Did I? That was very indiscreet of me!'

Agnes had laid her finger on the reason for the new prosperity of the Smith household. Not that it had ever been an impoverished home, for John Smith had never, at any time, been wholly dependent upon what he could earn by drawing up wills and conveyances, augmented by the occasional defence of some poacher or defaulting corn-merchant. He had other, and more profitable, sources of income – all connected with the gentleman with the peculiar nickname. (A 'holm' is the flat land bordering a river, 'caaf' is Scots for chaff: the nickname was doubtless ironical.) His real name was John Ferguson, and he had been a distant relation of John Smith's – the sort of relative that all men sigh for and dream of, but which few possess. When the twins had been born, fifteen years previously, Ferguson's wealth had already amounted to more than a million pounds; and since that date it had steadily augmented. With the administration of this vast sum, he could not be bothered; so he had entrusted its management to the only lawyer in the family, his cousin John. Smith had tackled this formidable assignment wisely, and was soon in receipt of a handsome 'retainer' for his services. Ferguson was delighted, and hinted broadly that a nest-egg of Arabian Nights dimensions might be expected to find its way to Irvine when he died. In this, he was as good as his word: he left Smith £200,000.

How in the world, it may be asked, did Ferguson come to acquire such an immense fortune? Was it by luck, or by brilliance? Certainly not the latter, for a contemporary has described him as 'an uninteresting man, of a somewhat ordinary character' (hence his nickname). He had been the son of the owner-skipper of one of Irvine's small coasters, and (happily for John Smith) had never married. The basis of his wealth he had inherited through his mother, who had been the only daughter of a Dalry meadow-farmer, one John Service, – an even less attractive man than his grandson, being 'of a narrow and contracted turn of mind, penurious in his habits and peevish withal.' Service had five sons who – father being what he was – had all emigrated to America at the earliest possible opportunity, and there had entered the employ of their Uncle Robert, who was 'doing very well' as a merchant in Boston, Massachusetts. Uncle Robert wasn't particularly easy to get on with, either – he was apt to be explosive at times, and indeed had been proscribed and banished from Canada shortly after his first visit to that country in 1776 – but at least he was, in the young men's eyes, an improvement upon Father, and much less parsimonious as an employer. Under his eye, the Service brothers prospered. Since their chief aim in life was to make money, their ideals corresponded exactly with those of Uncle Robert, who therefore thought highly of them as young men to be encouraged and promoted. How much he approved of them, they only discovered when he died: he left them not only the business but his entire fortune as well. This they quickly augmented . . . and then died, unmarried and intestate, in rapid succession. The lawyers dutifully searched for the next of kin; and one day, the uninteresting John Ferguson awoke to find himself with a million pounds to his credit in the bank. Small wonder that he was staggered by the prospect of having to cope with such vast assets! Racking his brains to think of someone who might be competent to deal with such matters, he suddenly thought of Cousin John – with the result that we have seen.

So it had come about that John Smith, with his handsome retainer and his distinctly rosy expectations, had been in a strong position, economically speaking, to leave his late wife in unchallenged possession of his affections. Money, while not bringing happiness, enables you to be miserable in comfort. It was true that the tragedy of her death left its mark upon his spirit, for never again was her name allowed to be mentioned in Hamilfield, and it was not until, in middle life, the girls visited maternal cousins in America that they learned anything about her at all; but in other directions, the comforts and consolations available to a man of means were certainly his. And when Holms o'Caaf died, he had been able to send the girls to a more exclusive and expensive school than Irvine Academy. Agnes had been right in linking the two events.

Now, as a kind of welcome home, and as a symbol of that more expensive life which Ferguson's death had made possible, he had had the whole house redecorated. As the girls stood at their bedroom window, they felt indeed content: behind them was the new expensive rosebud wallpaper, before them, through the window, the smoke from the ironworks blending pleasantly with the last glow of the setting sun – that sun which, on every free evening, touched with a dignified splendour the distant peaks of Arran. It was good to be home.

There are few days as exciting to contemplate, when one opens one's eyes in the morning, as the first day of the school holidays. After breakfast, the girls wandered down to the harbour – always a favourite stroll – where they could watch the coasters loading coal from carts which had rumbled their way into the town from the pits in neighbouring parishes. On the quayside, the skippers stood about in groups, transacting their business in leisurely fashion like farmers gossiping in the market; or, their vessels loaded, emerged wiping their beards from the public house, glancing at the sky to see if the breeze was favourable enough to forbid postponing their departure any longer. A traditional, sleepy scene, like the setting of a musical comedy. The twins wandered idly about, taking in the familiar activities and revelling in the fact that, while their five thousand fellow-citizens were all busily working, they alone had nothing whatever to do: the best part of any holiday.

On Sunday, it was pleasant to go with Papa, as usual, to the kirk – a marked contrast to the huge barn-like place of worship to which they were conducted in a 'crocodile' during term time, for it was a cosy little building situated in a back lane called the Cotton Row. The congregation to which the Smiths belonged was soon to move to a smart new building (with a new name to match: Trinity) on the banks of the river; but the one in which they now gathered was totally devoid of architectural pretensions, being, indeed, no more than a box within which the heavenly treasure could conveniently be displayed – square and simple, and ornamented only with two arched windows facing the narrow street. Between these, in a kind of wooden pen, sat the elders who watched over the collection plate into which Agnes and Maggie dropped their pennies as they entered.

A notable light, however, burned within this homely, unprepossessing candlestick in the Cotton Row: one from which many tapers were to be kindled, not only throughout Scotland, but even in England. 'Robertson of Irvine' (as their minister was generally known – it was his only parish) was a remarkable man, and to him the twins, no less than their father, were greatly devoted. He had, indeed, almost been promoted to the status of honorary uncle, and it was only a proper respect for his cloth which prevented them from addressing him as 'Uncle Willie' rather than as 'Dr Robertson'. One simply could not call a minister by such a familiar name, least of all one's own minister.

Robertson was noted for his learning and breadth of culture, even in a country and a communion which has, perhaps, always possessed the most highly-educated ministry in the world. A friend and protégé of De Quincey, upon whose prose style he modelled his own, Robertson had studied at Halle after leaving the Divinity Hall, had travelled extensively in Italy and Switzerland, was fluent in a number of European languages, had a passion for Renaissance art – a strange interest for a minister, in those days – about which he talked endlessly and enthusiastically, and possessed a wide circle of friends who had made their mark in literary, artistic, musical and scientific circles. How good it was, thought Agnes and Maggie as they took their seats once more in the box-like pew under the gallery, to be 'sitting under' – the somewhat oppressive phrase in those days – dear Dr Robertson again. The lazy hum of whispered greetings suddenly subsided, and there arose in the pulpit a little man in his late thirties, with hair already nearly white, who gave out the 'gathering psalm'. No, he had not changed (it was foolish of them to fear that he might have done; but that first term had seemed an eternity) – there was the same warm, vital personality; his dress was as untidy as ever, the linen bands beneath his chin still hopelessly crumpled, the undignified patch of snuff still decorating his upper lip. What a pleasant contrast there was between his silvery voice with its rippling burr, his vivid gestures and dramatic pauses, and the harsh drone and lifeless demeanour of his Birkenhead colleague! Yes, they were indeed fortunate in their minister – doubly so because, though a bachelor, he was devoted to children. Perhaps it was because he was a poet as well as a preacher that he possessed the imagination to enter into the feelings and interests of the young. Agnes could remember countless occasions, in her younger days, when he had carried on a charming conversation with her favourite doll, or with an imaginary playmate.

There was, in fact, a kind of elfin quality about Robertson to which every child instantly responded. So quickly, indeed, could he establish rapport with the young that it was his custom to avoid carriages containing children when he was travelling, declaring that the pain of parting from them at the end of the journey made the experience too harrowing. But it was not only with children that he was popular; his company was even more appreciated by adults. In those days, the minister's annual visit was invariably an occasion to be dreaded, for it necessitated donning one's best clothes, and setting out the best china, and keeping the children (under terrible threats) at least outwardly well-behaved – not to mention carefully primed in the answers to the questions in the Shorter Catechism. From the moment Robertson arrived in Irvine, he made it known that this starchy formality would be dispensed with: he would drop in unexpectedly, take them as he found them, and chat informally round the fire. He was a good talker, in the best sense of the word, and his

21

conversation sparkled with wit and humour. Ideas poured from him – ideas which he could never be bothered to systematise or work out in detail, so that such fragments of his writing as have remained give little indication of the range or fertility of his mind, or of the immensely stimulating quality of his personality. He was so full of life that others got a share of it, and, rarest and most blessed gift of all, he could listen as brilliantly as he could talk. With his gifts, his charm and his humour, it was not surprising that he attained distinction far beyond the borders of his parish and his native land. And this last quality, happily, preserved him from the spiritual perils of that lionization which the Victorians accorded to popular preachers, and which so often resulted in a regrettable distention of holy egos. To the end of his life, he remained unaffected and unspoilt, serious and devout but not solemn or stuffy – in some ways, a kind of Scottish Sydney Smith, with the same quick wit. On one occasion, he was showing a colleague round Irvine when a pretty girl, bearing a large lump of butter on a dish, ran out of a doorway, bid the minister good morning, dashed across the street and vanished into a house. 'Ah, a pillar of your kirk, Robertson?' enquired the visitor. 'No – just a flying butt'ress' was the quick retort. Conversing with a wealthy Jew on a channel steamer, he was asked whether he spoke German. 'Very imperfectly, I'm afraid.' 'O well, my dear sir, sovereigns are the thing – they speak all languages on the continent.' 'But they suffer very much in translation, I believe,' commented Robertson dryly.

Robertson had come to Irvine in 1843 – the year in which the twins were born – and a close friendship had sprung up between the minister and the solicitor. They had similar tastes – most of the Cotton Row congregation were simple working folk, with no interest in foreign languages, literature, art or travel. And when Smith's wife died, Robertson took to dropping in at Hamilfield rather more frequently – an escape from the dreariness of lodgings and the vicissitudes of a landlady. Agnes and Maggie had therefore seen much of him from their earliest years, and were very attached to him. Robertson's ideas were much in advance of his time. His sermons would be illustrated by references to Gothic architecture or the paintings of Raphael, making the point that all beauty had its source in God (a somewhat daring doctrine to expound in nineteenth-century Scots Presbyterian circles, where man-made beauty was decidedly suspect), and he stressed the importance of the worship element in church services, then usually dismissed as 'the preliminaries'. Similarly, in his Bible Class, he shunned the contemporary practice of long, dreary doctrinal lectures and made the occasion what today would be called a discussion group, training the young to think things out for themselves. It says much for his character and personality that he was able to carry his Elders with him in all these startling innovations (so that the Scottish national passion for secession was not, this time, indulged).

Agnes and Maggie were willing pupils, and it was from him, perhaps, rather than from their staid respect-for-all-institutions father, that they learned that sturdy independence of thought and action which was to stay with them decades later, when Irvine was visited only on holidays, and which was, as we shall see, to horrify the stuffier denizens of Cambridge University. A faith one had thought out and made one's own; an enquiring mind; an awareness of wider horizons worth exploring; an independent spirit, and a keen sense of fun* – what could be a better foundation upon which to build one's life? And how many small-town girls anywhere, least of all in the middle of the Victorian age, set off with such equipment? Robertson certainly deserves much of the credit for the twins' later extraordinary achievements. In essence, their characters were largely what he had made them: vigorous, adventurous, forceful, many-sided, able to distinguish between what is essential in religion and what is secondary, between unfortunate conduct which may be forgiven because of human frailty and inexcusable pomposity, conceit and self-righteousness or the indefensible betrayal of a friend.

---

* 'I often think that a frank, good-hearted laugh is a much higher attainment in spiritual life than a holy prayer or tear. Many get the length of the latter – few get so high as the former.' So wrote Robertson to Agnes during her first term at boarding school.

Soon they returned to school, attired by now in more suitable clothes. Thereafter, one term was very much like another. Holidays were sometimes spent at home, sometimes abroad – Dr Robertson often accompanying them on the latter, thus providing John Smith with adult companionship. When, the summer after they went to Birkenhead, Papa found it necessary to spend several months in America in connection with the Ferguson estate, the minister was left *in loco parentis*. All through the following term, he wrote the girls a weekly letter, giving them all the news from home. One such has been preserved. In it, he credits Agnes with having induced him to rise earlier in the morning, and continues with fifty lines of verse about his dog Fido who, he alleges, speaks fluent German ('Rauf! Herauf! Herauf! Rauf! This is the dogmatics Fido preaches.')

It was about this time that Agnes herself began to write poetry – spurred on no doubt by the wife of the Free Kirk minister (author of the hymn 'The sands of time are sinking') and perhaps encouraged by Robertson himself who, apart from light-hearted doggerel about Fido, was a serious poet of sorts, with some slight reputation in his day. Her verses need not detain us: they are the usual products of a schoolgirl of fifteen, bespattered with adolescent yearnings and moralisings. They perhaps tell us more about the author than about the subject, in much the same way as Shaw's book on Ibsen is chiefly valuable for what it tells us about Shaw. Alas, she was to continue to write verses for the rest of her life, curiously incapable of realising what rubbish they were; they were to be remorselessly inflicted upon her friends, year after year, in the form of Christmas cards and New Year greetings. Worst of all, this poetical jumble-sale was to be given an undeserved immortality, in her sixty-fifth year, by a publishing firm as reputable as Messrs Williams and Norgate. Here and there is to be found a line of real beauty, reminiscent of the jewel in the toad's head, but the volume as a whole is best forgotten.

Throughout this chapter, Agnes has dominated the stage, with Maggie lingering hesitantly in the wings. It was to be always so. Throughout the twins' long lives, Agnes was to be the senior partner – more strong willed and forceful, claiming as her birthright (for was she not the elder, if only by twenty minutes?) a double portion of the spirit. Maggie was altogether a gentler person, with less of the male in her emotional make-up. She was to become as capable a scholar and as intrepid a traveller; she had the same toughness of fibre, both in spirit and body; but in her case it was enveloped in a more feminine softness and gentleness. For eighty-odd years, the twins were to be together – so that it became as unthinkable for one to do something without the other as for a penny to have a head but no tail. But always, in the strange drama of their lives, Agnes automatically and without question took the lead: Maggie was content with a minor role, touched only occasionally and fleetingly by the spotlight, giving her loyal support, more often than not, from the protecting environment of the shadows. At school, as we have seen, Agnes was the essayist – the talented writer whose head was always full of vigorous ideas; Maggie's special talent, on the other hand, lay in the direction of water-colour painting. In later life, most of Maggie's achievements as a scholar were shared with her sister, the fruits of work done together, whereas Agnes had successes which were wholly her own. The writer/painter polarity at school was to continue: Maggie was to remain a kind of illustration to the book of her sister's life. In middle age, Agnes used to relate with gusto the judgment of their governess, who always maintained that though she was the more promising pupil, she often failed to fulfil her promise: whereas Maggie, who showed less initial ability, often outstripped her twin in actual achievement. There is perhaps some truth in this; but as the years go by, it becomes increasingly difficult to disentangle the work of one from that of the other. But when, at the age of eighteen, they left Birkenhead to go to a 'finishing school' in Kensington, it was already clear that the twins' talents, like their natures, were complementary; that here was a female Tweedledum and Tweedledee, clinging to each other through thick and thin, alternately quarrelling about a rattle and sharing the same umbrella in face of the storms of the world.

II

Agnes Routs a Wily Dragoman

Come travel: soon thy friends will be replaced.
Come work – and life's true sweetness thou shalt know.
Success and fame are never found in rest,
But cares are. Leave thy native land and go!

> – Epigraph to *Through Cyprus* by Agnes Smith
> (from the Arabic – her own translation)

Of the finishing school in Kensington, and of their life there, nothing is known. That they should go there at all sounds like another bit of Smith-Robertson planning. Transplanting the little seedlings from small town Irvine to fast-growing large-town Birkenhead would be, as it were, Phase I; but the two experienced men would realise that great as the change would be for the girls, they would, in reality, merely have moved from Small Provincial to Large Provincial, in terms of environment. What they now needed was some experience of life in London, between which and Birkenhead was a gulf as wide as that which separated Birkenhead from Irvine. Phase II, then, should be a year or two at a finishing school in the capital.

All we know about this interlude is that they formed a close friendship with one of the younger teachers, Grace

Blyth by name. She must have been in her late twenties – a big gap in age when one is eighteen, but considerably less by the time one is twenty or twenty-two. They 'kept up with Grace' after they left, and the polishing process was deemed to have been completed (what can have been the syllabus? It would be interesting to know); and she was to remain, for the rest of their long lives, their closest and most intimate friend.

In 1866, when the twins were twenty-three, Papa Smith died. The last time they had felt lonely and lost, it had been far away from home, in Birkenhead; this time, it was a comfort to know that Dr Robertson was just up the road, able to strengthen them and cheer them by his frequent visits. For eighteen months they mourned their father, to whom they had been very attached, and complied with the pattern of elaborate mourning – the black dresses and restricted social activity which convention then prescribed. It is difficult to understand why a generation which professed earnestly to believe that death was simply an unimportant incident – no more than the door by which the soul passed from one room to another in the Father's house – should make quite such a fetish of it, and should surround it with such an oppressive and melancholy ritual. But when the fantastically thick black edge on their notepaper had been reduced to the thin line permitted by custom, they set about planning their next tour abroad.

Their situation, apart from their loneliness, was an exceptionally fortunate one. They enjoyed a freedom which was rare in England at that time, and almost unheard of in Scotland. There were no relatives nearer than America to tell them what they must, or must not, do; they had inherited their father's substantial fortune, and so were, in the economic sense also, free to come and go as they pleased and to live wherever they chose; and they were well educated, not only in the narrow academic sense but equally in the wider sense of having gained self-confidence and a feeling of independence, of having had their minds stretched to embrace that wider culture of past and present civilisations to which Papa and Robertson had introduced them. All in all, they must have been the envy of their carefully-supervised female contemporaries; for John Knox's views on women who expressed their individuality were well-known, Burns had been more interested in the bodies than in the minds of females, and the Shorter Catechism gave no guidance at all as to what interests and activities were suitable for women. Hence North British society, lacking any other suitable mentor, had been compelled to fall back on the Old Testament patriarchs when it came to determining the role appropriate for Scottish girls. To Agnes and Maggie had been given all that the local Jeans and Jessies sighed for, but could not have: freedom beyond their wildest dreams, and the equipment, in mind and character, to make good use of it.

Given this freedom, what should they do? The answer was obvious: travel. To satisfy the local matrons, it would be prudent to take with them some older woman as nominal chaperon. There was no point, Robertson said, in giving unnecessary offence: it would only reflect on their father, and cause his admirable educational ideas to be reviled. Nor was it wise to run needless risks. By all means let them go abroad, but let them take some older woman friend with them. If, in spite of that arrangement, tongues still wagged, let them wag.

Where should they go, and whom should they take? As to the first, they had already visited France, Germany and Italy; was this not the moment to grow a trifle bolder, to strike off the beaten track and visit the Middle East? The twins thought it was. As to the second, there was no one in Irvine who was suitable. All the appropriately mature women had led very sheltered lives, and their mammas would certainly never have allowed them to venture even as far as Edinburgh without a male escort. Who, then? Why, Grace Blyth, of course! Only a few years older than themselves, yet A Teacher (the very title suggested someone experienced in the art of Curbing Youthful Enthusiasm, Giving Wise Guidance and Coping With Difficult Situations). They sat down and wrote to Grace, and began to make their plans.

Grace, however, never having done any travelling, was far from enthusiastic; but after a number of letters had passed between Irvine and London, and some judicious bullying and wheedling, she finally agreed to come. The friends of the three girls, both of their own and their father's generation, were unanimously horrified when the proposal was announced to them. They were shocked at Dr Robertson's approval of the expedition, and united in prophesying woe on a large scale. Whoever heard of innocent, sheltered girls wandering without male escort round such dreadful countries as Egypt and Greece? At best, they would all be murdered; at the worst, assaulted and 'interfered with' in ways that the appalled matrons preferred not to specify in any detail, even to each other. But Agnes and Maggie were unmoved by these expostulations. They were free agents now, and they proposed to exploit that delicious and enchanting situation to the full. Since Dr Robertson approved, what did the opinions of others matter? They set about working out their route.

It was agreed to dispense with the services of a courier: they would share the responsibilities of the journey between them. Grace would arrange the hotel reservations; Maggie would keep the accounts and attend to disbursements; Agnes would study the guide-books, plan routes and arrange excursions. What need of a courier? There would be nothing left for him to do.

The three friends left London on a dull morning in August 1868, travelled to Ostend and thence to Nuremberg. In the train to Munich, they shared a carriage with a celebrated German artist (Agnes does not give his name) and his wife. Almost at once, an argument developed as to whether women should be given the vote. Agnes held forth with Robertsonian logic on the subject, and the artist became very angry, writing out some verses of Schiller's for them, which he appeared to think settled the matter. His wife dutifully backed him up, declaring that such an idea never entered the head of a German woman. But when, exhausted by his arguments, the artist fell asleep, she whispered to the girls that they were quite right, and that German women were kept far too much in subjection.

They had planned to stay only a night or two in Vienna, but Agnes caught fever, and was very ill. It was a whole month before they were able to continue their journey. Maggie and Grace filled in the time teaching English to the waiter and making various preparations for the journey ahead – preparations which ranged from buying a good stock of insect powder (together with a small pistol, for firing it off) to acquiring broadbrimmed straw hats in readiness for the burning sun. Whenever they explained their plans to any of the Viennese ladies, they were met with looks of incredulity, swiftly followed by absolute horror; so much so, indeed, that even the resolute Agnes began to feel slightly apprehensive. However, the railway tickets had already been bought, and there was a fine smell of burning boats in the air. They left for Pesth as soon as Agnes was fit to travel.

This time, their travelling companion was a wealthy young Rumanian girl, returning home from a clothes-buying spree in Paris. She discouraged the girls' romantic imaginings of a rapturous reunion with her husband, by pointing out that her marriage had been arranged by her parents, and that her husband was thoroughly unattractive, interested only in drink and cards, and too stupid even to speak to her at dinner. Agnes considered that he should be firmly taken in hand, but the elegant bride considered this to be quite impossible.

From Pesth – where, incidentally, the Rumanian girl's aristocratic veneer had rapidly flaked off, and she had sworn horribly at both porters and cabmen – they embarked on the river steamer for Rutschuk, and there took another train for Varna. On this train, the discomforts (which is as near as most of us get to actual adventures) began.

The track was in such a bad state of repair that no trains were allowed to run after dark, for fear of a derailment. The coaches had little in the way of springs, and the girls were bumped and jolted for the whole journey. The carriages were icy, and a hole in the roof – where the lamp ought to have been – encouraged the wind to blow unceasingly on the travellers' heads. They had, of course, brought no winter clothing with them, so they just had to sit and freeze. The journey occupied an entire day and, though the train kept stopping – for no apparent reason and usually for more than an hour at a time – no food of any kind was to be obtained. Fortunately they had foreseen this possibility, and had brought with them some very cheap and tasteless wine and a half-boiled fowl rolled in paper. This last they had to eat with their fingers.

After Varna, they had to endure a very rough crossing of the Bosphorus, and entered Constantinople in a torrential downpour. There were no cabs, for porters carried the luggage on their backs, and they were compelled to trudge on foot all the way from the quayside to their hotel, 'following their trunks like elephants, through dirt of every description, spattered by passing horses and dodging snarling curs which snapped at them from the decaying rubbish heaps which bordered the road.' The girls were discovering, like others before and since, that adventure often proves less romantic in reality than in fireside dreams. However, by the time they had been an hour in the hotel and had dried their clothes and thawed out their persons round the open stove, it had all become fun again – even for the hitherto untravelled Grace.

The next day, they began sightseeing. First, they went to see some dancing dervishes, but found them an unimpressive spectacle. Their fixed notions of what dervishes ought to be like were, in fact, much more satisfied by the worshippers at some sort of Moslem healing service, their next 'sight'. Here (in Agnes' words) 'a number of grotesque objects writhed and yelled in close line', like the little children of St Vitus. 'Sometimes they cackled out from exhausted lungs a sound that we imagined might only be heard in severe bronchitis. We really expected them to drop down dead.' At the close of the dance, which increased in tempo and wildness, sick men were brought to the priest for healing: 'The priest touched the diseased spot and muttered something in a low voice. If the pain was in the back, the patient lay down and the priest stood on him,' Agnes records. After this somewhat drastic demonstration of Middle East physiotherapy, the girls climbed the hill above Pera, from which vantage point they could see not only the whole city, but also Scutari and its barracks, 'the scene of Florence Nightingale's labours.'

31

The next day, they left by ship for Cyprus. The vessel was crowded with passengers of every race, the poorer ones sleeping on mattresses laid on the decks. Agnes discussed theology with the Master, Captain Rollo, who had a low opinion of Greek priests – in his view a dirty, ill-mannered lot unworthy of respect. Maggie couldn't help wondering 'what some of our starched-up Anglican clergymen would say were that man [a priest gnawing a bone as he walked the deck] to address him as "Brother".'

In Cyprus, Grace insisted upon trying to ride a camel, amid cries of wonder and admiration from the rest of the party (all Germans). She succeeded in keeping her seat, as did Maggie; but Agnes fell off. She considered, however, that this served her right for laughing at a particularly pompous German who, scorning the advice to make the camel kneel before he mounted, took a flying leap at the saddle while the beast was still upright. Had he known more about camels, he would have been aware that the girth is rarely fastened tightly; the saddle instantly shifted, and he was compelled to scramble up on to the beast's neck to save himself from falling. There he sat, with his face to the tail ('in order that he might not turn his back on the ladies', Agnes explained maliciously), while the camel roared and groaned alarmingly and the rest of the party tried to conceal their laughter.

When they returned to their ship, they were afforded an insight into the problems of a ship's master in those waters. Among the passengers were a number of ladies in *purdah*, and for these, Captain Rollo had curtained off a corner of the saloon. Some of the European women who were travelling, however, considered that they were unnecessarily crowded because of this arrangement, and made a complaint to this effect. Captain Rollo, wishing to discuss with the purdah ladies some re-division of the saloon, had unthinkingly lifted the corner of the curtain which protected the harem – and had instantly been attacked by the enraged and indignant husbands. His officers, indeed, had had to rescue him from an infuriated Turk who had rushed upon him with drawn sword. The situation was tense and dangerous, and it took the expert diplomacy of the Austrian consul (hastily summoned) to convince the husbands that no offence had been intended. Eventually they calmed down and were persuaded to accept the Captain's apology. No doubt Agnes and Maggie felt it was all very different from the home life of our dear Queen.

So, by way of Port Said and Alexandria, they eventually reached Cairo where they had planned to take a river boat up the Nile, at least as far as Wady Halfeh. Agnes has left a description of the rascal who was to be their dragoman on this trip: 'We found Certezza *père* waiting for us at the station. Seldom have we seen a more handsome man. He might have sat for a portrait of bluff King Hal, after domestic worries had tinged that monarch's hair with silver. His face wore a smile which was meant to express the most artless sincerity; and each word as it fell from his lips seemed coated with sugar.' She mistrusted him on sight.

Certezza claimed that he would need a fortnight to make all the necessary arrangements, and the girls did not demur, for the delay provided them with the time to see the sights of Cairo, to taste the full flavour of the city and to enjoy the kaleidoscopic human scene which blended every colour of skin and every conceivable type of garment. Between peering into squalid dens in which craftsmen hammered away at trinkets and pushing their way through half-dark passages so narrow that two people could pass only with difficulty, they kept an alert eye for feminine fashions. Agnes was much amused to see an Arab woman 'of the better class' riding a donkey: 'Her loose pink silk dress and yellow over-shoes were covered entirely with a white veil, confined by a girdle, making her look exactly like a pillow tied in the middle.'

They did not see their river-boat until the actual moment of embarkation. True, the crafty Certezza had, their very first day, taken them down to the river and pointed out a magnificent craft which he alleged was to be theirs for the trip. But the reality was, shall we say, more of the genuine native type than of the luxury-for-foreign-visitors genre. Agnes has described it for us: 'Before the mast was the kitchen, where the cook was performing his operations in the

open air. The upper deck was partially covered with an
awning, and furnished with two high divans and two Turkey
carpets. At the stern was a great heap of slices of bread for the
sailors, a basket of oranges, and two coops of live poultry.
The helm was wrapped round with sheepskin, to prevent the
helmsman's fingers being chafed.' The girls' living quarters
were in the stern – a small dining room and four cabins, two
forward and two aft of the saloon, all narrow and confined
and totally lacking in drawers and cupboards for their
clothes. A curtain in a corner of the dining saloon concealed
the bathroom. It was all very primitive; and the bright green
and red with which the boat was painted was its most
attractive feature. However, they had come in search of new
experiences, and this dirty old ark was at least a change from
their usual well-appointed ocean-going liners. They sailed on
15 December.

Each evening Certezza entertained them with his guitar (or
the Cairo equivalent of one), and during the daytime poured
out endless reminiscences – which Agnes suspected to be
largely fiction – of his experiences as dragoman. They
reached Benisooef on Christmas Day, and were surrounded,
as they went ashore, by troops of excited children. The girls
proudly displayed their tattooed faces and arms and their
henna-stained hands, while the boys removed their only
garment and, holding it up in both hands, turned round and
round for the amusement of the visitors. Such impromptu
drama was perhaps not quite Irvine's idea of light entertainment. Agnes simply records the scene, but offers no
comment.

Christmas night was enlivened by the appearance of a
plague of rats, who darted, squeaking, round the heads of the
terrified girls as they lay in their bunks. Thereafter, Agnes
and Maggie squeezed into a single berth scarcely large
enough for one person. (Grace, presumably, was left to fend
for herself, as best she could, in her own cabin.) Certezza
promised to buy a cat at the next village they should arrive at;
but it was nearly a fortnight before he kept his promise –
during which time the girls frequently sat up all night, in
'watches'. Eventually two cats were added to the passenger-

list, and were tied one on each side of the girls' cabin. But these animals made almost as much noise as the rats, caterwauling and struggling, with many feline oaths, to escape from their rope. So the nights, though now free from actual danger, were scarcely more peaceful.

By this time they were beginning to near the Cataract, on the perils of which Certezza had expatiated for days, with many lurid details. Grace and Maggie became very nervous, and suggested leaving the boat before they reached it, but Agnes was adamant: she had planned to sail up to Wady Halfeh, and to Wady Halfeh she meant to go. Certezza, disappointed at being baulked of his desire for easy money – a boat without the inconvenience of any passengers to look after – tried another cunning gambit. He declared that they could not pass the Cataract unless they made themselves financially responsible for the boat. It was the usual custom, he argued blandly – their friend, Mr R., had readily agreed to be responsible for *his* craft. 'How much will it cost us, should it be lost?' asked Grace. 'Five hundred pounds, miss.' 'I shall not be responsible,' said Grace firmly. 'Nor I' echoed Maggie, 'you had better ask Agnes.' Agnes, when told, was torn between the duties of business and the obligations of strict Sabbath observance: 'I will say nothing today, as it is Sunday; but tomorrow Certezza shall certainly know my mind.' The dragoman interpreted her silence as timidity. When he waited on them at dinner, he assumed the air of a bully and waxed dogmatic: 'The thing is,' he said in menacing tones, 'those who become responsible get up the Cataract. Those who don't, don't.' Agnes said nothing; but next morning, taking their contract and the guidebook, she walked quietly over to Certezza's table. 'Certezza,' she said, 'I have heard what you said yesterday to Miss Grace and Miss Maggie about our being responsible for the boat. You will see from our contract, however, that in no case are we bound to be responsible for anything. And as Murray's Guidebook' – she waved it firmly at him – 'says that the Reis of the Cataract is the responsible party, it would be unfair to take his duties from him.' Certezza recognised that he had at last met his match. 'Yes, miss, you are quite right,' he answered in his most sugary tone, 'it is I who ought to be responsible. Don't be afraid: I'll take you up the Cataract.'

This incident, unimportant in itself, is worth recording as it makes clear Agnes' competence to deal with unexpected situations. Travellers in those days had to fight their own battles as best they could: there was no Travel Agency courier to smooth the way and take from their shoulders the burden of tiresome negotiations with local guide or dragoman. Certezza had made an understandable blunder. He had thought that three unaccompanied young women, with a month's sail between them and the nearest British Consulate, would be ideal victims for his little schemes. No doubt he had planned that the boat should sustain some slight damage while crossing the Cataract – damage which could be craftily magnified so as to give him a handsome sum in 'compensation'. But he had chosen his victims badly. The spineless Mr R. might capitulate, but Agnes, aged twenty-five, was made of sterner stuff.

Certezza, however, was not easily defeated. The main attack had ended in a rout, but an advance on the flank might yet succeed. Like Jeeves, he studied the psychology of the individual. Religious girls might possibly be vulnerable on religious grounds. It was worth trying, anyway. He opened the battle on the following evening by remarking casually that the Reis (the captain of the craft) had been very sulky all day. When Grace duly took her cue, and asked why, he replied that the following day marked the end of Ramadan, (the month-long Moslem fast) and he (the Reis) was believed to be apprehensive lest he should be unable to say his prayers in a mosque. 'But I thought Ramadan lasted much longer,' retorted Grace quickly. The smooth patter rose as easily to Certezza's lips as the reassuring rejoinder to the lips of an insurance salesman. 'So it does, miss; but for working people they allow a shorter time. If you would allow the Reis and sailors to stay here' (they were moored off a town at the time) 'until tomorrow, it would be better than giving them any baksheesh, and they'd work with much more spirit afterwards. The Reis has been trying to persuade me all day, but I said I couldn't do it without the ladies,' he added

36

unctuously. (Would he, wondered Agnes, get a contact-man's commission for his successful intercession? Probably.) 'Well, Certezza, do you think we should do it?' 'Yes, miss, I think you should.' They granted the request, not wholly free from the suspicion that it was simply another 'try-on'. It was. When, having strolled round the town all morning, they returned to the boat ready to resume the journey, Certezza renewed the attack. 'Oh miss, the Reis says he made a mistake in looking at the moon. It is tomorrow, and not today, that he has to say his prayers. If you'll only allow him to stay one night more, he'll guarantee your going up the Cataract.' By this time, Certezza and the Reis began to bear a strong family resemblance to the notorious Captain Goyles in Jerome K. Jerome's *Three Men on the Bummel*, who found a fresh reason every day for not putting to sea. The girls were suspicious – sailors were said to have a wife in every port: could this be one of the ports? – but the dragoman had been cunning to make the issue a religious one. It was hard for girls who were themselves devout to refuse a request lodged on such grounds. 'Very well, Certezza; we shall do it, as we think it right to respect everyone's religion.' Next morning, very early, the boat sailed, having been duly delayed forty-eight hours for the captain's prayers. They reached Assouan on the following morning, after eighteen hours sailing. They could not help feeling that the Reis might have been in time to say his prayers there.

Subsequently, they discovered – purely by accident and through a chance conversation with an acquaintance who was also waiting to go through the Cataract – the real reason for the two-day delay. Certezza's son, who was dragoman on their friend's boat, had contracted to take up his party within a certain time, and stood to lose £200 if he failed to adhere to his time-charter. Certezza, wishing his son to be first in the queue for the Cataract, had devised these excuses in order to give him a good start. They also heard on the grape-vine that the rascal had no intention of taking them up at all. The moment they learned this, they tackled him about it.

'What is the meaning of this, Certezza? Why have you been saying to everyone that we are not going to the second

Cataract? If you try to impose on us, we'll take another boat today – or we'll take the steamer and go down.'

'Oh miss, you're quite wrong, quite wrong!'

'You'll not find us so simple as you think,' said Grace sternly. She had not been a schoolmistress for nothing. Certezza began to shed tears. 'You've been so kind to me,' he wailed, 'how can you think that I would act traitor like that?'

'Ah,' said Maggie, 'we know you only stayed at Edfoo to let your Giacomo get first.'

'Oh miss, what you've said has hurt me worst of all. I'd rather have my hand cut off, or see one of my sons brought home dead, than hear you say such a thing.' The question, as Humpty Dumpty once observed, was 'who was to be master, that's all.' The girls considered that they had won the campaign. When they took a walk in the afternoon, the dragoman maintained a surly silence instead of his usual lively conversation, and looked at them with a face as black as Nile mud. But the next morning, they sailed promptly. Certezza was penitent and abject, now; and when they asked him whether they could row about the rapids in a small boat, he replied, 'If you like, miss, we'll do it. I'm ready to do anything you ask me, now.'

So they came at last to the Cataract. A thick rope was attached to the bow of the boat, and some fifty men on shore began to pull it. Other ropes were attached to other parts of the craft, and made fast round the rocks. In this way they were dragged over the first waterfall. But just as they were in the very centre of the current, with the whole force of the water beating against the boat, the holding rope broke. It was a dangerous moment; but another rope was quickly thrown ashore, and the boat brought back on to the crest of the fall just in time. Agnes, who alone had remained on board, was momentarily alarmed – as well she might be – and angry with herself for courting needless danger simply to have a new experience. Her fears, however, did not show on her face, and Certezza remarked admiringly, 'I think nothing can make *you* afraid, miss!' With bumps and jolts the boat was pulled over more rocks to safety, and Agnes was relieved to have escaped without accident from the wild waters and wilder hauliers.

The end of their journey was at last in sight. Ahead lay Wady Halfeh, beyond mountains of bright-coloured sand, interspersed with streaks of black granite, which reminded the fanciful Maggie of custard sprinkled with cinnamon. In consequence of the Prince of Wales' visit, food was everywhere very dear, so they lived for several days on pigeons which Certezza shot. Their dragoman seemed to have worked with the British for so long that he had acquired one of the less admirable British habits, for every antique monument and statue which they visited in their shore excursions seemed to have his name carved upon it. Above Silsilli, they passed the Royal boats, but no one was on deck, and even Certezza's efforts to attract Royal attention by firing pistol shots in the air proved singularly unsuccessful: a curtain was raised for a second and then dropped, but no face appeared.

The return journey to Cairo was uneventful, save for a glimpse of a boat filled with slaves (recruited in the Sudan) on their way to be sold, *sub rosa*, in the capital – for the trade was by then illegal. Cairo to Alexandria, Alexandria to Jaffa: uneventful journeys by rail. From Jaffa, they rode to Jerusalem on horseback. This sounds quite a simple operation; but in fact it could be described as an expedition, for there was so much to transport – a kitchen tent (presided over by a Nubian cook, who could get up a first-rate dinner in half an hour, afte.˙ a ten-hour ride), a sleeping tent (complete with small portable iron bedsteads 'and every convenience except a looking-glass.'), and a little square tent which was always pitched for luncheon; stores of food, cooking utensils, fodder for the horses, and so on down to a Union Jack and a flagpole from which to fly it. To carry all this luggage – and themselves, dragoman, and servants – they had six horses, twelve mules and two donkeys. There was a staff of five (augmented each night by armed guards from the nearest village), headed by Armanous, the dragoman, 'a man with a very dark complexion and a very long Roman nose, whose clothes always looked as if they had been thrown on with a pitchfork. His full Turkish trousers were so long as often to make him stumble.' The girls always rode with their umbrellas up, and with white cambric scarves, put on like Turkish veils, below their white-turbaned straw hats. It sounds a remarkable entourage, suggesting a cross between a British military mission and Chipperfield's Circus. But it must be remembered that the only alternative sleeping places along the route were monasteries – which of course would not have extended hospitality to women – or tiny village inns, unlikely to have been able to cope with a party of that size and probably not safe.

Their reaction to Jerusalem and its Holy Places was much the same as that of any modern tourist, but their final expedition is of more interest: they essayed the still-hazardous journey down the lonely road from Jerusalem to Jericho. From all accounts, conditions had changed little from the days of the Good Samaritan; only the previous week, an American acquaintance of theirs had been set upon by robbers – though he had succeeded in beating them off with no more casualties than a wounded muleteer and one dead bandit. Somehow, it seemed hardly a suitable journey for three young women, but Agnes, as usual, was quite determined to go. She argued, first, that they might never again have the chance to make the trip; second, that the British Consul would certainly have forbidden them the journey if there had been *real* danger (but was he aware of their plans, one wonders? It seems unlikely); and thirdly, that a second American party had not been molested at all. When it was pointed out to her that the tourists, on that occasion, had all been men, she retorted that 'gentlemen who are unacquainted with firearms are as helpless as we.' The logic of this argument was perhaps not quite up to Agnes' usual standard; but, like most human beings, she was adept at making out a good case for a course of action she had already decided upon. Maggie sighed apprehensively, and gave in. Grace, however, absolutely declined to come. She had fainted when they had visited the Cave of Adullam (which they had been compelled to enter on hands and knees, after a long and uncomfortable ride over rocky country occupied by 'a turbulent tribe') and still felt very unwell. She did not feel up to bandits, that week.

The party, when it set out, was certainly formidable enough to give any but the most stout-hearted robbers ample cause for hesitation. First came three soldiers on foot, armed with guns and pistols, who peered into every bush and around every mound in search of bandits; next, the sheikh and the dragoman, mounted on horses and carrying guns 'at the ready' (the sheikh had a sword as well); then Maggie and Agnes, armed only with a sense of the rightness of their cause and a firm trust in Providence; and finally the chief muleteer and his assistant, each with a cocked pistol in his hand. Whenever the party came to any slight eminence, Armanous and the sheikh rode to the top ahead of the main expedition; and when they came – as they frequently did – to places where the track ran through overhanging rocks and by dark caverns, there was more careful reconnaissance, accompanied by much impressive firing off of rifles.

After all this impressive build-up, however, the journey itself proved disappointingly uneventful. If the twins had hoped for a mild adventure, with which to make the Irvine ladies' flesh creep at a later date, they were to be disappointed. As it happened, they were unaware of the most dangerous moment of the trip until after their return to Jerusalem. This was when they were encamped for the night on what was supposed to be the site of Gilgal, where the Israelites had once pitched their tents before attacking Jericho. Armanous had prudently concealed from them the fact that a party of six Arabs had been set upon there the previous night, and two had been killed. On his arrival at the site, he had found the corpses, and had hastily dragged them off into the scrub before the main party arrived (for a dragoman still rides on ahead 'to prepare a place' for his party at the end of the day: see John xiv.2, R.V. margin). He and the sheikh spent some anxious hours, and in fact had sat up all night, their guns on their knees, while the rest of the party dreamed untroubled dreams. No attack, however, occurred: perhaps the bandits spotted the 'watch'.

The only other outing worth mentioning was their visit to a harem – or, to be exact, to two – escorted by a doctor whose wife kindly took them inside. Climbing a flight of steep stairs, they were shown by a black slave into a room furnished with low divans against the walls. There, they were received by three ladies, who wore (Agnes noted) 'prettily-made gingham dresses and pearl necklaces – and, in the case of the principal wife, a handsome diamond star.' They were given sherbet and coffee, and Grace was offered a cigarette which she not only accepted but (to the indignation of the twins) smoked down to a stub without offering her companions so much as a puff. They discussed the education of women with the Effendi, and Grace hinted that European ladies, though favourably placed in some respects, were less happily situated in the matter of smoking.

They then moved on to the second harem, which was at the house of the Mufti of Jerusalem. This dignitary also had three wives, who lived in greater style, as befitting his rank. Each wife had a separate house which (as Agnes delicately expresses it in her journal) 'had the honour of lodging him by turns.' They were conducted to the home of the principal wife, 'a very lively lady, somewhat negligently dressed in scarlet muslin drawers and a yellow padded short jacket, fastened round her waist by a girdle. Her hair hung down in thin plaits, and she wore a coloured veil.' This matron informed the girls that she 'wished to be civilised', and offered them lemonade and nargilehs (hookahs). She opened an immense chest, and brought out most of her dresses for inspection. As far as they could gather, the room 'served the united purposes of sleeping, cooking and lounging.'

At this point in her book, Agnes passes to another subject. We hear no more of the harem, and are not told whether the dresses in the chest were likewise of see-through muslin; nor are we told whether Grace, emboldened by her previous experience, had a puff at the hookah.

That interesting day seems to have been the climax of the tour. Thereafter, Agnes appears to grow suddenly tired of writing. The remaining thirty pages of her book consist of rather dull descriptions and desultory conversations with fellow-travellers. The final chapter takes the reader from Damascus to Greece in sixteen pages, and from Venice to Paris in four lines. It is the experience of all who travel extensively that a day comes when, suddenly, one has had enough and wants to get home as quickly as possible. The abrupt and perfunctory ending may perhaps be thus accounted for; or perhaps she said nothing about the journey home because her scrupulous mind felt it would be improper to describe European scenes in a book entitled *Eastern Pilgrims*.

She provides us, however, with an entertaining account of an adventurous tour. It is a pity that the book is not more widely known, for it supplies an interesting contrast to the once immensely-popular writings of Lady Brassey, whose *A Voyage in the Sunbeam* (1881) went through innumerable editions, was presented as a school prize to every Victorian boy, and yet is absolutely unreadable today.

III

'Shedding one's Sicknesses in Books'

He married Agnes Smith, a writer of novels.

— *Dictionary of National Biography*:
entry for the Revd. S.S. Lewis

It has now become the fashion to assert that no work of fiction can be successful if it is written with a purpose. We think that the whole history of literature teaches something contrary. Had Milton no serious purpose when he penned *Paradise Lost*? Nor Dante when he wrote the *Divine Commedia*? . . . Did not the humour of Molière chastise a thousand follies? It matters not that some of these great writers missed their purpose: the fact remains that we should never have possessed their masterpieces had the purpose not impelled them to write as they did.

— Agnes Smith: article in *The Presbyterian Churchman*,
June 1883

Back in Irvine once more after their prolonged jaunt, what were their feelings as they slipped back into the old life? It is always pleasant to be home; but is hard to believe that they settled in happily. A decorous fling, to celebrate one's new freedom, was splendid; but what now? Long years of life

44

(presumably) stretched out before them, to be filled with . . . what? They cannot have been anything but restless and impatient to find themselves once more back in an environment where tongues would find ample material for a week's conversation in the fact that the minister had preached for twenty minutes longer than usual, or that the grocer's assistant had absconded with ten pounds from the till, or that Mrs McSumph's washing had been so spattered with smuts from the new-fangled railway engine that she had been compelled to do the whole lot over again. Apart from Dr Robertson, who would have been keenly interested to learn all the details of their trip, there can have been scarcely a person in the town with whom they could hold a conversation on topics that interested them. They could not see themselves contentedly resuming – and devoting the rest of their lives to – the activities proper to their sex and station: passing their days in endless social calls, visiting the 'poor' in their crofts and hovels, teaching in the Sunday School, assisting the Ladies Knitting Party for Deepsea Fishermen – varied, in their case, by a little learned reading in foreign languages, an occasional week in Edinburgh, and perhaps a month or two each year at some continental spa. The prospect, frankly, appalled them. If this were all they had to look forward to, their father could have dispensed with Birkenhead and London as means of stretching their minds and widening their outlook. The vociferous opponents of education for women were right in at least one respect: it certainly caused girls to become discontented with the small, restricted world in which their mothers had lived without the faintest stirrings of discontent. Agnes and Maggie were not at all clear, as yet, what precisely they wanted to do with their lives; but they were quite clear what they did *not* want to do with them. They had no intention of hibernating in the drawing rooms and Ladies' Guilds of Irvine – fond though they were of the place – now that there was no longer any filial duty to require them to do so.

They found themselves envying Grace, who already had a career of sorts and had returned to her teaching at the finishing school. Always fond of her, their shared experiences over a protracted period had drawn the trio closer still: Grace was now practically another sister. Life without her was at least one-third less fun. Since it was impossible for her to come and live with them, why should they not move to London? After much deliberation, they decided to do so. Hamilfield was accordingly disposed of in the direction of their father's junior partner, who had now become head of the firm, and they took a house in Pembridge Square, near Kensington Gardens. Such a location was convenient for Grace, who would now be able to spend much of her leisure time with them.

The girls were not averse to a social life as such, provided that it did not become a whole existence. They began, as most people did in those days, by linking up with a church. It so happened that a close friend of Dr Robertson's, a Dr Alexander MacEwan, was minister of the Presbyterian Church in Clapham Road, so this was the one they joined, and from among the congregation there, they began to build up a little circle of intimates. They conducted Sunday School classes – somehow more interesting a task than it had been in Irvine – and assisted in a soup kitchen which the kindly ladies of the church organised for the neighbouring poor. Through Grace Blyth, they met other congenial people, including her cousin, James Young Gibson, a shy gentle man in his fifties, who had recently suffered a breakdown in health which had necessitated his retirement from the ministry of the United Presbyterian Church.

But all this, though pleasant, was, of course, not enough: they needed work to do. For a time, the twins toyed with the idea of becoming scientists of some kind – science was a subject which had always interested them keenly – but the scientific world received their advances coldly. Such interests were for men, not for women. They racked their brains to think of some niche for themselves, some occupation which would turn to good account the intellectual training they had hitherto received, but, despondently, could find none. They were the wrong sex: that was the trouble. Doors which opened readily for men remained obstinately closed to them. Mulling over the problem, and in desperation for something to work at, Agnes exhumed her youthful poems from a trunk in the attic and, stimulated by re-reading them, embarked upon an enormously long (and, alas! completely unreadable) poem on the life of Queen Margaret of Scotland. It was neither an urgent nor a particularly worthwhile task; but at least it would occupy her mind until something better should turn up. By 1871, she had completed this saga, though she was not to give it to the world (greatly to the world's advantage) for another forty years.

Any hopes of marriage which the girls may once have entertained had by now faded. A contemporary of theirs, Mary Paley Marshall (the wife of the Economics Professor at Cambridge) has recorded that, in the seventies of last century, 'if a girl did not marry, or at any rate become engaged, by twenty, she was not likely to marry at all'; and the twins were now twenty-eight. Agnes, with her heavy features and somewhat forceful manner, had perhaps never cherished any very high hopes of a suitor; but Maggie had thought, at one time, that her chances were considerably greater than those of her sister – and was, indeed, even now, daydreaming a little about that nice Mr Gibson. However, it was evidently not to be, and they must make the best of it.

Leaving aside the question of age, part of the trouble, of course, was that, from the eligibility standpoint, the girls fell between two stools. In Irvine and Ayrshire generally, they were sufficiently educated and cultured to qualify as good prospective wives for some of the 'county'; but as the daughters of a mere solicitor – worse, one whose wealth had been acquired (albeit indirectly) through 'trade' – their names would hardly be on the 'eligibility list' of the local aristocratic mammas. Socially, they were only out of the middle drawer – if that. On the other hand, their own vigorous intellects would never have been satisfied with a marriage on their own social level – to some personable young farmer, perhaps, or to the son of the local bank manager. In Ayrshire, too, their wealth was an awkward factor. How could they be sure that the young men who paid them some attention were not more interested in their bank balances than in their persons? And in London, they were in no better case: obviously, they did not have the *entrée* to upper class circles – and even if they had, the same disqualifications would have applied as in Scotland. The only young men whom they did meet all belonged to Clapham Presbyterian Church. These would certainly be of their own station in life – junior partners, perhaps, in their fathers' solid and prosperous businesses, or rising lawyers at present 'devilling' for some eminent barrister, and hoping, in a year or two, to have chambers of their own – but such young gentlemen could be forgiven for eyeing the twins a little askance, as slightly formidable young women. They would hesitate to see too much of girls who, instead of sitting demurely at home doing needlework and embroidery under the eye of mamma, already spoke four or five languages and had been gadding about Europe and the Middle East *on their own*! No, sighed Agnes and Maggie, there was no doubt about it: they must abandon all thoughts of marriage. They were on the shelf for good – and a high one, at that.

What, then, should they do with their lives? Maggie had no ideas at all; but Agnes, once her poem was completed and laid aside, decided to try writing novels. If Jane Austen and the Brontës could do it, under far more discouraging conditions, surely she could. (At least she had that 'room of her own' that Virginia Woolf was later to insist upon.) She would not, of course, be able to do it with anything like the same skill – Agnes was always ruthlessly honest with herself – but, nevertheless, she ought to be able to make some sort of showing at it. So she set to work. Her first novel, *Effie Maxwell*, was published in three volumes by Hurst and Blackett in 1876, and was followed, three years later, by a second 'three-decker', *Glenmavis*, from the same publisher. Her third story, *The Brides of Ardmore*, appeared – in one volume this time – in 1880.

There is nothing remarkable about these books (though all three received favourable reviews at the time), and they are unlikely to be mentioned by any historian of the minor nineteenth-century novel; but they are of interest here, since they provide us with indications of Agnes' developing mind, and reveal the personal and social problems which were then occupying her thoughts. The first two deal with contemporary life, and would today be labelled mildly left-wing; the third had a historical subject: it deals with twelfth-century Ireland, the period in which the Papacy took over control of the Celtic Church and, among other 'reforms', compelled its priests to renounce their wives and become celibate. This book has obviously involved its author in much historical research, and so gives the first hint of Agnes the embryonic scholar. The scholarship is exact and detailed; and any statement in the text at which the ordinary reader might be expected to raise his eyebrows, is fully supported in an appendix which contains lengthy quotations from medieval writers, mostly in Latin.

We have already seen, from *Eastern Pilgrims*, that Agnes possessed some of the necessary qualifications for a novelist. She could describe a scene sharply and evocatively; she could write excellent and lifelike dialogue; had a sharp eye for idiosyncrasies of character; and could, on occasion, summarise a person very neatly in a single telling phrase. Unfortunately, she was less happy in her choice of plots and in her handling of them: these tend to be extremely involved (and, at times, improbable) and are inclined to rely overmuch upon Hardyesque coincidences and sudden deaths. What is of interest here, however, is neither the plots nor the dialogue, but the themes and the types of character which she chose to portray, the interplay between the individual and his social environment, the cramping effects upon personal freedom and personal happiness of fixed conventions and inherited traditional codes: subjects still being worked over today by novelists. There is a noticeable preoccupation, both in *Effie Maxwell* and in *Glenmavis* (and to some extent in *The Brides of Ardmore* also) with a society in process of change; a society in which old patterns of life are breaking up and giving place reluctantly to new ones; a society in which one or two individuals, spurred on by the fact that their own future happiness is at stake, fight spirited actions against an 'old guard' which clings tenaciously to the old ways, will not yield more than an inch at a time, and still possesses the power to enforce its outdated mandates. In all three novels, the central characters belong to the largest fictional group in the world: the people who are determined, whatever the opposition, to 'form liaisons out of their class' – that group which spans the history of literature, from *Cinderella* to *Lady Chatterley's Lover*. The love that inconveniently flowered between the high-born and the honest humble was, of course, a special problem of the nineteenth century; for the rising bourgeoisie, enriched by trade, was now able to buy educational* and other advantages for their children, might even manage to collect a title and a country house, and generally began to consider themselves the social equals of the decaying aristocracy, which viewed the advance of this class with disfavour and its matrimonial aspirations with dismay.

Effie Maxwell is a rich and lonely middle-class orphan (as Agnes herself was) who falls in love with the brother of a 'county' schoolfriend – a union which the landed gentry do everything in their power to prevent. In *Glenmavis*, Katherine, the only child of an 'old' family, is in love with a young baronet, fresh from Oxford, whose father is a good and generally respected (but, alas, self-made) man. The match just won't do; and, in order to prevent it, her father goes to lengths of which Mr Barratt of Wimpole Street would certainly have approved, – even to the intercepting and destroying of correspondence. Her cousin Marion is being forced into marriage with the son of the Castle, an empty headed but well-connected young man, of whom a candid friend remarked 'There are dozens of fellows in shops who would cut quite as good a figure if they had his money.' Discovering, a few days before the wedding, that he has a discarded mistress (who has borne him a child) in the village, Marion runs away to London and there marries a radical M.P. with revolutionary ideas as to how landowners should behave towards their children and tenants.

Katherine, too, marries her baronet, but at the price of forfeiting all claim to her father's estate. The same situation appears even in the medieval Ireland of *The Brides of Ardmore*. Sorcha, the granddaughter of a farmer, marries Ardal

---

* Compare Chesterton's remark that the Public Schools are not for the sons of gentlemen, but for the fathers of gentlemen.

O'Brien, a young priest of royal blood, (in the Celtic Church, priests were allowed to marry) thereby antagonising the Abbot's aristocratic wife, who had privately earmarked him for her own daughter, Mòr. This girl, who was 'too well brought up to fall in love without sufficient encouragement,' marries, in secret, an ambitious, silver-tongued cleric of proletarian origin, who thinks that his career will be greatly advanced by securing his superior's daughter. The rest of the story concerns the experiences of Sorcha and Mòr (the brides of the title) in view of the differing political and ecclesiastical loyalties of their husbands during those unsettled times. Ardal fights for the spiritual independence of the Celtic Church and the continued political freedom of Ireland (and becomes an outlaw with a price on his head), while Fergus (Mòr's husband), with his resolute eye to the main chance, goes over to the Papal invaders (who are backed by an army of mercenaries from England – 'barons more given to hunting than to holiness'), accepts re-ordination according to the Roman rite, and, to ensure the best of both worlds, passes off his wife as his sister.

It is worth pausing here, and speculating – for there is no evidence either way – whether this fictional preoccupation arose out of some personal experience in Agnes' own life. It is curious, to say the least of it, that she should return repeatedly to this theme. *Effie Maxwell*, at least in the early chapters, is quite plainly autobiographical: the loneliness of a gauche orphan, her rather remote father, engrossed in his business, her surroundings (Irvine is thinly disguised as Kilronan), Effie's experiences at boarding school – all these have obviously been written up from the inside, as is the way of first novels. Can it be that the same is true also of Effie's thwarted love-affair, of the problems facing Katharine and Marion in *Glenmavis*, and of Sorcha and Mòr in *The Brides* – save that, in fiction, all these girls achieved the happy ending which Victorian readers demanded, and which, for all we know, may have been a kind of wish-fulfilment for the author? Was she, one wonders, here recalling with some bitterness her secret love for the scion of a noble Ayrshire house, a romance which his family successfully killed – or, more likely, which the lovers themselves realised could have no future? It seems highly probable – doubly so, in that Agnes' other preoccupation in the first two novels is so manifestly a personal one: namely, the problems raised by the ownership of wealth in contemporary society. 'One sheds one's sicknesses in books,' D.H. Lawrence once wrote to a friend, apropos of his own autobiographical novel, *Sons and Lovers*, 'repeats and presents again one's emotions, to be master of them.' One is encouraged to think that Agnes is effecting a similar catharsis by the fact that she employs the Lawrentian technique: like Lorenzo, she begins not with characters who will later encounter problems and perhaps solve them, but with a problem which the author – unsure, as yet, of the 'right' answer – proposes to try and work out in terms of a group of characters. Not having his genius, she does not do it very successfully, but she makes a spirited attempt.

Her second obsession (if that is not too strong a word) is with the problem of the wealthy individual in a far from wealthy society. What, in this situation, are his or her duties? Is it enough to be vaguely benevolent, to 'do good to' the poor in a desultory and patronising sort of way? Ought such a person, really, to get rid of his money as quickly as possible – see the advice of Jesus to the rich young ruler – lest, in John Wesley's words, it should find its way into his heart? And with wealth goes ownership and power: what are the duties of landlords toward their tenants? Are these responsibilities adequately discharged when the landlord has taken the rent and has effected the absolute minimum in the way of necessary repairs to their hovels? Is not the basic trouble this, that the well-to-do simply do not realise – or realise insufficiently deeply – the responsibilities attached to the ownership of wealth? Or that, if apprehended in a vague sort of way, they are generally evaded through lack of imagination; through a certain fatal incapacity to see tenants, servants and 'the poor' as *persons*, with certain basic rights and feelings not dissimilar from those of the landlord himself? So often, it seemed to her, such dispossessed groups were viewed merely as useful appendages to an estate, like a full stable or a good kitchen

garden or a well-stocked wine-cellar, or were simply neglected because of the landlord's enslavement to money as
an end in itself (rather than as a means to usefulness in
society), or because his natural humanity was smothered by a
too-great subservience to established conventions and to
'what the neighbours will think'.

All these questions are raised in the novels, especially in
Glenmavis with its Ayrshire 'county' setting. Katharine
Leslie, the heroine, has a keen social conscience, and is
considered by her old-fashioned father to be dangerously
radical in outlook. She is profoundly shocked by the
condition of one of the tenant farmhouses, the walls of
which are running with damp even near the beds in the
kitchen:

> 'There's damp over the whole place – why not have a drain
> put round the whole house and make it thoroughly dry?'
> Mr Leslie looked up astounded. 'Why, what a turn-up that
> would make,' he said. 'It would have to be very deep.
> Davidson himself [the tenant] did not propose it, though
> of course it would improve the property.' 'And the
> family's health,' added Katharine. 'I was sorry to see the
> children's weary faces, and to hear that the mother has lost
> two of them. It seems strange that they should not be
> stronger in such fine air. I fancy if the house were dry . . .'
> 'That's Davidson's lookout!' he exclaimed, 'Let him think
> of his family. I'll take care of my property.' 'Perhaps he did
> not propose the drain,' said Katharine, 'because he was not
> aware that it could be done.' 'Then let him alone,' said Mr
> Leslie.

She discusses the problem further with Marion, when they
are preparing for bed that night:

> 'What would you like to do?' Marion asked. 'I would like
> to pull the whole thing down and build it up again,' replied
> Katharine – 'on a dry foundation, of course. It would not
> cost more than three or four hundred pounds, for one
> could use the old stones. Papa is going to spend as much on

the new conservatory. I have had a great many thoughts about these things of late. Would you like to hear some of them?' 'Certainly,' said Marion. 'Well, it seems to me,' continued Katharine, 'as if God has given us something more precious than even money or land. When people had slaves, they knew these slaves were their own, and they had a duty to them. Now of course we think of our servants' welfare . . . but there are whole young families as dependent upon us as possible for the influences under which they are reared, and yet we only think about how it will suit with our getting a fair income . . . It seems to me that people always take care to keep philanthropy out of the way of their incomes. Our own tenantry come first morally. If I am to help my neighbour, it isn't so much by making him richer as by giving him freedom to develop himself mentally and morally, so as to rise higher in the scale of being (I don't mean in society). And how can this spiritual part of anyone be developed if he is weighed down by physical ills?' 'Can't they afford a doctor?' asked Marion. 'Yes, of course,' replied Katharine. 'He can cure disease, but it's we who can prevent it by insisting on their living under healthy conditions.' 'But if you spend money on the farms,' said Marion, 'you won't have so much to give away.' 'Giving away is a luxury,' answered Katharine.

– and she goes on to point out that handsome donations to the infirmary could be better employed as she suggests, for they would considerably reduce the number of patients there.

Katharine tackles her father next morning on the subject. Asking what he proposes to have done at the farm in question, and learning that he plans no more than 'new stones in the dairy floor, and perhaps the kitchen,' she asks, 'Would you do as little if we had to live in it?' Papa can't see that that has anything to do with it, and becomes angry when she presses her question: 'Katharine, once for all I tell you, the people's health is a thing we have nothing in the world to do with. You don't know how to deal with the working classes. Be kind to them in every way you can, but keep business by itself. Once let these people think that you'll be easy in the matter of rent, and you'll see how you'll be imposed upon.' Katharine plays a trump card: 'And who is my neighbour?' she demands. Mr Leslie is momentarily shaken, but falls back on the traditional closure applied by outmanoeuvred parents: she does not know enough about the world. She goes into breakfast feeling very discouraged, but the practical Marion points out that she should not have expected her father's instant conversion, for 'to begin your ways would have been to confess that his old ones were wrong till now.'

Sir John Abbot, with whom Katharine falls in love and whom she ultimately marries, is sketched as the antithesis of her father – perhaps because, having grown up the hard way instead of being born into the aristocracy, he has a better appreciation of ordinary people's struggles; indeed, it is this imaginative quality in him which first attracts her. The two are agreed that those with coronets must also have kind (as distinct from charity-giving) hearts, or it will be the worse for their tenants:

> 'I have often thought,' said Sir John, 'that we are very impertinent to preach to the lower classes as we do. They perform their duty to us twenty times better than we do ours to them. To speak the truth, the standard we are mostly guided by is our own selfishness. It seems to me that nobody should put a spade into his neighbour's vineyard till his own is thoroughly in order. And even then he should do it with modesty, for he neither knows what weather his neighbour has to fight against, nor if a keen eye may not detect weeds in his own.'

After these admirable, if meteorologically somewhat confused sentiments – for not even in Scotland do next-door neighbours have different weather to contend with: but Sir John's mind was doubtless upon Katharine (whom he had just met for the first time) and not on his analogy – he continues:

> 'Your father is a landowner, I understand, Miss Leslie. So I hope you won't think what I am going to say is anything

55

personal. It does seem wonderful that an individual can look over a piece of this beautiful earth and say, "These fields and hills are mine." Mine? What for? Do I merely claim proprietorship over these acres to grow turnips and corn? Does the soil produce nothing else? Has not my position given me a certain power over human life: a responsibility to Providence for its due development? . . . We put property before men.' 'I have often thought,' said Katharine, 'that statesmen might learn many lessons by going among the poor.' 'Yes, if they went to learn, and encouraged the poor to talk,' replied Sir John. 'They would at least find out where the shoe pinches. But your fine ladies, who do it principally for their soul's salvation, do you think *they* learn anything? Not they!'

These opinions must have seemed dangerously advanced in 1876, especially the attack on the benevolent ladies. Such a passage is plainly very far removed from the urbane world of, say, Charlotte M. Yonge, where the *status quo* is accepted as natural and proper and of Divine ordering; and where the only revolutionary figure, in that lady's vast gallery of characters, is Dr Spencer in *The Trial*: a man with an unaccountably cranky notion that defective sanitation is the cause of disease, a view which is dismissed with contempt by his medical colleagues and by everyone else (including, it would seem, the author). This outburst in *Glenmavis* may possibly have been provoked by reading Disraeli's *Sybil* or Mrs Gaskell's *Mary Barton*; but it is more likely to be simply the fruit of her own observation and her own reflection.

If Agnes is revenging herself on the Ayrshire gentry, she is certainly doing it very thoroughly. Mr Leslie, with his scholarship in Greek and Latin, his absorbing interest in archaeology, and his tireless collation of facts about the statues he unearths, is a not unsympathetic figure (it is amusing to note the close similarities between his interests and those of the man Agnes was later to marry); but it is plain that he lives in a bottle (as the Border saying has it), in a remote world of culture and wealth and comfort, isolated from the struggles experienced by ordinary people. Never for one moment does he think of his tenants as human beings. As such, he is very unfavourably contrasted with Abbot, who has both a social conscience and imagination; who, suitably disguised, sleeps one night each week in a workhouse in order to identify himself with the poor (anticipating a best-seller of twenty years later, Whiteing's *No. 5 John Street*); and who celebrates his wedding, not by giving a ball for the bored gentry but by taking a trainload of slum-dwellers into the country for the day, and feeding them at his own expense. He at least realises that the great Victorian doctrine of Progress must be applied also to the ideas which indwell men's minds, especially at a time when the horizontal barriers of society are beginning, imperceptibly but inevitably, to crumble. Abbot does at least try to get the 'feel' of the vast social problems of Industrial England from within, and to think himself into the shoes of those whose exhausting labour and often unspeakable living conditions enable the rich, and even the comfortably-off, to have such an enjoyable time. It is clear that Abbot is the mouthpiece for Agnes' own idealism: in contrast to the 'romance' theme in these novels, where she seems to be shedding her own sicknesses, here she is (as it were) shedding her healthfulness – outlining some kind of positive philosophy of 'caring' which shall assuage the guilt she clearly feels because of the Ferguson inheritance. It seems probable that her general uneasiness, her doubt and questionings, had been increasing in pressure since she had taken up residence in London. There would be plenty of poverty in Ayrshire crofts, and in Irvine itself; but this would be nothing in comparison with what she would have seen in London. The world of Dickens and of Mayhew had not passed; and the number and condition of the patrons of the soup-kitchen run by the Clapham ladies would be of a very different order from those she had encountered in Irvine. The contrast between her own comfort and the lack of it in those who dwelt in the 'mean streets' would be immeasurably sharpened when one moved daily about a large city. Why should she have so much, and they so pitifully little? How could she exercise her growing sense of responsibility? The charity that merely hands out money to every passing beggar and then feels that duty has been done, might satisfy some: never, throughout her life, was it to satisfy Agnes. One must devise some way of giving oneself, of replacing negative handouts by a positive, person-to-person caring. As soon as one began to probe, to ask searching questions, to study what today would be called sociology-type books, one was faced with a further area of horror: working conditions. She does not explore this subject in any depth; but she notices it. When a friend of Effie Maxwell's goes into raptures over some superb home-made lace, Effie can think only of the unhappy poverty-ridden workers, becoming 'more and more feeble in health and stunted in growth, till at last their eyesight fails them, and they sink into premature and peevish old age.' And when her uncle sneers at the railway company's chairman for sitting in Parliament instead of enquiring into conditions (by which he means the conditions of safety for passengers) on the railway, Effie retorts:

'Yes, and ask the engine-driver and the signalman how long they've been working . . . What is Parliament about, that they don't pass an Act forbidding railway servants to work more than eight or nine hours out of the twenty-four? Extra pay is not the question, it's the physical balance between waste and supply. A driver can no more attend to his engine without proper intervals for food and sleep than his machinery can work without coals. I'm sure we should all travel up to London more comfortably if we knew that both driver and stoker were changed at Preston.'

It must not be thought, however, that these novels were simply left-wing propagandist tracts, as perhaps the extracts quoted tend to suggest. Most of the propaganda is implicit in the characterisation and the plot, and she is clever enough not to overload her story with didactic material, such as might induce readers – especially high-born or well-to-do readers – to fling the book aside, and so miss the broadside which she has reserved for the next chapter. In between her brief 'lessons' there are sharply-etched character studies. Observe

Katharine's mother, for example, in *Glenmavis*: here seen at the moment when she has a delicate and distasteful task ahead of her – that of breaking the news to her daughter's suitor that, if he marries her, he will be required to take the surname of Leslie for the sake of the Glenmavis estate:

> Mrs Leslie felt herself in a painful position; she felt that an explanation about some things was due to all parties. Yet how to introduce the subject she did not very well see. She wished her husband had been there; men were accustomed to the directness and explicitness of business communications, and it was always a little hard when such communications devolved on a woman. Mrs Leslie was one who had taken life very easily. She had been nursed in the lap of prosperity so long that she had scarcely felt her own weight, as it were, and had lost the power, in a moral sense, of progressing with the aid of her own feet. Her taste was rather to smooth over difficulties than to encounter and overcome them. She did not see why life should not flow easily with everyone. Most people's troubles were of their own making, she thought, and as she had never exerted herself sufficiently to create any, she fancied she had an undoubted claim to be vexed by none.

In *Effie Maxwell*, there is a quick vignette of Effie's Uncle Robert – in whom we may perhaps catch a glimpse of Holms o'Caaf? 'He was of a somewhat meddlesome disposition . . . When he entered a room, a throb went through the heart of every picture which was not hanging quite straight; and the gas flowed through the pipes with a presentiment that its purity would soon be put to the test.' And a slightly bitter description of Effie's father, which may well be a study of Papa Smith. At the time of writing, the latter had been dead for ten years; and though Agnes had been very fond of him, her ruthlessly honest eye would be perfectly capable of observing his faults:

> My father was a man who had apparently seen fifty summers. His hair was of a bright brown, his whiskers

59

red, and his eyes of that indescribable tint between grey and blue, which betokens keenness of observation without much depth of reflection . . . It seemed as if a shadow had settled down upon his face, a shadow through which one might read the tale of legitimate hopes disappointed. It was the look of a man who had not succeeded in life, and was ready to impute the blame to others rather than to himself. My father was one of the numerous class of professional men who have been satisfied with attaining to the degree of proficiency in the technicalities of law or medicine which just qualifies them for practising these arts, and who makes no further effort to enlarge their mind by the acquisition of further knowledge . . . My father was in the legal line of business, but in a very small way. Whether it was want of talent or want of opportunity, I never found out – in fact I fancy it was the former. He had never managed to compete for custom with Mr Rose, an able solicitor, who likewise resided in Kilronan. Perhaps his presence there had even been an element in Mr Rose's success. Lawyers are proverbially lost when alone. One will starve where two would thrive; and in this case, fortunately for Mr Rose but unfortunately for my father, the two were of different dispositions, and my father took up the lawsuits which Mr Rose had done his best to discourage. Some fishes must unquestionably have come to his net, for we lived in comparative comfort.

The character of Effie, with her plain looks, her intense loneliness and gaucherie, and her repeated complaints that she derives no real companionship from her preoccupied father, and the character of Mr Maxwell himself, are drawn so much more 'in the round' than are the other characters in this novel, that it seems highly likely that here we have an authentic fragment of Agnes' own childhood: a further 'shedding of her sicknesses.'

The other type of character to which she returns in each of these three novels is the careerist: the able, ambitious man of humble origin who will stick at nothing in order to further his own ends. Agnes' ironic eye is at its best when describing this type. The go-getter, whether in society, profession, business or University, is a type which naturally emerges in greater numbers from poorer countries and Agnes would accordingly have had many opportunities for examining the specimen – perhaps, in the first instance, among her male contemporaries in Clapham Presbyterian Church? It cannot be denied that the high road to London has tended to become uncomfortably crowded at times, at least when viewed through the possibly jaundiced eyes of Saxons; and her portrayal of these characters is, perhaps, a commentary upon some words which she put into the mouth of Ardal, in *The Brides of Ardmore*, spoken at the time when Ireland was becoming flooded with worldly Roman priests: 'The failings of good men have done more harm to the cause of truth than has all the malice of wicked ones.'

Olrud, the ambitious priest in *The Brides*, may perhaps be allowed to represent this type, as Agnes sees it:

> His movements were governed in the first place by self-interest. He had a notion that he might possibly triumph over these disadvantages [i.e. of low birth] by attracting some great man's notice. Nor did any constitutional timidity stand in the way of his doing this. No matter who might be present, Olrud's voice was always the first to be raised . . . To have a sense of one's own superiority is a great step towards impressing it on others, and one result of Olrud's efforts was that a vivid conception formed itself in his mind of the intensity of admiration with which everyone regarded him. Another was that . . . many of his brethren entertained towards him a dislike which they would have found it difficult to account for.

Even the advantages of marriage present themselves to him in terms of the main chance:

> A superficial observer would have found it no easy task to discover whether or not Olrud possessed a heart; yet a closer examination might have convinced him that such an organ actually existed. It was not capable of great expan-

sion, but there it was, making up for what it lacked in the way of bulk by exceeding tenacity of fibre. And it was altogether an ill-used member. It was not allowed a word until its intellectual colleague had decided on several interesting points, viz. that matrimony was an honourable estate; that it was distinctly enjoined on bishops in the Epistle to Timothy; that thirty-seven was an age when a man ought to be competent to make a wise selection; that a Christian young woman would be a help rather than a hindrance to his career; and that he, Olrud, would be neglecting his plain duty were he not to admit such an one to the valuable example and instruction to be derived from his society. After a careful scrutiny, it was resolved by all his faculties in solemn council that Grainné Ni-Ahern was likely to fulfil all the requisite conditions.

G.K. Chesterton says somewhere that the essence of the novelist's craft is the art of sympathy and 'the interplay of personalities in private . . . the study of human variations',. and that in the nineteenth century, the women novelists were more successful at achieving this than were the men. Whether or not we accept this characteristic wild generalisation – and it need not be considered inappropriate or presumptuous to quote it in the present context, since Chesterton bases his judgment, not upon the masterpieces only, but upon the whole field from Jane Austen to Ouida – it is interesting to take it as a convenient yardstick against which to measure Agnes' work. Her novels are little more than prentice efforts, revealing a very moderate talent: it does not need saying that they plainly lack the subtle interplay of emotion which is found in *Pride and Prejudice*, or the smouldering passion of *Wuthering Heights*. But it is at least equally obvious that they rate far above the comic heroics of Ouida. Whatever other defects a trained critical intelligence may detect in Agnes' work, at least there are no hairbrushes with diamond-studded backs or other palpable departures from reality. Her characters may sometimes seem a little lifeless, but even where something is lacking there is no actual falsity in what is described. One has to sink a long way down the scale before one arrives at the cheap emotions and fifth-rate melodrama of many Victorian bestsellers. Agnes may have been, at times, a little out of her emotional depth; but she was not emotionally illiterate. She was, perhaps, saved from the worst excesses of degenerate sentiment and overblown romanticism by the strong rational element in her psychological make-up, which helped her to see life as more than simply a mixture of lilies and languors, roses and raptures: that streak in her which not only gave her an intense and perhaps slightly male preoccupation with the structure of society, the limitations of accepted convention, and the unrealised responsibilities of the wealthy, but also made her capable of understanding, and sympathising with, those who took their stand upon abstract matters of principle. Duty, for Agnes as for the agnostic George Eliot, was something of overriding importance; and it was better to fight under the wrong banner – as Mr Leslie did, for example, in his harsh treatment of his daughter's love affair – than to imagine that banners were of infinitely less importance than the arrows of Cupid. Whether the issue at stake was one which she felt to be right (as in the resistance of the Ardmore community to the Papacy), or one she felt to be wrong (as in the totally unreasonable demands which Mr Leslie made of his prospective son-in-law), Agnes could understand it and make it seem compelling: something at least equal in importance to the claims of the heart's affections. She could even appreciate, and make plausible, that stubborn pride in the family honour which could be entertained even by the son of a self-made man such as Sir John Abbot, and could contrast it favourably with that empty, exaggerated, merely conventional 'family pride' of the county families.

It would be foolish to overrate her achievement: from the extracts quoted in this chapter, the reader will have been able to 'place' her in the novelists' form-list. The passage dealing with Olrud's musings on the subject of matrimony provides a fair sample of her strengths and weaknesses. The amateurish, roundabout opening, and the slightly arch continuation – these are weak; the ironical development, stage by stage as Olrud ponders, from scriptural beginning to selfish end, from biblical injunctions – observe he is already aiming at a bishopric – through career prospects to the egotism which takes it for granted that he will be conferring a great blessing on some female – this is much more skilfully done. If Agnes abandoned novel-writing at this point, it was almost certainly for two reasons. First, she had done what she had set out to do – to clear her own mind about the duties of the moneyed, to say certain highly critical things about the snobbish judgments and outdated codes of the "old families', and to say them in a medium which would ensure that her views reached the womenfolk (who all read novels, but would certainly never have read articles in serious periodicals) of that stratum of society to which she had, she felt, certain important things to say. And secondly, because her mind was sufficiently critical and honest to realise that, for all her talent in the handling of words, she was plainly insufficiently gifted to make this particular form of intellectual activity her life's work.

What field she should choose in its place had not yet become clear to her; but at least she had "shed her sicknesses in books', was now much more aware where her duty lay in the administration of her large fortune (and what principles should guide that duty), and was rather closer to a solution of the problem of vocation than Maggie was. But then Maggie had other things on her mind: she was not drawn to attempt descriptions of imagined emotions for the very excellent reason that her own heart was, by this time, busily trying to cope with ones that were alarmingly real, and which left her in a state of considerable uncertainty and no little confusion.

PART TWO

Mrs Lewis and Mrs Gibson (1883–1891)

IV

The Broken Column

At game of chess a gallant Scot I see,
A gifted lady is his *vis-à-vis*;
His knowing smile appears the game to slight,
He thinks it pastime, and no earnest fight.
Yet in the picture, lo! a *third* I find,
Who hovers gently and unseen behind.
It is the God of Love, on mischief bent,
Who eyes the players with a sly intent.
He marks the play, and then begins to think,
He wags his head with many a roguish wink;
And so contrives the game, in curious whim,
That she must 'mated' be, yet conquer him!

> – Lines written by James Young Gibson under a
> photograph of himself and Maggie playing chess.
> The picture hung in Maggie's study in Castlebrae

For the time being, then, travel and private study continued to be the two focal points of the twins' lives. Agnes and Maggie had none of the easygoing hedonism which so swiftly corrupts the wealthy. They had not yet discovered their *metier*, but they had all the puritan horror of idleness: the time of waiting must be profitably used. In 1878 they wintered in Mentone, not, as most of their contemporaries did, in order that a butterfly existence might be continued under a more azure sky, but so that they might be sufficiently free of social engagements to learn Spanish; and, on their return to London in the spring, they proceeded to embark upon the study of Greek under Mr Vice of King's College. Mindful of their father's principle that, when one had acquired some knowledge of a language, one should forthwith visit the country where it was spoken, they set about planning a trip to Greece.

In this instance, however, there was a slight complication: the pronunciation of modern Greek happens to be quite different from that of the written, classical language. Mr Vice, like all good classicists, viewed with horror the suggestion that this sacred tongue should be bracketed with mere living languages like French, German and Spanish; so they set about obtaining an introduction to Professor John Stuart Blackie (he lived less than a mile from their house) who had just been appointed Professor of Greek at Edinburgh, and who had been known to dismiss the notion that Greek was a dead language as 'an Oxford superstition'. From him, the girls duly acquired the modern pronunciation, and, their appetite already whetted by a brief visit to Athens at the close of their Middle East tour, they sailed for Greece in the New Year of 1883, bent on a more leisurely and detailed study of the country and its antiquities. Grace Blyth (who apparently experienced no difficulty in obtaining leave of absence from the finishing school whenever she wanted it) went too.

The Bay of Biscay is notorious for its skill in reducing the size of the human ego. On this occasion it lived up to its reputation by providing the twins with the worst storm for many years. Their vessel – the Orient liner *Iberia* – had a very unpleasant time; but at least the ship did not founder, the fate of a vessel with which they kept company for two days. It was fortunate that their previous travels had inured them to a little hardship and discomfort, for they were surrounded by broken skylights, wounded stewards and hysterical women passengers. However, they derived great comfort from the fact that the Captain was a Scot – and therefore, in their patriotic eyes, a man who might be assumed to be equal to all emergencies – even, if necessary, shipwreck.

The gale raged with a fury unparalleled in the experience of the ships' officers; but the girls remained unflustered and cheerful. Their luggage careered wildly about on the floor of their cabin, as the vessel rolled and pitched; and a small crate of wine with which they had provided themselves shuttled from one end of the room to the other, fetching up with an alarming thud every time it hit the bulkhead. Whenever they entered or left their cabin, they had to dodge this dangerous missile, and to watch its contents being steadily reduced (after the manner of the nursery song) from twelve green bottles to seven. The scene recalled to their minds Victor Hugo's description of the loose cannon in the hold of the man-of-war. One night, Maggie, exasperated by the bangs and crashes which rendered sleep impossible, leaped angrily from her upper berth and tried to secure the crate. She had just succeeded in pinning it in a corner, and had lifted it up preparatory to wedging it under the berth, when a sudden heave of the ship precipitated her and the claret on top of Agnes, who experienced an alcoholic's dream of a rain of bottles. Eventually, however, they managed to secure it, and returned to bed, tossing uncomfortably about until the dawn showed them, through the thick glass of the porthole, the waves looking 'like gigantic alps of ice'. After forty-eight hours, during which the Captain turned the bows of the ship to face the storm – so that they headed temporarily for New York instead of Gibraltar – the gale blew itself out; and they were able, at last, to sit down to a meal served by pale, bare-footed, shirt-sleeved stewards, some with bandaged arms and heads, and all red-eyed from lack of sleep. It was a matter for thankfulness that they were still alive: that the saloon was somewhat draughty because all the skylights were broken was a very minor inconvenience. Two days later, with the sea like a millpond, and the blue Mediterranean sky overhead, and the passengers lazing beneath awnings on deck, it all seemed as remote and improbable as a nightmare.

At Naples, they transferred into an ancient Messageries Maritimes vessel, thanking their stars that they had not been called upon to weather the gale in such a decrepit tub. A few days later, they sailed peacefully into the Piraeus.

From then until the beginning of June, they travelled round Greece in their usual tireless fashion. They spent some time with the Schliemanns, Sophie helping them with their 'modern Greek' pronunciation while Heinrich prepared for his next excavation, on the island of Nera in the Bay of Salamis. They climbed Hymettus (Agnes overdid it, and was compelled to rest for a whole week), inspected innumerable monuments and antiquities, and were regularly peered at (during meals and even when they wanted to sleep) by the entire female and juvenile population of the various villages in which they stayed. In fact, in order to eat at all it was frequently necessary to lock the door of their room. In the smaller villages, their beds were invariably alive with bugs (later satisfactorily stupefied with Keatings' powder), and their sleep disturbed by barking dogs, who performed tirelessly until it was time for the dawn chorus of cocks and doves to begin.

Their peasant hosts, however, were friendly and kind, qualities which more than atoned for their unfamiliarity with soap and water. The trio visited several monasteries, discussing theology with the Priors, and at one were touched to find a little rosebud placed by each of their plates at dinner. Adventures, somehow, always seemed to come their way. Riding everywhere on horseback, they were forever fording dangerous streams; and one day, on a narrow mountain track, Grace's horse took fright, attempted to bolt up the steep hillside, threw her, and rolled over on top of her. But such incidents did not disturb them; they merely provided them with sensational material for their diaries. When it was time to leave Greece, they came to the conclusion that the popular conception of the Greeks as a lazy, feckless lot, and Mark Twain's insistence that they were simply thieving rascals, were both very wide of the mark.

They returned home by way of various continental watering places, where they 'took the waters'. Agnes was already having twinges of that persistent rheumatism which was to prove, in later life, such a nuisance to her. This seemed a good opportunity to do something about it. Marienbad they found to be full of matchmaking Jewish mammas, all proudly displaying their wares and furtively inspecting those of other middle-aged couples. It was also full of a great number of very stout people. 'Whatever other virtue there may be in its waters,' Agnes writes, 'there can be no question as to their efficacy in reducing corpulence. The Russian princess who is daily to be seen at our one o'clock *table d'hôte* claims to have lost no less than thirty pounds during the three weeks that she has partaken of the Kreuzbrunnen . . . As you take your morning stroll along the Promenade, you cannot help observing some specimen of humanity who looks as if he had just been disinterred from the depths of a wine-vault. His flabby form has become as round and ponderous as one of his own musty casks. He is quite unequal to the task of fetching his own glass from the fountain, and may be found at any hour of the day helplessly reclining in the same chair. In a week's time he has disappeared . . . But after two days he suddenly starts up under his favourite tree, somewhat diminished in bulk, and actually trying to balance himself in a slouching sort of way on his feet . . . By the time he leaves to seek his 'after cure' in the Upper Engadine, you could scarcely recognise his former ponderous figure in that of the strong active man who steps so briskly into the hotel omnibus.'

At Toeplitz, they were shocked by the sight of peasant women carrying heavy loads while their husbands stood around doing nothing; and at Ischl, by 'human beings doing the work of donkeys' – carrying stout patients for miles in a sort of sedan chair called a 'sessel'. This spectacle raised Agnes' temperature almost to the level obtaining in the 'Inhalation Room', where men and women, enveloped in stout mackintosh mantles and hoods and 'looking like familiars of the Inquisition', dutifully perspired amid whirling funnels of steam.

So, at the beginning of September, they came to Wildbad, a small town nestling amid the pine-clad hills of the Black Forest, secluded and romantic. 'Romantic' is certainly the operative word, as far as the trio were concerned: for, here, they were met by Grace's cousin, James Young Gibson, who, entering wholeheartedly into the spirit of the place, married Maggie on September 8th.

Who was this James Gibson, so far glimpsed only in passing, that he should enter the story in so abrupt and unexpected a fashion? It will be remembered that when Grace had introduced him to the twins, he had been in process of regaining his health after his premature retirement from the United Presbyterian ministry. At that time, he had been in a very depressed state of mind, weighed down by a sense of utter failure; and it may well have been that he had found Maggie's sympathetic, understanding nature provided exactly the balm he needed for his wounded spirit. The two had, indeed, become engaged for a short time, but the engagement was subsequently broken off, James feeling that, with his precarious health and persistent melancholia, he was no match for a young and vital girl some seventeen years his junior.

Gibson was a man of extremely sensitive and highly-strung temperament. In order to understand him, it is necessary to know a little of his personal history. He was the fourth son of a prosperous grain merchant in Edinburgh, and had been delicate from birth – so delicate, indeed, that his mother, despairing of rearing him in a city, had sent him when only fourteen months old to the home of an uncle in the country, in the hope that a long stay there might strengthen his slender hold upon life. He remained with this uncle until he was six, when she brought him home; but she herself died when he was ten, and his father did not remarry. James was sent to the Academy at Bathgate, an arrangement which necessitated his being 'boarded out' with strangers for the remainder of his schooldays. It will therefore be seen that Gibson had had the same kind of lonely, love-starved childhood which Maggie herself had experienced. But whereas Maggie had Agnes, James had no one. The lonely, hyper-sensitive man, lacking the tough hide of his more fortunate rough-and-tumble contemporaries and devoid of all self-confidence, had never recovered from this experience of childhood rootlessness; in those years, after all, a person's emotional pattern tends to be established, and it is in that period that he gains, or fails to gain, that sense of security and that practice in loving and being loved which is the basic need of every human being. As he grew older, his health varied from indifferent to very poor indeed, and he was periodically subject to moods of the blackest depression.

That he entered the ministry at all was the result of his father's strongly-expressed wish. It was not easy to go against Papa's wishes in the forties of last century, least of all in Scotland; and perhaps he sensed, behind this command, an affectionate desire to protect him from the hurly burly of a business life. So, after a year at David Livingstone's old school in Essex, and the necessary training at Edinburgh and Halle Universities, he was licensed as a preacher of the Gospel in 1853. His troubles, however, were not yet ended: to be licensed was one thing, to be called to a parish was quite another. Like so many pathologically shy men of his time (and many exceptionally dull ones, too) he became a 'stickit minister': year after year went by, but always he failed to commend himself to congregations as a suitable person to be entrusted with a cure of souls. This experience naturally sapped still further his small stock of self-confidence. Eventually, however, after several years delay, he was called to a parish in Melrose.

By this time, the puny, weakling child had grown into a huge man, six feet tall and correspondingly broad of shoulder. His portrait reveals a well-shaped intellectual brow and a wealth of curling light-brown hair which fell on his shoulder in waves, giving him the appearance of an Old Testament prophet. (He was once stopped in St Margaret's, Westminster by a total stranger who commented upon his remarkable likeness to Shakespeare.) To his ministry, for all his unsureness of himself, he brought considerable gifts: a sound College record as a scholar, a well-stocked and deeply-cultured mind, a fine poetic instinct, a gentle, sympathetic nature, and genuine religious convictions. His temperament was naturally mystical, as is evidenced by his translation of the seventeenth-century Latin poem *O Deus ego amo Te*, which contains much more warmth and feeling than the more familiar version by Edward Caswall. He had clearly found in those lines an echo to his own thoughts, a summary of his own experience.

But more than such furnishings of mind and spirit are needed, if a man is to become a useful minister, and to find satisfaction and enjoyment in his work. He requires a certain toughness and resilience of spirit, a sturdy indifference to criticism, misunderstanding and foolish gossip, a fundamental confidence in himself which remains unshaken in the face of opposition to his ideas and decisions. These qualities James Gibson did not possess. His congregation thought highly of him – nor was this appreciation confined to those hopeful young ladies who, admiring from afar his handsome appearance, and feeling their maternal instincts deeply stirred by his known delicacy of health, crowded into the choir in hopes of a special smile or encouraging word. But the demands of the ministry in sheer nervous and physical energy proved to be more than his frail constitution and psychological make-up could stand. He hated being so much in the public eye; and he found the conduct of services, and the constant preparation and delivery of sermons, a very heavy emotional strain – particularly as his scrupulous determination to give of his best often drove him to sit up the whole of Saturday night, re-writing, revising and re-polishing his material. With his strong literary bent and his fastidious artistic conscience added to his strongly-marked sense of responsibility towards those who would be his listeners, he put far more work into his sermons than their necessarily-ephemeral nature required: to paraphrase Wilde's epigram on Pater, at midnight he would insert a comma, and at 3 a.m. he would take it out again. A congregation composed, not of Edinburgh University students or literati but of small-town shopkeepers, farmers and housewives, hardly needed such scrupulous ways of working. These good, plain folk might, admittedly, be much more educated, reflective and discerning than their English counterparts at that period; but they were plainly not the kind of congregation to which, say, John Donne had preached – people with a fastidious literary ear, alive to phrasing and critical of every cadence. Their concern would rather be for theology, solid and sonorous and with sound practical applications for the market or the wash-tub, preferably set forth under three heads. Given such fodder, they would have been quite satisfied.

But one who, by his temperament and training, has become accustomed to giving exact expression to his thought and a high literary polish to his work can no more go back on that way of composition than a chartered accountant can revert to counting on his fingers: stylistic padding, hasty writing, threadbare religious clichés, empty rhetoric – all these belong to a stage which he has long outgrown. For his fastidiously high standards, James Gibson paid the inevitable price. Not even an iron constitution could have stood up indefinitely to such late hours, scanty sleep, and constant over-driving of a too-sensitive nature. It is scarcely surprising that he broke down. His nerves were too close to the surface, perpetually exposed to the wounds inflicted by well-intentioned but blunt-spoken people, accustomed to the rough forthrightness of the market-place. Opposition, even of the slightest, he took far too much to heart, ever ready to believe that his judgment was faulty and his vision of the truth mistaken; criticism – the lot of any man in a public position – plunged him into the blackest despair and self-pity, so that the sore place festered for weeks. There is a story of his meeting one of his congregation, a tough blunt farmer, on one occasion, and being told that his advice was wanted on a matter of conscience. 'Supposing I send a sample of grain to your father,' began the man, 'and he agrees to buy so many quarters: am I bound to send according to sample?' 'Of course,' replied Gibson. 'Well, when you stood as a candidate here, you preached without the paper,* but now ye've ta'en to it: is that according to sample?' The farmer departed in triumph, chuckling heartily at the way in which he had caught the minister. But Gibson was deeply upset and, in the lowest of spirits, brooded anxiously upon the matter for days.

A man of that type always suffers inwardly and in silence. A wife might have saved him, for she could have banished his loneliness, built up his self-confidence by her love, and have put into proper perspective the trifling setbacks of the

---

* i.e. without any manuscript in front of him. It was considered a weakness, in those days, for a minister to deliver his sermon from a prepared script. The view was that such a method revealed an unwillingness to rely upon the Holy Spirit.

daily round. But he had no wife, and was not to have one for another quarter of a century, by which time the Melrose years had become no more than a scar on the surface of his spirit – healed, but still tender to the touch. He had to fight his way through, alone, as best he could – conquering 'sturdy doubts and boisterous objections', as Sir Thomas Browne had done, on his knees. It is greatly to his credit that he stuck it out for three years.

At the end of this period, his father died. Feelings of filial sorrow struggled in Gibson's heart with regrettable emotions of joy at the prospect of release from his bondage. His father's death meant that he was no longer under any obligation to fulfil his wishes – or, perhaps, to do him justice, that his resignation could no longer bring pain and disappointment to the old man. So he resigned from his charge, and for weeks revelled in the sense of freedom. Through his head ran the words of that Metrical Psalm which he had so often sung with his people:

Even as a bird
   Out of the fowler's snare
Escapes away,
   So is our soul set free;
Broke are their nets
   And thus escapéd we . . .

From his father he had inherited a comfortable income, which would enable him to pass the rest of his days in pleasanter and less demanding occupations. But his exhilaration and relief were soon succeeded by the most extreme depression. He was burdened by a sense of failure; he felt an apostate; he had set his hand to the plough, and then had turned back – a course of action condemned by Scripture in the very strongest terms. He saw an emblem of himself in the broken column which adjoined his family's grave-plot in the Dean cemetery in Edinburgh – beginning to rise to a height, and then snapped off short.

But after a few months, the mood passed and he set about finding something pleasant to do. In the spring of 1865, he went with some friends to Cairo, and thence embarked on a somewhat adventurous expedition through the Long Desert to Jerusalem and Damascus, spending three days in the Monastery of St Catherine on Mount Sinai. Though his engagement to Maggie had been terminated, he remained on very friendly terms with the Smith girls and wrote regularly to them from Palestine urging them to visit the same scenes. It is interesting to recollect, as one of the strange ways in which the pattern of our lives is woven out of stray threads, that it was his enthusiasm for the Sinai Monastery which, twenty-seven years later, prompted Maggie and Agnes to make their remarkable trip there, with the discovery that followed from it. To return, however, to James. He thoroughly enjoyed his long holiday – collecting wild flowers, making innumerable sketches, acquiring a little Arabic, and being thrown from his camel.

For the next few years, his inner restlessness kept him continually on the move. After visiting Italy and being present at the opening of the Suez Canal, he made his way, in 1871, to Spain. The Spanish visit was the result of gentle persuasion from an old friend of his, Alexander James Duffield, the translator of *Don Quixote*. Duffield, who had learned Spanish in South America while working as a mining chemist, dragged Gibson all over Spain and talked endlessly about Cervantes and the jouster at windmills. Gibson began to find himself sharing his friend's enthusiasms, and, when Duffield was suddenly summoned home by telegram, he remained behind, settled in Madrid and began to learn Spanish. Soon he was trying his own hand at translation. After six weeks work on *The Despairing Lay of Chrysostom* from *Don Quixote*, he had achieved quite a passable translation. He wrote to Maggie: 'It was capital practice – it is certainly the crabbedest bit to translate in the whole book, and it gave me such a headache at the time that I declined afterwards having anything more to do with it. And so there it stands, with all its uncouth rhymes hanging about it in indelible print.' But Gibson, as usual, had underrated his own ability. His translations had considerable merit, and his subsequent renderings of *The Cid Ballads* for long remained the standard ones. These, however, were to come later; at the moment, he concentrated upon translating all the songs in *Don Quixote* as a help to Duffield, who at that time was engaged upon his three-volume rendering of the whole novel. These verses (says Duffield in his preface) 'are of great difficulty. They are not of the ordinary kind of poetry which authors of fiction incorporate in their writings: the Spanish critics pronounce them to be unintelligible, perhaps for the reason that they are the productions of various kinds of madmen.' So James had found a small field – or perhaps it would be more exact to say a window-box – of usefulness.

In the autumn of 1880, his engagement to Maggie was renewed; but all his hesitancies and doubts about such a commitment returned at the same time. In her Memoir of her brother-in-law, Agnes writes: 'The marriage was delayed until Mr Gibson's health should be in some measure re-established: and he seldom allowed himself to look to the future with any degree of hope. His life was to be, in his opinion, a short one, and at the best but a struggle against increasing pain and weakness.' This statement, however, should not be taken at its face value. It is certainly the official version, given to interested friends at the time and reinforced by Agnes with the dignity of print. But there exists another explanation, written in old age by a ministerial friend of his, which suggests that the real reason for delay was that Gibson was so sunk in melancholy and self-pity that he failed to realise that his continual postponement of marriage was placing his fiancée in a very invidious position: one that was, not unnaturally, causing her considerable mental and emotional distress. Maggie (reports this friend) 'felt the indefinable delay'; and, to 'put all doubts at rest', commissioned Dr MacEwan (the twins' Clapham minister) to interview Gibson with the object of discovering how the land lay and precisely what his 'intentions' were. One seems to see the hand of Agnes behind this bold and unconventional course of action. She was always one for grasping the nettle.

Dr MacEwan bravely undertook this delicate diplomatic mission, taking with him, for moral support, the minister to whom we are indebted for the account of the incident.

MacEwan saw Gibson alone, while his colleague interviewed the doctor-proprietor of the hydro where he was staying, with a view to collecting precise information as to the state of the patient's health. Evidently the doctor's reports were reassuring, and Gibson was made tactfully aware of his duty, melancholia or no melancholia: for the outcome was, as we have seen, a wedding at Wildbad. Dr MacEwan, for all his diplomatic skill, must surely have spoken very plainly, or Gibson would hardly have gone rushing across Europe to annex Maggie instead of waiting to be married by the good Doctor in Trinity, Clapham, when the girls returned home.

Such, then, was James Gibson, and such the curious circumstances of his marriage: a marriage which, though not by any means to be called a shotgun wedding, had, at least, a little friendly pressure behind it. Apart from his Hamlet-like indecision and his acute neurosis (for such it evidently was), he had much in common with Maggie: the same lonely childhood, the same gentle sensitivity, the same artistic and linguistic interests, the same religious allegiance. In spite of the great difference in their ages, the marriage proved to be an extremely happy one.

They lived for a year at a hotel in London, alternating with a Spa at Tunbridge Wells; and in the spring of 1884, took a lease of a large house called Swaynesthorpe on Ditton Hill, near Surbiton. It stood in four acres of ground, and had previously belonged to C.T. Studd, a well-known cricketer and evangelist of the time. What was to become of Agnes? There was never the slightest doubt about that: naturally, Agnes would go and live with them. 'Whom God hath joined together, let no man put asunder' may be said to summarise Maggie's attitude.

Marriage clearly did James a great deal of good. Feeling secure and loved for the first time in his fifty-seven years of life, he came out of his shell and left behind him for ever his depressed moods. Agnes, indeed, says that she found one of his chief characteristics 'his faculty of looking at things from the humorous side . . . not in the jovial fashion which compels attention, but unobtrusively . . . as if the speaker delighted in fun for its own sake,'

With all-embracing charity to move
A listening world to laughter and to love.

– to quote from a poem which he wrote about this time.

The James of Ditton Hill is a very different person from the James of Melrose days. He had left the storms behind him, and had cast anchor (as he no doubt would have expressed it) in the quiet peace of his domestic harbour – wandering contentedly about his garden, playing daily games of chess with his wife, and translating, first, Cervantes' *Numantia* (which he published in 1885) and later the *Cid Ballads* (published posthumously by the twins). There was, indeed, only one thing he did not do which, from our knowledge of his character, we might have expected him to do: attend church. Though both Agnes and Maggie joined the Presbyterian Church at Kingston, and attended worship every Sunday, James never accompanied them – though he was on excellent terms with the minister, a frequent and welcome visitor to his home. Did he fear, perhaps, the possible effects of the familiar metrical psalms upon his lightly-sleeping conscience? Of all the arts, music is the most powerful at evoking the past, the most insidious and adroit at moving the emotions; and perhaps the slow, measured beat of the Old Hundredth constituted a threat to his peace of mind which he could not face. Was he afraid that, caught up in the old once-loved rhythm of worship, some division of the sermon, some verse of a lesson, some phrase in the Prayer of Confession, would bring him suddenly face to face with the accusing angel with the flaming sword, who would demand to know why he had deserted his post and abandoned the souls committed to his charge? He felt, probably, that he could not afford to risk imperilling his new tranquillity of spirit, vainly sought for so long and achieved finally at such a heavy cost.

Marriage seems to have suited Maggie, too; although as a spinster of forty, it must have entailed a considerable revolution in her habits. But there is in existence a photograph showing her seated on a fine chestnut horse outside the front door of Swaynesthorpe: her light-coloured riding habit is relieved by a dark scarf at her neck, and, from under the topee-like hat which is tilted over her face, her expression is peaceful and contented, though it has not entirely lost the Smith severity.

As for Agnes, she was now, technically speaking, a guest in her sister's home. The Victorians took very seriously the priority of status accorded to married women; and her new circumstances reduced her from her previous position of half a householder (or perhaps three-quarters of a householder, since she took the lead in most affairs) to no position at all. No doubt she took her full share in the ordering of provisions, in controlling the domestic staff, and in planning what entertaining they should do; no doubt she was consulted by Maggie upon all important matters, from the diet of the dog to the renovation of the kitchen range; neverthless, the final responsibility for such everyday affairs was no longer hers. It had passed to a Man. For the first time in her life, and in spite of Maggie's tactful efforts to make her feel that nothing was changed, she felt a little out of things, with rather more leisure than she was able to use.

This state of affairs she set about remedying. Her first move was to bring Grace down from London. It was time she gave up that school job anyway. The twins bought a house for her in nearby Kingston, and installed her in it. She would be excellent company for Agnes, who could now go for long walks with her along the Surrey lanes and over the Surrey hills. But, delightful though it was to have their 'honorary sister' (as they called her) once more close at hand, more was needed: fresh intellectual activity. Agnes began to take lessons in Hebrew from the Presbyterian minister at Kingston, the Revd. Thomas Anderson. (It is interesting to reflect that, but for Maggie's marriage, Agnes might never have tackled the language in which she was to become something of an authority.) Her next step was to set herself to write a book about their tour of Greece, a task which occupied much of her time during the second half of 1883 and the early months of 1884. This was published by Hurst and Blackett towards the end of the latter year, under the title of *Glimpses of Greek Life and Scenery*, and illustrated by some of

Maggie's sketches. It was very well received by the critics, and was at once translated into Greek by a certain Dr I. Perbanaglos, whom they had met on their travels. The Greek edition sold very extensively, and had a good deal to do with the cordial reception which the sisters subsequently received in cultured Greek circles; for it vindicated the Greek character, praised the virtues of the Hellenes, and generally helped to offset several savagely-critical books which had recently appeared about that country, such as that by M. Edmond About. As further practice in Greek, Agnes then embarked upon the translation of a little book on *The Monuments of Athens*, by P.G. Kastromenos. This book, she felt, would be very useful to European travellers who might have only a few days in which to inspect that city's antiquities. It had the virtue of combining the maximum of information with the minimum addition to their luggage.

It should not be imagined that Maggie allowed marriage to put an end to her intellectual activities, either. While James was busy with his Spanish poems, and Agnes with her guide-book, she set herself to translate *The Alcestis* of Euripides. James could help here, for not only was he a sound classical scholar, he also had some experience of the special problems involved in translating poetry. Lines which obstinately declined to 'come out', or which, after endless recasting and repolishing, still stubbornly refused to sound like anything but a metrical psalm at its worst, she submitted to her husband.

In mid-September, when they went away (without Agnes) for a little holiday at Ramsgate, they took the manuscript with them to work on in the evenings. They were both tired, and ready for a break; August had been especially hot and enervating that year, and James' brother Willie and his family had stayed at Swaynesthorpe for a visit which had been protracted far beyond the expectations of their hosts – so that they had got practically nothing done on the *Alcestis*.

They were delighted to find that their room at the Grand Hotel was spacious and airy and, the first evening, they set to work on the play, in which they had reached line 379. This particular line, where Alcestis says to Admetus

82

O children, when I should have lived, I die

particularly defeated Maggie: her translation, as it stood, was cumbersome and prosy. James agreed to have a look at it, but could suggest nothing better than

Children, when I should live, I go

– which really wasn't much better. They agreed to sleep on it, laid the manuscript aside, and went to bed. This was on the thirteenth of September.

The next day there was an autumnal chill in the air, and the wind blew cold. By the time they returned to the hotel, it was evident that James was not well. He retired to bed, and the doctor, hurriedly sent for, diagnosed a touch of pleurisy, though not a serious one. The following day the patient seemed to be recovering satisfactorily, but towards the evening he had a sudden relapse and became unconscious.

Agnes was wired for, and came hurrying down to Ramsgate. The doctor's second diagnosis was more grave: he inclined to think, now, that the symptoms might be those of tuberculosis. Mr Gibson's condition, the twins were told, was serious, but not desperate; there was no immediate cause for anxiety. On the Saturday, however, while Maggie was snatching an hour's sleep after being up all night with him, and Agnes was out shopping, he had a sudden spasm and, shouting 'I'm dying – fetch my wife!', lasted only long enough to die in her arms. On the table by the bed, among the medicine bottles, lay the manuscript of the *Alcestis*, still open at the page of their last revision:

O children, when I should have lived, I die

– at which Admetus exclaims

Alas, what shall I do alone without thee?

It was all too apt.

V

Satan – and the Sorrows of Satan

We are all in part weavers of our own destiny. Although the warp of our surrounding circumstances may be prepared for us, it is we who unquestionably form the pattern of it. The process is carried on, for the most part, unconsciously: we are not aware what important issues may depend upon our most trifling actions. But certain times come when the pattern must be definitely chosen, when the shuttle of our desires stops a moment from its incessant darting, and we hesitate before we let it slip forth to form the first stitch of a new design.

Agnes Smith: *The Brides of Ardmore*

Maggie was completely broken down by her loss. To have waited so long for happiness, and then to have it snatched away again after such a brief period – it was too cruel. She could understand, now, the feelings of her father when she and Agnes had been born, and the excitement of their arrival had been followed almost at once by their mother's death: the sun had burst forth from behind clouds, and then had been instantly eclipsed, leaving him in perpetual darkness. Perhaps there flashed into her mind a phrase from one of Dr Robertson's sermons: 'a gloomy day, fit for the funeral of a hundred kings.' Yes, the darkness was as impenetrable as that: small wonder that her father had been silent and preoccupied and moody for the rest of his days, living as he did under perpetually louring skies. Bereavement did strange and terrible things to you: part of you died, and stayed dead – and what remained alive was alive only in name, for you lost all capacity for feeling. The nerves and the heart, exhausted, sank into a kind of coma. It took the full drive of the will to go on living at all, and there seemed little purpose in making the effort; for life without James was futile and meaningless – and, unlike her father, she had not even a baby to care for, by which to remember the one who was gone. Her father must often have seen his dead wife momentarily resurrected in some gesture or sudden smile or toss of the head on the part of one of the girls: but she had nothing. Those lines in the *Alcestis* – the last which she and James had revised – kept running through her head: 'Alas, what shall I do alone without thee?' – and Alcestis' reply: 'Time will console thee.' Never, she thought, never, never, never.

'I hardly left Maggie a moment for months after James Gibson died,' Agnes was to write, years later, to a friend, apropos of a suddenly-bereaved mutual acquaintance who, in her view, 'should never be left alone. She is very much broken down, but she may recover if she could interest herself in something fresh.' She was recalling, at that moment, her own desperate efforts to bring Maggie back to life. Facing her sister's drawn white face across the oak dining-table, she racked her brains to think of something that would 'take Maggie out of herself.' It was clear that she was in no fit state, as yet, to undertake a long continental tour; it was equally clear that she had lost, for the time being, the power to concentrate upon study (the *Alcestis* had been pushed away in a drawer of her desk, where it was to remain for more than a year). Where could they go? What could they do?

Suddenly, just after Christmas, she had an inspiration: Cambridge! It was easily accessible; it was a historic and beautiful place; and among the manuscripts and treasures of the ancient colleges, they would surely find *something* that would quicken Maggie's sluggish pulse? When Agnes put forward her idea, Maggie displayed no interest at all; but she agreed, apathetically, to accompany Agnes, who had hastily invented something she wished to look at in connection with her Hebraic and Hellenic studies. Accordingly, the last fortnight of January 1886 found them installed in The Bull Hotel in Trumpington Street. They spent most of each day visiting acquaintances or being escorted round the various colleges by the Revd. J.F.E. Faning, the Chaplain of King's College. The shuttle, though they did not know it, was 'slipping forth to form the first stitch of a new design.'

On the 31st – the last day of their stay – Mr Faning, aware of their scientific interests, led them to the Geological Museum. This, however, proved to be closed that day, so, after a moment's rapid thought, he suggested the Library of Corpus Christi College as a possibly acceptable substitute, pointing out that it contained much of interest, including a unique collection of manuscripts and early printed books which had been bequeathed to the College by Archbishop Parker in 1575. Arrived at Corpus, they found that they were once more out of luck: the library, too, was closed and the door locked. Mr Faning's reputation as a guide, which had hitherto stood high, plunged as violently as that comet which had startled the world a few years previously (and about which, incidentally, Maggie had written a sonnet). But he was determined not to be defeated twice in the course of a single afternoon, so, murmuring excuses, he went in search of the Librarian, leaving the twins somewhat uncomfortably perched on the topmost of the twenty-odd steps which led to the Library. He was away for nearly half an hour. Maggie and Agnes grew impatient; and not only impatient, but also bored and cold. They were extremely tired. They had tramped dutifully round Cambridge for a fortnight, absorbing knowledge, and, had they at this point felt the need for a period of quiet meditation, the cold hard stone step of a draughty College staircase in mid-January provided neither 'the time nor the place nor the loved one,' to misquote Browning.

They had just come to the point where they felt these objections were, so to speak, fundamental, and had decided to abandon their guide to the wrath of the Librarian – who would certainly not be in the best of tempers when he found he had been fetched for nothing – when Mr Faning returned, accompanied by a Corpus scholar bearing the key. Bringing up the rear of this procession, and at a distance that served to enhance his importance, like an archbishop about to consecrate a cathedral, appeared the Librarian himself, his features bearing plain marks of reluctance and impatience: like all scholars, he was not partial to interruptions. However, he managed a charming smile when Faning introduced him to the twins as the Reverend Samuel Lewis.

He was an ugly little man, whose most conspicuous feature was a large black beard which was the very reverse of closely-trimmed, and which, indeed, reflected to the full the prevailing doctrines of individualism and *laissez-faire*: every single hair could be observed striking out resolutely on its own, and being allowed full liberty to do so. He looked, indeed, more like a Nihilist conspirator than a don. His dress, too, was unusual: when not in cap and gown, Mr Lewis invariably wore a suit of black cloth and a broad-brimmed hat and – disliking the white tie of a clergyman – replaced this on weekdays by a little black one. This last item (for his was a punctilious and exact mind) was intended to make clear the fact that, though a clergyman, he held a lay office. Not everyone, however, was astute enough to draw the correct inference: he was often mistaken, by library visitors, for a College servant (and rewarded with a half-crown tip – which he accepted with aplomb, and put into Library funds) or even, when away from Cambridge, for a Wesleyan minister (the ultimate insult for an Anglican clergyman).

But to return to Mrs Gibson and Miss Smith and their aching feet. The Librarian gave them a courteous welcome and, leading the way inside, began to explain the Library's treasures. The first showcase contained the Canterbury Gospels, said by tradition to have been given to St Augustine by Pope Gregory and the copy upon which Archbishops of Canterbury still take their vows at their enthronement. Here, a lively argument began as to the true method of pronouncing Greek. The discussion, of course, was inconclusive, but led to the discovery of mutual tastes and interests – classics, archaeology, travel — and a number of common acquaintances in cities abroad. It took them a long time to get past the first showcase. When the twins finally took their leave, Lewis invited them to visit his rooms the following morning, so that they could be shown his private collection of antiquities. In the gathering dusk, they said goodbye to each other in Greek (no doubt variously pronounced, according to their respective principles) and went their way.

Nine o'clock next morning found the twins being piloted by the porter across Old Court, under an arched doorway and up a low wooden staircase to Lewis' 'set'. 'Come in: wipe your feet!' was the unexpected reply to their knock. When they entered, Lewis apologised, explaining that most of his visitors were undergraduates, who lacked a proper respect for his excellent carpet. The sisters looked around them in astonishment. They had been prepared for the rooms of a scholar, but hardly for a museum. The walls of his study were lined with bookcases, every flat surface of which was crammed with Greek and Roman vases. In the centre of the room, on a large table, was set a model of a prehistoric lake dwelling, almost engulfed by a tide of papers which had, indeed, overflowed onto every available chair. Windows on one side looked out onto Old Court, where undergraduates were strolling, and on the other onto the graveyard of St Bene't's Church, enabling Lewis (as it were) to keep an eye on the future and the past simultaneously. He led his visitors through the rest of his 'set', part of which consisted of an immensely long gallery which, it appeared, had been built in the late fifteenth century to connect the cloister of St Benedict with the adjoining church. This, too, was laid out like a museum: pictures of ancient Greece and Italy crowded the walls, interspersed with plaster casts of intagli, bronze plaques of cameos, statuettes of Greek marble and, on the desk below the window, an illuminated missal of great beauty. He led them down a little stone spiral staircase, past a window which looked directly into the church, to a sort of crypt lined with shelves on which were ranged Greek vases, terra cotta lamps, spears, knives and fishhooks. His bedroom contained five large cabinets of coins — another of his interests

– and vast quantities of signet gems, some stuffed into jamjars, others scattered over the windowsill and even the dressing-table. (The gems, today, are more decorously arranged in showcases in the Library.)

Samuel Lewis was very much the don. Living in what Caroline Chisholm was then describing as 'the demoralising state of bachelorism', he had been a Fellow of Corpus for more than twelve years, after a youth so troubled by ill-health and failing eyesight that he had twice been compelled to abandon his studies and go and work in the open air on farms. He was almost thirty before he completed his studies and took his degree. The son of a leading London surgeon, and the grandson of a Principal of Brecon Theological College, he was a quiet and studious man, with that fussy pedantry and slightly old-maidish air which is so easily acquired by bachelors after the age of forty, particularly when they inhabit academic groves. Showing some American visitors his treasures on one occasion, he gently reproved them for referring to him as an antiquarian: 'What have I done that you should consider me an adjective?' he exclaimed, 'I thought I had some claim to be a substantive!' His method of giving a tip to a tradesman was equally characteristic. Whenever a man came to regulate his gas-fire (a new-fangled invention: his was one of the first in Cambridge) he would ask, 'Are you interested in coins?' The man, puzzled but suspecting this was 'a question expecting the answer Yes,' as the Latin grammars say, would confess that he was. 'And do you collect?' On being assured that he did, Lewis would hand him a five-shilling piece, saying, 'Then add that to your collection!'

If he was eccentric, it was only mildly so by Victorian standards. His oddities, apart from the black tie, took such innocuous forms as invariably wearing white socks (fully displayed because surmounted by half-mast trousers), and filling all his pockets with loose signet gems of considerable value, which invariably fell out at an inconvenient moment – for example, when a railway porter was carrying his overcoat, or as he was passing through Customs. He was noted for his kindness to impoverished students, and he would adopt transparent little devices in order to help them, such as borrowing an undergraduate's book and returning it with a twenty-pound note concealed in its pages. When the alarmed student came rushing back with it, Lewis would blandly disclaim all title to it and express himself as completely mystified as to how it had got there.

The Corpus undergraduates nicknamed him 'Satan', less by reason of his ugliness than because of a remarkable legend which is recorded by the historian of the College. It seems that, in the course of a wedding in St Bene't's Church, the bride suddenly shrieked out 'Satan!' and fainted. When she revived, she pointed with trembling finger and horrified eyes to the small window which looked into the church from Lewis's staircase and declared that she had seen the devil peering down at her. The story got around, and from then on he was 'Satan Lewis'.

Like the twins, Samuel was an indefatigable traveller. His favourite opening to conversation, when abroad, was to produce picture postcards of Cambridge and show them around, explaining (by signs if necessary) that this was where he lived. With educated fellow-travellers, this was invariably a successful gambit and one that clothed his insignificant figure with a new dignity; but among the lower orders it was less successful, and only once did it elicit an excited response. A French shepherd recognised the word 'Cambridge' with enthusiasm, embracing Samuel warmly and explaining that this hallowed town was the domain of a noted sheep-breeder.

Lewis' college was to have one very tangible reminder of his travels. From one of his visits to the Middle East, he returned bearing a palm tree, which he persuaded the College authorities to plant in Old Court. The undergraduates, however, disapproved strongly of this exotic addition to the local flora. Under cover of night, they uprooted it and replanted it upside down, affixing to the trunk a card bearing the legend 'PALMA SATANICA BOTTOMUPPERMOSTICA'. The tree was discreetly removed (probably to the Botanic Gardens) and was never seen again.

Such was the twins' new acquaintance. The friendship ripened with such speed that before they took their leave that morning, they had invited him to come and stay at Swaynesthorpe for the first part of the Easter vacation. In the course of this visit, they discovered that their respective families were acquainted; that the twins had spent six months of their childhood at Wrexham with people who proved to be his cousins; and that his sister Jane had for a short time been one of their schoolfellows at Birkenhead. When he left, he invited them to come up to Cambridge for the University Musical Society's concert at the beginning of June. Thereafter, as Agnes put it with Caledonian delicacy and reticence, 'events led to our engagement' (which took place on August 4th). The next month, Samuel joined Agnes and Maggie for a holiday at Entretat, on the Normandy coast.

As is so often the case with those who fall in love late in life, Agnes had fallen hard. Samuel spent only five days at Swaynesthorpe, that Easter vac., but in that time she had written a schoolgirlish poem on her lover's eyes:

Oh, what is the hue of the windows two
Whence the captive soul doth peep?
Lo! some, like the sky, are a gentle blue
And some are like violets deep;

Some (the poem continued, taking the reader upon a kind of conducted tour through a museum of lovers' eyes) are like grey clouds, some brown as the nuts and leaves of autumn, some black as the 'coals that wait/ To burn with a wondrous fire'; but Samuel's

. . . have the sparkling sheen
Of the calm yet restless sea;
So clear and bright, I have never a sight
Of all they would say to me.

Miss Buss and Miss Beale might not feel Cupid's darts, but Agnes (to the reader's astonishment and incredulity) was, it seems, more vulnerable.

They make a curious pair, these two, viewed down the vista of the years: far more curious than James and Maggie

Gibson. For James Gibson, in spite of his neurosis, was plainly a lovable and even attractive man, whereas Samuel Lewis (one would have thought) was equally plainly *not*. What had our lovers really in common, beyond unusual plainness of feature, a fondness for travel, and strong views on the proper pronunciation of Greek? Agnes, for all her forty-five years of spinsterhood, was quite free of those fussy, old-maidish ways which were Samuel's most noticeable characteristic; though her interests were scholarly, she was no pedantic splitter of hairs, as Samuel plainly was; she did not live more in the ancient past than in the vigorous present, as this man, seven years her senior, seemed to do; above all, she had a lively sense of fun, whereas he, it would appear, was totally devoid of any sense of humour.

Two sentences from one of Agnes' novels possibly suggest an answer to the enigma: 'Modern science', she writes in *The Brides of Ardmore*, 'has taught us that substances are capable of very unexpected combinations; a component part of one material being sometimes inexplicably attracted by some component part of a neighbouring one. Human beings, perchance, have the same capabilities of adjustment.' The inference is that she considered their identity of tastes as sufficient basis for a marriage. But more significant is the other quotation: 'There is a gratitude for being loved which most women feel, and it is often quite sufficient to marry on.' Was Agnes, perhaps, deeply affected by the sudden and overwhelming devotion of this insignificant little man? And did the old maid in him respond to the strong male streak in her, so that together they made up male and female, but in a different way from the usual combination? Perhaps she was a kind of mother-substitute, with her taller stature and her more ample proportions and her obvious competence to deal with everything and everybody.

But possibly the explanation is much simpler: they were both lonely people, who desperately wanted to be loved. It sometimes happens that, when two such people meet, each releases something in the other which has hitherto been imprisoned – so that a relationship which begins in mutual interests and kindly attentiveness passes swiftly into love.

Each responds to the warmth which the other bestows and in gratitude and release pours out more warmth and love, so that each, for the first time, feels secure – and, in that security, the whole personality suddenly blossoms, like a rose transplanted from a windswept bed to a sunny and sheltered corner. What might be called a virtuous circle is set up, to the benefit of both parties. In the end, we must be content to leave the mystery unsolved. But, though physical attraction in the accepted sense – such as often promotes strange unions among the young – must surely have been absent in view of their riper years, yet it cannot have been wholly an intellectual relationship, fashioned exclusively out of mental affinities, or Agnes would never have burst forth with those romantic poems on Samuel's eyes, nor would Samuel have contemplated abandoning his pleasant, independent bachelor routine at the age of fifty-two. In view of their respective ages, they could simply have remained close friends, even in those days; wagging tongues would surely have found little scope there.

Agnes and Samuel were married on 12th December 1888 by the Master of Corpus, Dr J. J. S. Perowne, in the parish church of Long Ditton. The benediction was pronounced by Archdeacon Philpot who, at ninety-seven, was the oldest clergyman in the Church of England, and who might perhaps be said to symbolise Samuel's antiquarian interests. As they drove away from the church, Samuel made only one remark; but it was highly characteristic both of himself and of his age: 'Agnes, let us try to distribute happiness, and then we shall be happy ourselves.' Not even the bitter weather of a December day could damp their spirits: 'there are some days' (Agnes had written in one of her novels) 'so bright as to efface all recollection of a hundred cloudy ones that have gone before. It is a happy instinct of our nature to be impressed by these, and to treasure them up so as to extract sunshine from their images in the midst of after darkness. Such a day had been this one.'

From the day of her marriage, Agnes signed herself 'Agnes Smith Lewis' (in full) and Agnes Smith Lewis she remained, on the title-page of all her subsequent books, and on her death certificate too.

It was at this point that the inseparability of the twins took a new and startling turn. When the newly-weds set out for a honeymoon tour of Greece, Maggie went too. Even Agnes could not fail to recognise that this was an arrangement which would occasion raised eyebrows among their friends, for she writes: 'It was my wish that she should do so, for I could not bear the thought of leaving her in her desolate home.' One wonders what Samuel's views were; but as he had already invited her to share their home in Cambridge, it was merely antedating an agreed arrangement.

Thus began a curious three-cornered establishment. The Corpus undergraduates did not need to rack their brains for long in order to find a suitable sobriquet for their don's household, for Marie Corelli was soon to publish a novel with the very title for their purpose. Agnes and Maggie were forthwith labelled 'The Sorrows of Satan'.

Some five years previously, when the University had made a new (and in the opinion of many, a dangerous) departure from the custom of centuries by permitting dons to marry, several enterprising local builders had been quick to turn the situation to their own profit by erecting streets of roomy houses to accommodate the newly-domesticated Fellows. One of the pleasantest of these was Harvey Road (respectfully named after the discoverer of the circulation of the blood), which ran from busy Hills Road, by which Cambridge is entered from the south, to Gresham Road and the wall of Fenners Cricket Ground. It was a quiet enclave, lined with spacious flat-chested houses of yellow brick (since weathered to a dirty grey by ninety years of fen fogs) with large solid front-doors approached up flights of wide stone steps. Samuel and Agnes moved into No. 2.

A distinguished colony was already in occupation of this road, for it was still relatively on the edge of the town and, to the south, only a sprinkling of houses stood between Harvey Road and the distant Gog-Magog hills. At No. 6 lived Dr and Mrs J. Neville Keynes, whose little boy Maynard had just begun to attend the Perse School; other residents included Charles Villiers Stanford, the Professor of Music; Sir Richard Tetley Glazebrook, the eminent physicist;

Professor and Mrs Alexander Macalister, who were to become close friends of the twins; Mr and Mrs F.C. Burkitt, whom we shall meet again later; J.P. Postgate, the classical scholar; Mr Boughey, a Fellow of Trinity; and Mrs Bateson, widow of a Master of St John's.

For all its air of studious calm, Harvey Road had its enlivening moments. Residents were regularly entertained, for instance, by the spectacle of the Professor of Music, standing at the top of his steps and shaking his fist and swearing savagely at the itinerant organ-grinder, who insisted upon distributing his canned music, *urbi et orbi*, – encouraged to remain by the pennies which the children of the various dons threw down from their nursery windows. On fine summer afternoons, a more solemn spectacle would meet their eyes, as the Reverend Augustus Austen-Leigh (the 'Austen' came from Jane's family: she was his great-aunt) proceeded down Harvey Road on his way to Fenners. Being both Provost of King's and also President of the University Cricket Club, he sought to do honour to both offices by invariably wearing, even on the hottest day, a top hat and morning coat whenever he watched a match.

The Harvey Road families formed a closely-knit little community. 'We had a common tennis ground,' (writes Mrs J.N. Keynes, recalling those days) 'now covered with houses and small gardens, but then a field where we had two grass courts which subscribing families had on certain days, and to which they could invite friends. We also had a book-club: any member could order any book, and when a fair number had returned from circulation we held a club meeting and the books were put up to auction. Both these clubs were due to my husband's initiative, and the book-club meetings always took place in our house.' Professor Macalister's daughter recalls a form of exercise which supplemented the tennis, but which, however, was confined to the garden of the Lewis house: the twins bought a trapeze and a set of parallel bars, and on these objects they were wont to disport themselves whenever they felt they needed exercise – an astonishing and unforgettable sight, surely.

Agnes' marriage did not disturb the twins' close friendship

with their 'adopted sister', Grace Blyth, any more than Maggie's had done. The Giblews (it is time we began to use their Cambridge nickname) were not like those women, sometimes encountered, for whom friendships with their own sex are no more than a *faute de mieux*, a convenient stopgap until such a time as the appearance of a husband relegates their former intimates to the list of those whom one 'simply *must* have to dinner sometime'. Grace had been part of their life for twenty years now, and continued to be so. They had transplanted her from Kensington to Kingston when they had set up house in Swaynesthorpe; now, she must come to Cambridge that they might continue to see as much of her as formerly. As her means were slender, the twins bought a house for her in Trumpington Street (Douglas House, it was called: it is still there), installed her in it, and settled £10,000 on her, that she might be able to live in comfort. Thereafter, she was always in and out of the Harvey Road house, and was to be, subsequently, a frequent visitor to Castlebrae. If she appears little in this chronicle henceforth, it is not because she was quietly 'dropped' – far from it – but because there is nothing special to report about her (there were no more holidays together) until old age rendered her slightly eccentric, and a 'Grace saga' of anecdotes was added to the Giblew saga of oddities.

One of the curious features of Agnes' marriage was that Samuel was hardly ever at home. It was as well that she had her sister and Grace to keep her company, or she would certainly have felt desperately lonely; for by the terms of his Fellowship, Lewis was required to reside in the College for five nights of every week, and almost every weekend he was away taking duty for clerical brethren in distant parishes. The couple could be sure of a daily hour and a half together, (for he always came home for lunch) and, twice a week, a second hour (when he also came to dinner): but that was all. This was scarcely married life as Agnes had envisaged it, and she quietly set about making discreet alterations in his timetable. She suggested that it would be pleasant if he came home to breakfast on the days when he had slept in College. This he gladly agreed to do, arriving precisely at eight o'clock (so precisely that a family in Regent Street used to regulate their watches by his passing), and departing in time to be in his rooms again by 8.45. Agnes' next plan was that she should accompany him on his weekend visits, for the rectories were usually empty; but some of the parishes were so inaccessible that an exhaustingly early start was necessary on Monday morning, if he were to be back in Cambridge in time to do a full day's work. Elsewhere, there were clergymen's wives who did not care overmuch for the idea of a strange woman being given the run of their home in their absence. Eventually, a compromise was arrived at: he would accept engagements only on alternate Sundays, and then, for preference, in reasonably accessible villages to which he could take his wife. 'Our Sundays in country rectories are almost the only reminiscences of married life which I have now to look back upon,' writes Agnes, a trifle bitterly, in her Memoir of her husband; with his month's annual holiday in September (which they always spent abroad), these weekends provided the only opportunities for 'that interchange of thought which is so desirable between married persons.'

Was Agnes disappointed with her marriage? She must have been, though she was too loyal to admit it. At this distance, Samuel's behaviour seems unbelievably selfish; but, if we are to be fair to him, it must be remembered that, at fifty-four, a man can be very set in his ways and resent any disturbance in his pattern of life. It is common for bachelors of long standing to imagine that, after marriage, life can go on as usual, with the comforts of a wife simply added to all those activities with which one has hitherto filled in the lonely days. And, in Lewis' further defence, it would be charitable to point to his over-developed bump of conscientiousness, and his absolute obsession about time. To him, time was precious, a God-given gift, and to waste it was a grievous sin. He once rounded angrily on a man who was slightly late for an appointment, exclaiming 'You have made me waste four minutes of my life!' It was not merely that he had much to do: it was, rather, that in the forefront of his mind loomed, always, the memory of the long wasted years of his youth, when ill-health had kept him marking time over such a protracted period – a debit balance which he could only work off by driving himself over-hard in the span that remained to him.

For work he certainly did. We have seen that, after walking the three quarters of a mile from Corpus to Harvey Road for breakfast, he would be back in his rooms by 8.45. At 1.30, he would be home again to lunch, but back in College by half past two, dealing with his foreign correspondence. Out again to catch the 3.30 post; back to College in order to show visitors round the Library; out again at dusk, to look up some bachelor acquaintance, returning for College dinner at six – or, if he dined at home, he would be in College again by eight o'clock, to dictate letters to an amanuensis, with whom he would work until ten. Out to post these letters, then back to his desk to write more letters until the small hours. He was secretary of the Cambridge Antiquarian Society, a responsibility which involved him in a heavy mail. This society met on Monday evenings, an additional burden after a weekend of travelling and preaching. Samuel's strength was further sapped by his being a poor sleeper. His wife thought this affliction might well have some connection with the state of his College bed, and an inspection confirmed this. The spring mattress proved to be so dilapidated that there was a hole in the centre 'the size of a large fish-kettle' (Agnes' description) which allowed only a narrow ledge as a resting place. For years he had absolutely forbidden his bedmaker to have it repaired, but Agnes would brook no arguments, and it was replaced by a new one. If he were to lie awake for half the night, let it as least be in comfort.

In the year after their marriage, the Lewises and Maggie spent their September holiday in France, visiting Lourdes among other places. An article which Agnes wrote on her return reveals that, beneath her stern Presbyterian principles, she possessed a catholicity of spirit which enabled her to appreciate the good in ceremonies with which she was otherwise out of sympathy. She was as greatly touched by the piety of simple people – 'the spontaneous outcome of a living zeal' – as she was unimpressed by the officiating priests, who were 'not remarkable for the intellectual expression of their faces'; and as for the theology of their sermons, anyone trained, as she had been, by Dr Robertson would inevitably be repelled ('the most ingenious perversion of the Gospel we have ever heard': this in reference to the constant theme that the Virgin gave her Son to appease the wrath of an angry God). They made the acquaintance of a French priest, who kindly acted as their guide and introduced them to some of the invalids and ex-invalids. With an acuteness of perception that anticipates the psychosomatic discoveries of a later day, Agnes notes that 'the cases which are most often cured at Lourdes are those of paralytics and blind people. The former we can well understand, seeing that the nerves which govern locomotion are so much affected by mental emotions.'

In December, they went to Algeria for the whole of the Christmas vacation, inspected Roman remains and had one or two mild adventures. They came close to sharing the fate of Shelley when out at sea in a boat which was struck by a sudden powerful gust of wind. Samuel, who was holding the sheet, took too long to work out what the old fisherman (who was steering) meant when he shouted 'Arrivez!', and the boat, which had heeled over dangerously from pressure on the sail, was on the point of capsizing when Maggie snatched the sheet out of his hand and slackened it a split second before disaster. On another occasion, more amusing, they had been given the wrong departure time of a steamer they had planned to take from Algiers to Bougie. They arrived to see the ship departing. Their boatman put out in pursuit . . . Agnes jumped for the gangway steps and landed in a heap . . . Maggie, scared to leap the widening distance, let out a wail 'not unlike that of a cat which has lost its kittens' (Agnes' words) . . . and it looked as though Agnes were going to Bougie alone. Characteristically, she marched to the bridge and demanded to see the captain, waving aside imperiously the officers and crew who tried to bar her way. The captain was in a bad temper, not improved by the sight of a woman invading his private territory; but our heroine, as usual, carried the day and the ship put back for the others.

Agnes and Maggie had to share a cabin with a nun, who absolutely declined to open the porthole, even for an inch. But, outnumbering the enemy like the rabbits in the fable, they got their own way – and were thanked in the morning by the nun, who had slept more soundly than usual. This holy woman slept in her habit, and her morning toilet consisted of rubbing her face with a dry towel. The twins were perturbed to discover that she was a nurse, on her way to take charge of the hospital at Bougie. Plainly Florence Nightingale's reforms had not yet percolated down to religious communities.

On this holiday, Agnes assiduously collected snails for the wife of a Cambridge professor who was making a special study of them. These she housed in a small basket, furnished with semolina. Her French friends, for all their national devotion to snails, thought her enthusiasm peculiar, as well they might – particularly as the creatures kept escaping and wandering around in unsuitable places. But she managed to bring some back to England. It makes a pretty picture to imagine: Samuel and Agnes, in their smartest clothes, calling one crisp January afternoon on the wife of the eminent professor, carrying between them a basket of live snails which were subsequently released in the drawing-room. Quite a conversation piece.

Their strenuous life, in which holidays were as exhausting as work, continued for several years, but the details of their activities would be tedious to read. Let us therefore skip on to March 1890, when a fourth character was added to the group in the shape of their newly-built house, Castlebrae. Samuel had chosen the site (which was at the opposite end of the town from Harvey Road, on the lower slopes of Castle Hill) shortly before his marriage, and the house was partly of his own designing – though he scarcely set foot within the gates until the building was completed. There will be more about this roomy mansion, standing just past St Giles' Church in Chesterton Lane, later; for it is with the twins in their long years of widowhood, rather than with Samuel, that it is naturally associated – and it is their spirits which brood over its lofty rooms still, in spite of the fact that it has been a

College hostel now for almost sixty years. 'Lampada tradam' [Let me hand on the torch] was the motto which they caused to be set, carved in stone, over the baronial front door: in view of its present usage, they may be said to have succeeded in doing so – a kind of apostolic succession which would certainly not have been maintained if it had passed, like so many large houses in this century, into the possession of the Borough Treasurer or the Regional Gas Board. Beneath the Latin motto was hung a huge wrought-iron lamp, which they had brought back from the Holy Land and had previously hung over the door of Swaynesthorpe. It is still in the porch of Castlebrae to this day.

Shortly after they had moved in, the Lewises travelled to Normandy to attend the wedding of the brother of a French agriculturalist whom Samuel had befriended, many years previously, in the days when they had worked together on the Royal Norfolk Farm. Agnes returned home convinced that there was more to be said in favour of arranged marriages than Saxons were willing to admit: for one thing, the system eliminated 'outrageous flirtation and evident husband hunting by *jeune filles* guests at the wedding breakfast', and on similar social occasions; for another, 'the French system gives more of a chance to girls whose lot is cast in lonely places, in remote districts destitute of congenial society, or in attendance on invalids.' There is surely a note of wistfulness, a faint undertone of bitterness, here. Such a 'lot' had been hers. In retrospect, she wished the English custom had been for Papa and Dr Robertson, perhaps, to select some pleasant young man for her, and thereafter (in Lin Yutang's phrase) to allow the cold kettle to become slowly warmed up by the stove. It was comforting, of course, to have dear Samuel, even if it were only for two hours a day and for alternate weekends, but she had had to wait until she was forty-three before she met him – and but for Gibson's death would never have met him at all. Looking at the bride and bridegroom who, even if they had been brought together by a go-between, obviously delighted in one another's company in more than an intellectual way, Agnes must have felt that this was an experience she had missed: an experience of which she had been deprived by a society that did not care that she had missed it, and saw no necessity for changing its customs. From this deprivation flowed others, even worse. She, like Maggie, was childless.

By the time the Long Vacation came, Samuel was very tired indeed; but he declined to take his usual brief June holiday and, instead, carried his 'Sorrows' off to an Antiquarian Congress in the South of France. The weather was intensely hot; they were involved in endless exhausting expeditions to remote excavations; their stomachs were compelled to cope with buns out of bags during the day and huge formal banquets in the evening; and there were, of course, interminable papers by scholars to be endured. No sooner were they home than they had to cope with entertaining visiting pundits, in Cambridge for some conference, and with arranging and leading a long-distance expedition by the Cambridge Antiquarian Society; then, in September, they dragged themselves, utterly weary, to Cologne for the Old Catholic Congress, from which they returned only in time for the beginning of the Michaelmas Term. The Christmas vacation, which should have been a rest, had been earmarked some months previously for an Asia Minor tour.

By the end of the Lent Term, Samuel was beginning to look, and to be, thoroughly exhausted. Agnes grew uneasy. Though Samuel drove himself as hard as ever, and retained his enthusiasm for every undertaking, it was plain that his reserves of energy were fast dwindling. Only when there was a dinner-party did he spend an evening at home; and even on these occasions, he was often too tired to make pleasant conversation, but would excuse himself and retire upstairs to rest, leaving the Sorrows to entertain the visitors. But he declined to abandon his weekend preaching expeditions, and nothing could turn him from the early start on Monday morning which would enable him to put in a full day's work on his return – even though his Sunday had invariably involved him in taking four services single-handed and preaching three times. His obsession with the stewardship of time increased rather than diminished, and he could not be induced to slacken his pace.

At Easter, they went to stay with friends at Somerton Rectory, near Oxford, where he was undertaking duty. On Good Friday and Easter Day, he preached at his best and, though obviously very tired, was in exceptionally high spirits. On Tuesday, they began their return journey, which they broke several times in order to see friends or inspect local antiquities. At Oxford, there was a forty-minute wait for the connection. Samuel installed Agnes in the refreshment room with a cup of tea, and dashed off into the town to see an acquaintance. Agnes drank her tea and read her newspapers (several of which were in Greek and Arabic) until Samuel returned. At the last possible moment, just as the train was leaving, he rushed into the station and flung himself into the carriage. Agnes opened her Arabic newspaper, and asked him if he could identify the place shown in one of the illustrations. He glanced at it for a moment, then made a gesture of impatience, and leaned his head on the back of the seat. An expression of uneasiness came over his face, and he closed his eyes; from his throat came a low gurgling sound.

It was the end: the indefatigable traveller had set out on his last journey. The punctilious steward of time had been rewarded with 'desarts of vast eternity'.

PART THREE

Dr Lewis and Dr Gibson
(1891–1926)

VI

The Case of the Remarkable Butterdish

Isn't it fun when you can quote from something no one else has access to?

– Agnes Smith Lewis:
letter to Rendel Harris, 17 July 1894

So Agnes returned, alone, to Maggie and to the vast empty house in which, like two eighteenth-century patrons of scholarship and letters, the twins were to hold court for the remainder of their lives. '*Vae victis*!' Samuel had written in his diary on the very first night that he slept in 'the hillside hut', as he always ironically called Castlebrae. Who, one wonders, were the vanquished to whom woe was vowed? Agnes, who came upon the entry some months after his death when she began collecting material for a memoir, always maintained that he had been referring to his own carefree, untidy bachelor habits – those bohemian ways which were henceforth to be as strictly regulated as any stream which dares to enter a German park. He had always insisted that his wife had 'destroyed the Spartan simplicity of his life', as wives will. But had this been his meaning, surely his wedding day would have been the fitting occasion on which to make the entry? It seems more probable that he was thinking of himself and his 'Sorrows' in the context of their new surroundings. Life in Harvey Road had been quiet and uncomplicated, whereas now they must grapple with all the complications of a large establishment: increased entertaining, new problems of staffing – at one time, there were as many as eight 'below stairs' – and the planning and oversight of a large garden.

But viewed from the Olympus of ninety years later, the words take on a more ominous meaning – a meaning pregnant with that dramatic irony which Maggie at least, as the translator of Euripides, would have appreciated: the victim, though he did not know it, was Samuel himself. Even while he pronounced a mock doom upon the twins, the Fates had observed his untidy figure and had begun to sharpen their shears. The victors of the darkling plain were to be, once again, Agnes and Maggie; within a year of writing that entry in his journal, Samuel was to slip away for ever – vanquished, like James Gibson before him, by that abiding passion of the sisters for each other: a subject, perhaps, upon which the two husbands may have exchanged rueful reflections, as they leant together on the golden bar of Heaven.

With the death of Samuel, Agnes, who had always taken the lead in everything, now found herself the pupil and Maggie the teacher in what their contemporaries would certainly have described as 'the school of sorrow.' She had shared Maggie's grief, and now Maggie was to share hers. For all the little time that Samuel had spent in Castlebrae, his spirit brooded over its sombre portals. Had not the Greek texts painted over the doorways of the dining-room, drawing room and kitchen been of his composition? Lunch became an oppressive meal, now that the shaggy beard was no longer bent over the soup. Agnes' eyes wandered to the intertwined initials 'A & S' which were carved on the oak mantelpiece. (They are still there.) For the first forty years of their lives, the sisters had been alone together; and now, after eight brief years in which each had tasted marriage in turn, they were alone again. The wheel had come full circle.

Years may roll, like rivers by us,
Death and change may come too nigh us;
 Oh may trouble only tie us
  Two in one

– Agnes had written to Samuel, in a poem composed on their first wedding anniversary. Well, it was still her prayer; but the 'two' were now the original two. Samuel had gone; but Maggie, thank God, was still there, a strength and a comfort, as she had always been. They must try to resume the old ways, enriched in spirit by the new experience of darkness and desolation.

How should they set about this? Well, thought Agnes, leaning back in her desk chair and gazing through the study window at the empty drive, she must take her own medicine – the medicine which she had prescribed for Maggie a few years back: new sights and scenes, fresh interests that would wholly engage the mind. Another tour abroad, and a good long one at that, and to some place where there would be opportunities for concentrated study: that was what she needed. Why should they not make the long-projected and long-deferred trip to Mount Sinai, now that there was no longer any necessity for them to be back in Cambridge in time for the beginning of Term? She had often broached the idea to Samuel, but he had always replied with a smile, 'You may visit it after I am gone.' But ever since their girlhood days they had dreamed of walking, one day, in the steps of Moses and the Israelites. She had fully intended travelling thither in 1866, when she and Grace were in Egypt. But though James had insisted for years that they simply *must* visit St Catherine's Monastery* at the foot of Sinai – so full of interest were the contents of its library for the studiously-inclined – he had, on that occasion, written strongly discouraging the trip, pointing out that Cousin Grace lacked the immense stamina of his sister-in-law; so the idea had been

---

* Agnes always gave it its proper title of 'Convent'; but since that word, in popular usage, has come to be used exclusively to describe a community of nuns, I have ventured to replace this word by the more usual one.

abandoned. But the place had continued to exert its fascination; and their dormant interest had, indeed, been awakened only two years previously, when Samuel's Quaker friend, Rendel Harris, had returned triumphant and excited from a stay of a few weeks in the Monastery. He had shown them copies of several interesting manuscripts which he had discovered in a neglected corner of the library, including his transcription of a Syriac codex containing *The Apology of Aristides* which the monks had not realised was in their possession. He had said at the time (she remembered) that in his opinion there was a rich mine of material to be found in the place, much of it quite unknown to the world of western scholarship: some of it uncatalogued, even, by the monks themselves. So taken had Harris been, indeed, with the possibilities of making further discoveries there, that he had asked Agnes to teach him the art of photography in preparation for his next visit. Mr Harris was a sound man and a first-rate scholar: his judgment was to be relied upon, and his excitement at the time had been infectious. Yes, they would go.

But, she reflected, it would take at least a whole winter to prepare for such a trip. There was much preliminary reading to be done, if they were to get the most out of such a visit. And they could do with another language, or even two. Thanks to Mr Anderson, in their Swaynesthorpe days, her Hebrew was pretty good; but from what Mr Harris had said, a working knowledge of Arabic was almost essential, and some acquaintance with Syriac highly desirable. Well, thought Agnes, Maggie already possessed some knowledge of Arabic: that could be polished up in the coming months, while she herself set about tackling Syriac. That would give her an immediate task with which to occupy her mind. Six months, say, for all these preparations? That would mean they would be ready to leave for the Middle East in the New Year – from the point of view of climate, the ideal time for travel in such parts. She resolved to put this plan before Maggie, and to see what she said.

Maggie, remembering how much benefit she herself had derived from the Cambridge visit after James' death, became quite enthusiastic. And so it was decided. The twins felt that, with their fluency in modern Greek, they should be able to establish rapport with the custodians of the St Catherine's library – all the monks there were Greeks, Harris had said – and to decipher any manuscripts that came their way. Their attention, they decided, should be given in the main to Biblical documents – the field in which, as devout women, they were mainly interested.

Agnes began to carry out her preparation plans. She called upon the Reverend R.H. Kennett of Queens' College, one of the leading Syriac scholars in the University, and enquired whether she might be allowed to join his regular class. Alas, that would not be possible: it was against all precedent in the University for a woman to engage in such studies. She therefore enquired about the possibilities of private tuition; and the upshot was that Kennett agreed to come to Castlebrae for lunch every Monday, and thereafter to give her a lesson. He also arranged for her to practise the writing of Syriac under the guidance of the twins' former Harvey Road neighbour, the young and brilliant F.C. Burkitt. When she began her studies, Agnes was pleased to find that the language proved to be 'quite easy', no doubt by reason of its affinities with Hebrew. Kennett expressed himself as delighted with her progress, and was subsequently heard to remark to a colleague that she had 'acquired a marvellous knowledge of that tongue in a very short space of time.'

In January 1892, the twins packed their bags, collected various introductions which might prove useful (including one from the Vice-Chancellor, Dr Peile), and departed once more on their travels. Rendel Harris went with them as far as London, to see them off. He would have liked to join the party, but the problem was time. The Christmas vacation was too short, as to reach Sinai involved a long and tiring journey by camel; and the heat was too great for an expedition in the Long Vacation, the obvious time. Hence the twins were entrusted with various commissions by senior members of the University: the Regius Professor of Divinity asked them to try and collate two manuscripts for him, for example, and the Professor of Geology wanted a specimen of granite graphites, a kind of hornblende. Other dons contented themselves with offering gloomy forecasts: Bensly (the Professor of Arabic) thought it very unlikely that two women would gain admission at all to the monastery, and was supported in this pessimistic view by other Eminent Persons; but Agnes and Maggie were confident of success, and their only fear was that they might be insufficiently skilful at photography – for they planned to photograph any manuscript of interest – to do justice to their opportunities.

In Cairo, they engaged a dragoman (with the Alice-in-Wonderland name of Hanna) whom friends had strongly recommended as reliable; and, through the good offices of Lady Scott-Moncrieff, obtained further introductions to the chief dignitaries of the Greek Church, particularly to those who had jurisdiction over the Monastery. Discovering precisely who these dignitaries were, however, proved a fatiguing task for two Presbyterians, unaccustomed to princelings of the Church. They called upon the Patriarch, but he was away; they were referred to his Vicar, the Metropolitan of Libya, who received them but felt obliged to point out that they ought to have addressed themselves to the Archbishop of Mount Sinai (how in the world could they be expected to know that Mount Sinai, hardly an over-populated spot, had an archbishop all to itself?). Eventually, however, they tracked him down and he proved to be friendly and encouraging, though he was more impressed by the seal on the Vice-Chancellor's letter than by its contents, and clung perversely to his opinion that the chief object of their journey was to further a plan by which the English might be persuaded to pronounce Greek properly. However, he provided them with an introduction, and gave them his blessing ('we probably ought to have knelt but, being Scotch, we stood' Maggie wrote to a friend), so that at last they were able to cross the Gulf of Suez and begin their journey.

Their caravan consisted of eleven camels, and the journey took ten days. Camel-riding has few delights in real life – or not until one is an experienced rider, which the twins, at this stage in their careers, were not. The constant jolting induces a stiffness akin to, but far worse than, that which one experiences when one resumes cycling after a long interval. Six years later, Agnes was to write an entertaining page on the nature and eccentricities of camels, with various hints on how to ride them:

A camel becomes an intensely interesting being when he is carrying you. You observe that the light yellow hue of his skin is exactly that of the sand, whilst the dark brown of his shaggy mane and the hairy fringe of his tail match well with the rocks in the wadys. You regard the elastic spring of his spongy foot, the not ungraceful twists of his long massive neck, with as much interest as you are wont to bestow on the telegraphic column of your newspaper at home, and all his humours become as important for the moment as the latest piece of gossip in your visiting circle. . . . His supreme virtue is his patience, and his ability to subsist on the dry desert herbage at which even a thistle-loving donkey would turn up his nose. There was one little plant which grew straight out of the sand, without any mould about it, and it had not a single leaf, but only a green stem and little branches furnished with spikes as strong and sharp as two-inch nails. My camel would actually turn from the bunch of tempting herbs which his master was holding before his nose, to crunch up this dreadful thing, and he would pick it out in preference to anything else when he was unheeded. I have even seen him devour actual wood – the leafless branch of a palm tree – and look as if he considered it a treat.

Camels are, as is well known, not responsive to kindness. You cannot caress them, for the least touch on their heads or necks when you are dismounted will bring their teeth into your arm.

The saddle on which you have to sit is not far removed from a common baggage one, and in many cases actually is one. It has two horns, one of which is meant for a rough support to your back, but if it is too short, will act rather as a prod. Your knees ought to rest on either side of the front horn, and you ought to be able to cross your feet in front of it, but sometimes from the angle at which you are sitting you find this an impossibility. The animal's back is protected from the rubbing of the saddle by a pad filled with rough straw, whose points are as sharp as nails if they come in contact with your ankles. On the saddle itself, a gay-looking quilted cover is generally placed; its looks are the best of it, for the stuffing is of the thinnest cotton, and quite half the fatigue and discomfort of camel-riding is due to this. Also, to keep you steady, your toe is thrust into a rope stirrup, and whether it be long or short, your whole leg gets cramped, for you are unable to change its position or that of its fellow at will.

It was a great day when we discovered how to remedy all this. The rule is simple. *Observe what your dragoman has got for himself, and adopt it.* After all, the structure of his bodily frame does not differ greatly from your own, and why should he have four folds of a thick bed-quilt (and a pillow to boot) beneath him, while you have only one fold of a thing whose stuffing is of the scantiest?

But this 'simple rule', like all human experience, had to be learned the hard way, and it was not until their third journey to Sinai that they discovered it. For the moment, they had to resign themselves to being very uncomfortable indeed. As their caravan advanced along a track that had been in use for several thousand years, Agnes tried to get into the spirit of the country by reading a Psalm in the original Hebrew; but the jerky motion of the camel caused the type to bob up and down in a way that was fatiguing to the eyes, and this work of *pietas* had to be abandoned.

The pleasure of eavesdropping on the men's conversation was severely hampered by their ignorance of the local dialect. In the tiresome manner displayed by the natives of every country, the spoken word seemed to bear little relation to the standard language which one has painfully mastered with the aid of teachers and grammars. The twins could not follow more than an occasional word. Aching in every joint, they were not sorry when the time came to camp for the night at 'Ayin Mousa. The sleeping tents were pitched – an operation that took far too long for their taste – but even then, there

114

Agnes Smith, novelist

'Robertson of Irvine'

Hamilfield, Irvine, Ayrshire: childhood home of the twins

James Young Gibson, Minister of the United Presbyterian Church

Samuel Savage Lewis, F.S.A., Fellow and Librarian of Corpus Christi College, Cambridge

The twins on their camels. 'Like resuming cycling after a long interval'

Maggie
(observe black box on camel's rump,
containing camera)

Agnes

Maggie's sketch of St Catherine's Monastery, Mount Sinai

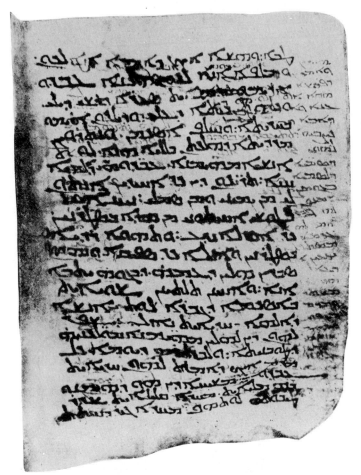

A page from the Sinaitic Syriac Palimpsest discovered by Agnes and now
known as the Lewis Codex. It is of Matthew XV, 12–27. The
underwriting can be clearly seen in the right-hand margin

Agnes Smith Lewis, Ph.D., D.D., Litt.D., LL.D., M.R.A.S.
This photograph probably 1901, aged 58

Margaret Dunlop Gibson, D.D., Litt.D., LL.D., M.R.A.S.
This photograph probably taken at the same time

A rest on the way to Sinai, 1893.
From left to right: Mrs Amy Burkitt, F.C. Burkitt (with handkerchief over face), Mrs Bensly (holding early-model Ensign camera), Agnes, Rendel Harris, Ahmed the dragoman

In the Monastery garden, 1893. Galakteon (now Prior) with Bensly (wearing fez) and Burkitt. Galakteon died a fortnight after the party left Sinai

Castlebrae, Chesterton Lane: the twins' Cambridge home. (Dining room with the french windows; Agnes' study between that room and the porch; Maggie's study masked by left-hand pillar of porch; drawing-room extreme left, with twins' bedroom above.)

Westminster College, Cambridge, from the 'Backs'. Agnes and Maggie bought and presented the site and laid the Foundation stone on 25 May 1897

Maggie with Father Nicodemus and unidentified (perhaps German scholar on her last visit to St Catherine's, 1906

Agnes and Maggie on Commemoration Day at Westminster College Sometime during the 1914–18 war (Maggie on the left)

was little rest for them. A gale sprang up which made sleep impossible: indeed, they expected the tent to blow down any minute. At half-past six, they crawled out, preferring an early start to further tossing about in their sleeping bags. But they had reckoned without the leisurely habits of the bearers, and it was nearly eleven before the procession was ready to move off.

The second night, at Wady Sadur, (the spot where Cambridge's Professor of Arabic had been murdered, ten years previously) proved no less squally, and again they got hardly any sleep. Next day, they set off on foot soon after six, leaving the caravan to follow at its leisure. At lunch time came the first of many tiresome disputes with Hanna. It had been agreed, when he was first engaged, that the ladies should choose the resting-places, and that Sunday should be a day on which there should be no travelling at all. But when Sunday came, Hanna became obstinate and insisted upon a twelve-hour ride – much longer than usual – to a wady of his own selection. Tired and irritable, the twins' anger was not wholly sabbatarian, for, among other inconveniences, this long trek meant that the last hour of the day's journey had to be accomplished in total darkness – a hazardous undertaking in a country where the only indication of the 'main road' consisted of the footprints of previous travellers. Their dreams of a pious Scottish Sabbath had to be regretfully abandoned, and the most they could do, by way of marking the day, was to refrain from taking photographs: a somewhat inadequate obedience to the commandment enjoining rest.

On the Monday, they again set off on foot, ahead of the camels; and thereafter, one day was very much like another, with nothing to relieve the monotony save occasional variations in the scenery of the desert. The level country gave way to a terrain broken by sandy hillocks ('dreary as a dustheap', according to Agnes), with a prospect of red sandstone mountains in the distance; then into a valley strewn with bits of black flint, then more sandy mounds, and finally a ride along the seashore. One day, they encountered a young girl ('in a graceful blue garment, well worn, and with nothing betwixt it and her person') who exclaimed 'Are not these *women*?' – a remark prompted by their unaccountable lack of veils: see-through shifts were one thing, bare faces quite another. To this shocked young woman (aged twenty-five, married, with three children, Hanna explained in an undertone), Agnes showed Samuel's portrait, perhaps in an attempt to convince her that they were, after all, respectable females, properly equipped with husbands (well, until recently, at any rate). This encounter prompted Hanna to assume the role of lecturer, perhaps in revenge for Agnes' disquisition on the Sabbath; he explained that Bedouin women have no desire for their husbands to grow rich – and actually try little tricks to prevent them from earning too much money – fearing that, if they should grow too prosperous, they themselves would rapidly be supplanted in their husbands' affections.

So the long journey dragged on, for five more days of discomfort, weariness and inadequate sleep amid windblown sand. More than once, they finished their day's journey by the light of the moon and the stars. On February 7th, they climbed the pass of Nugb Hawa on foot, ahead of the camels, and stood at last before the mountain, sharp as a knife and red like old dried blood, where the voice of God had once been heard in thunder by the multitude beneath.

It is easy to imagine Mount Sinai as a huge, gaunt mountain, rising sheer above the surrounding country, with the cluster of St Catherine's monastic buildings set squarely on its summit, like a gigantic limpet clinging to the bare rock. Such was my own mental picture – one reinforced by a pleasant little sketch which Maggie drew on the day of their arrival: a sketch which concentrates upon the buildings and the garden of cypresses, and gives no more than the slightest of hints as to the background. No impression could be farther from the truth. The Monastery, in actual fact, nestles in a narrow valley, surrounded by a walled garden and overlooked by gigantic cliffs on one side and a mountain on the other. H.V. Morton likens it to a child's toy on the floor of a room.

The Monastery had had a long and chequered history since its foundation by Justinian in the fifth century – a history reflected in the varied style of its buildings which, even in

1892, seemed to have a somewhat provisional air. Strongly-built, low-roofed vaulted passages led into a courtyard, where modern rooms of mud and plaster opened onto wooden galleries. At one time, the foundation had been under the protection of Mahomet himself: the monks, alarmed at a resounding victory for his arms in the neighbourhood, had made a tactful and Vicar-of-Bray-like gesture of homage to him, in order to save the place from pillage. One result of this submission was that a mosque (which is still there) had been built inside the walls, adjoining the Church.

But we left Hanna supervising the erection of the tents beside the little well amid the flowering almond trees, olives and cypresses of the monastery garden. While he was thus engaged, the sisters were formally received by the grey-headed Prior and by Father Galakteon, the librarian. To the latter, they presented a letter of introduction from Rendel Harris, which he read with eyes sparkling with pleasure – everyone liked the Quaker scholar – exclaiming, 'The world is not so large after all, when we have real friends in such distant lands.' It was not, perhaps, a very original observation, but at least it allayed the twins' anxiety as to the degree of cordiality with which they would be received. They might well have endured all those privations for nothing, as prophesied by their Cambridge friends.

The learned Father at once bustled them off to have a preliminary look at his library, after which Agnes and Maggie felt it their duty to attend the afternoon service in the Church. Agnes, in her journal, does her best to be charitable about this, but it was obviously not to her taste. For one thing, it lasted a full two hours, which was a little excessive even for those accustomed to 'sitting under' long-winded Scottish ministers, and doubly so when coming at the end of a prolonged and exhausting journey. Aching in every limb and growing increasingly sleepy, the twins tried not to fidget on the uncomfortable stone benches, and occupied their time in examining such parts of the Church as were visible from where they were sitting. The building blazed with light from the gold and crystal chandeliers which hung from the blue, star-spangled roof. Tall Byzantine granite columns divided the Church into two side aisles; ikons glowed on every side. In the dome of the apse was set the superb Justinian mosaic of the Transfiguration, with its dark blues, greens and browns against a background of gold and silver. To the right of the altar stood a marble shrine containing the relics of St Catherine, the virgin-martyr of Alexandria in whose honour the Monastery had been re-named in the Middle Ages; while, across the roof, along one of the beams, ran the inscription: 'For the salvation of our pious Emperor Justinian.' Eventually the long service ended, and the sisters emerged, cramped and exhausted, into the clear evening air. 'It was the last of their services we attended,' Agnes writes laconically.

The next day, they began work in the Library; and thereafter, from nine in the morning until seven at night, they were hard at their researches. The place seemed to them to be pretty disorganised, some Greek manuscripts being in the Show library and the Arabic ones partly there and partly in a little room half-way up a dark stair. The Syriac ones, together with those manuscripts supposed to be most ancient, were either in this stair room or in a dingy closet, approached through a small sunless anteroom. In the cupboard, the said 'treasures' were simply stuffed in two boxes, so placed that it was impossible to examine them without the aid of a candle. It was just as well that the original writers had employed the best parchment for their copying task; for whenever the monastery had been threatened with attack, all valuable manuscripts had been stored for safety in the vaults, which were extremely damp. Consequently they were not, to put it mildly, in the best condition.

However, the twins kept their shocked surprise to themselves as Father Galakteon bustled round, friendly and anxious to help. The obvious knowledgeability of Agnes and Maggie filled him – and indeed all the monks – with admiration and amazed respect. Here, indeed, was true piety – to go to such immense pains in order to possess a correct version of the sacred writings! Truly the English must be a holy nation!

Galakteon, however, was not always easy to get on with. He had 'all the instincts of a despot' (wrote Maggie to her

Cambridge friend Mrs Tillyard, after three weeks of his constant company): 'I got three scoldings in one day from him – one for coming to the Library a quarter of an hour later than usual, the second for perusing a book without first having asked his permission, and the third for suggesting that the great boulder which another monk had showed me as the one Moses struck might possibly not be the true one. To make amends, he sat down beside me and read the book – an illustrated manuscript of Job – for two whole hours.' Though they did not know it at the time, the Librarian was on the verge of a fatal illness, which may well have accounted for his occasional touchiness and irritability.

The only drawback to the work was the intense cold. Because of its location – analogous to that of a lump of sugar at the bottom of a teacup – the monastery caught the sun only for an hour or two each day. The Library windows were unglazed, and the twins became so frozen by the bitter wind that blew through them that it was essential, from time to time, to go for a smart walk out of the narrow wady into the bright sunshine of the plain. At night, too, the temperature in their tents was invariably below zero, so sleep was once more at a discount. Only women with an iron constitution – and an inflexible will – could have stood up to several weeks of such a life; but it does not seem to have bothered them unduly, for Agnes' journal contains no more than a passing reference to such inconveniences, and any entries that are not concerned with scholarship are devoted to lush descriptions of the beauties of the locality. Each evening, when the day's work was done, they would stroll in the monastery garden, where the tall cypresses towered above the massed almond blossoms against a background of bare granite cliffs, all touched with the gold of the sunset. Later, they would sit by the fire outside their tents, while the moonlight made the olive boughs look like fairy lacework, and the ground beneath the trees, strewn with fallen almond blossoms, gleamed like snow.

The first Saturday of their stay, the twins decided to take a day off in order to climb Sinai. They set off at seven in the morning, an early start by European standards, but late by the customs of a monastery with its choir offices. As they set out, accompanied by a blue-robed lay brother named Euthymios who was to be their guide, they encountered a straggly procession of monks returning from their service in the cemetery chapel, which happened to be close by the twins' tents. It is to be presumed that the procession was so lacking in order and dignity, and so characterised by genial informality, that Agnes and Maggie assumed the monks were 'marching at ease' (or its ecclesiastical equivalent, if any), or perhaps they declined to admit any religious significance to such popish goings-on as outdoor ceremonies. Anyway, the twins 'said good morning' to their particular friends among the monks, and, perceiving the Prior in the rear, Agnes 'deemed it courteous' to advance and shake hands with him. The holy man was slightly taken aback; but, recovering himself quickly, and concluding that this gesture must have some religious significance in the Scottish Church (akin, perhaps, to the kiss of peace at the *agapé* in the catacombs?) 'sent a shower of holy water from the vessel he was carrying' over the startled Agnes. Her manners were equal to the occasion, however, for she politely said 'Thank you.' But the last laugh (if one may use such an irreverent expression in connection with pious acts) was definitely with the Prior, for he suddenly held up a small silver cross and commanded Agnes, 'somewhat peremptorily', to adore it. The monk who was walking immediately behind the Prior, foreseeing a tiresome and delicate contretemps analogous to the old deadlock between the irresistible force and the immovable body, swiftly murmured behind his hand, 'Her form of religion is different from ours.' But the Prior was disinclined to bother about such niceties, and repeated, very firmly, 'Adore it!' Who, after all (he may have felt) held the cure of souls in that place? If the head of a religious community, properly elected and inducted, were to be compelled to modify ecclesiastical protocol for the benefit of some cranky foreign woman with a fancy religion and an over-endowment of 'scruples' – even if that woman were a remarkable scholar, as indeed she certainly was – where would the matter end? One would be in the clutches of heresy, if not of downright unbelief, before one knew where one was. 'Adore it!' repeated His Beatitude, with even greater firmness. 'I saw no way out of the difficulty but that of suppressing my predilections', confesses Agnes in her account of the incident, 'so I kissed the cross and said, "I adore the Saviour, Who died upon a cross."' One of the blessings of education is that it trains one in the art of selecting, at a moment's notice, a form of words that will meet the demands of an unexpected occasion without violating one's conscience or giving offence: the classic example is that of Disraeli who, when presented with an obviously boring book by a proud author, said with a charming smile, 'I will lose no time in reading this.' Agnes had been trained in the same school of politeness. Indeed, she recognised (for she was, after all, a woman of imaginative understanding and kindly heart, for all her firm Protestant principles) that, had she done otherwise, she would have thrown the poor Prior into a state of great perplexity. He would certainly have thought her an atheist, for (as she puts it) 'his intellect was not capable of understanding my notions.' She adds, in chastened tones, 'It was a lesson to me never again to approach a Greek ecclesiastic when walking in procession.'

After this somewhat shaky start to the day's outing, the sisters began their climb. The lower slopes of the range are called Horeb, the name Sinai being reserved for the upper section. Passing the spot where Moses was supposed to have watered the flocks of his father-in-law, they came to a cluster of cypresses which surrounded the chapel of Elijah, situated at the foot of the peak named Jebel Mousa. This was traditionally the spot where Elijah was fed by the ravens; and the chapel precincts enclosed the cave in which he is said to have slept. Already the view was superb. Range upon range of mountains lay below, looking like a rough sea that had been suddenly turned to stone: some ridges resembled waves about to break, others akin to the spent wave as it regathers itself – a savage and desolate scene. Often they were compelled to scramble up on hands and knees, with eyes smarting from the dust of an evil-smelling plant called sphaka, which it was necessary to grasp in order to gain a foothold on the innumerable boulders. Eventually they reached the foot of the inaccessible rock which crowns the summit of the Ras Susafseh. They sat down to eat their lunch facing a magnificent view of the whole plain, and sheltering as best they could from the strong wind which threatened to sweep them over the precipice.

As they munched their bread and cheese, Brother Euthymios told them his life story: how he had worked for fifteen years in a tailor's shop in Athens and, being childless, had come to the Monastery after his wife's death – no doubt his celibate colleagues considered him to have had the best of both worlds – and how he had often attended the services of the Greek Evangelical Church in Athens, and hence had a better understanding of Reformed worship than most of his brethren.

It was on the way down that Hanna (yes, they had taken him along too) suddenly saw an opportunity to settle old scores. Agnes who, as usual, had all potentially useful information stored ready in her mind, was aware that there were three possible routes by which they might descend; but as they scrambled down she foolishly asked Hanna which track they were on, thus disclosing her ignorance of their exact whereabouts. The dragoman quietly drew Euthymios to one side, and represented to him that the sisters had specially asked to be conducted home by the longest route, in order to see as much of the country as possible. The unsuspecting Brother fell into the trap, and duly led the party into a wady on the side of Jebel Mousa that was farthest from the Monastery: a detour that necessitated a five-mile walk home from the base of the mountain, and which involved a half-circuit of Horeb. The twins were furious, and relieved their feelings in a large-scale row with Hanna; but there was nothing they could do about it, and the long trek had to be faced, exhausted though they were. Long after the moon had risen, they were still walking, Agnes being compelled to stop and rest on a boulder at frequent intervals. It was eight o'clock before they finally reached their tents. The excursion had occupied thirteen hours, for twelve of which they had been climbing over the roughest of rocks. For women of fifty, cumbered with heavy Victorian clothing, and with their strength depleted by a fortnight's hard camel-riding, three weeks of scanty sleep, and a single meal of bread and cheese, it was a remarkable performance. The following day, spent freezing in the Library, must have seemed quite a lotus-eating holiday by contrast.

But what precisely was this 'work' upon which they spent most of each day? Were they simply browsing vaguely among the endless manuscripts on the shelves, savouring their antiquity and hoping that something unusual would catch their eye? A profitable week or two might certainly have been spent thus; but this was not, in fact, what they were doing with their time. It will be recalled that Rendel Harris had spoken to them about certain uncatalogued Syriac manuscripts which (he had said) were stored in damp chests in one of the dark cubbyholes which adjoined the main library: being feminine enough to have a nose for a 'bargain', the twins had, after the first few days of general browsing, headed for that cubbyhole and those chests. Many of the musty documents there housed proved to be palimpsests of great age. It should perhaps be explained exactly what a palimpsest is. In bygone centuries, when papyrus had become scarce and paper was not yet invented, the monks used to write on vellum – that is, on the finely-prepared skins of animals. From time to time vellum also became scarce, especially in out-of-the-way places like Mount Sinai. In such circumstances, the practice was to take vellum which had already been used, and to erase the existing writing by scraping it with a knife or with pumice-stone. When the page was reasonably clean, the scribe would use it for its new purpose – indifferent to the fact that the writing which lay beneath was probably of great value. Such a twice-used sheet is called a palimpsest. It is often possible to see traces of the earlier underwriting on the margins and between the lines of the page; and naturally it is the older script which is of principal interest to scholars. The various dark and airless cupboards of the Library were full of such: they had been relegated to this obscure and undignified position because the upper, or more recent, writing was no longer of interest.

It was in one of these store-chests that Harris had discovered the Syriac Codex containing the translation of the *Apology of Aristides*. The twins' first task was to photograph this document. It consisted of one hundred and ten pages, so the undertaking does not sound very formidable. But the problems of photography in 1892 were immense, especially when grappled with by two amateurs who had no more to guide them than vague memories of the advice of the Kodak salesman in London, supplemented by a few random hints offered by fellow-travellers on the boat. Agnes may be allowed to describe their first attempts in her own words: 'The sharp points of the camera's legs [i.e. of the tripod] could never be coaxed into keeping steady on the marble floor, and the legs of Mr Harris' manuscript stand would not fit. I am not a mechanical genius myself, and the monks knew nothing about such contrivances: so I summond Hanna to my aid . . . He said he could not be expected to help with a thing whose like he had never seen before, to which I replied that I had never seen one in use myself, but that it might well be the delight of clever people like him to overcome difficulties. How I longed for a single pair of European male hands to help us, for neither of us had the strength to fight with these things for any length of time, and I feared that the monks would get worried and tell us to take the whole thing away. At length it was tied up, somewhat awkwardly, with ropes and we screwed on our ten-inch lens. The pictures which we took with it, after many attempts at focussing, were far inferior to those given through the six-inch lens, which happily we tried a few days later. Mr Harris had told us to expose for twelve seconds, in that room, with the ten-inch lens; and we developed a few that night with Eastman powders in a rough way, pinning them to the sides of our tent to dry. We thus ascertained that we had got on the right track; but the films became so parched and ready to crack in the dry desert air that we decided to keep the rest undeveloped until our return home. Hanna took advantage of our absence in the Library to have our tent swept out: this raised a storm of dust from the garden mould, which settled into the gelatine of our damp films.' So the whole task had to be done again. It is not surprising that this first undertaking kept them fully occupied for several days. Thereafter, taper in hand, they began to rummage on their own account in the manuscript boxes.

But their notable discovery was not to be the result of diligent burrowing: it was to be the result of one of those curious accidents which look so improbable in the pages of fiction. Hospitality in an all-male community, though cordial, is apt to be of a somewhat rough-and-ready kind. At St Catherine's, meals tended to be served on the firm principle that one eats to live, and no more. Butterdishes, for instance, were scorned: when, at breakfast, butter was required, it was simply planked down on an old sheet of discarded manuscript, and put thus on the table. After all, vellum is a tough material, and will resist grease for at least the period of one meal; and its use reduces the washing-up. Such, at any rate, was the monks' normal custom, and they saw no reason to vary it for their feminine visitors. They had been so long out of the world that they had forgotten that women attach considerable importance to such trifles. So the butter for the twins' meals appeared on the same ersatz tableware. Our heroines were somewhat disconcerted but, as well-bred women, naturally made no comment.

Agnes, indeed, saw in such unusual arrangements an excellent opportunity to combine study with eating, to blend intellectual refreshment with the somewhat clumsy methods prescribed by the Lord for refuelling the human frame. Hence it soon became her custom to scrutinise the 'butterdish' with an unobtrusive scholarly eye, to see whether it offered anything of interest. As a rule it did not; but one morning the grubby sheet proved to be a fragment of a palimpsest, and at the edge of the 'dish', disappearing under the lump of butter, was a line or two of the underwriting – clearly visible – which she at once recognised as a verse of the Gospels. This happened to be in Syriac, Agnes' newly-acquired language (and therefore one in which she happened to be especially interested at that moment). Tactful and casually-worded enquiries, after the meal, led her to a certain basket in the glory-hole where they had been working.

There, she found a complete Syriac palimpsest of three hundred and fifty-eight pages, the leaves of which were mostly glued together by dirt and damp – so firmly, indeed, that the least force used to separate them resulted in instant crumbling. Its relegation to this dusty corner no doubt resulted from the fact that none of the monks – not even Father Galakteon – knew any Syriac. Hence no one at Sinai had any idea of its possible value.

The problem was how to investigate it, so frail was the condition of the codex: even the most delicate and careful manipulation with the fingers resulted in immediate damage to the vellum. Suddenly Agnes had an inspiration. Of course! – her tiny tea-kettle, that indispensable item of luggage for any British traveller. The very thing! Maggie was dispatched to the tent for it; the little spirit lamp was lit, and the kettle put on to boil. As soon as it began to steam, they held the leaves in the vapour; and to their satisfaction, the pages separated easily. The British passion for tea had once more paid dividends.

When the pages were dry enough to examine, Agnes scrutinised them carefully under her lens. After a few minutes, she straightened her back and reported excitedly that while the upper (or more recent) writing seemed to contain an account – very well-thumbed in places! – of the lives of certain rather frisky women saints, the underlying and more ancient script was evidently a copy of the four Gospels of a very early date indeed. The headings 'Evangelium', 'da Mathai', 'da Marcus' and 'da Luca' could be clearly seen, free of the overwriting, on different pages. It was difficult to determine the date of the 'Lives of the Saints', for the hole through which the binding had once passed had destroyed part of the lettering of the actual year: but it looked like A.D.698. (subsequently, she modified this to 778). This meant that the underwriting would be very much earlier, for vellum would be unlikely to be re-used before a century – or perhaps even two centuries – had passed. This gave a probable date for these gospels as (at least) fifth century, possibly fourth century.

There was no doubt about it: she had accidentally stumbled upon a document which might well prove to be of the utmost importance for Biblical scholarship. Father Galakteon and Maggie, sceptical at first, soon began to share her excitement. If she were right in her assessment, this was indeed a 'find'. She would, of course, need to consult some more experienced scholars before she could express an opinion on its exact value, or 'place' it in relation to existing versions: such enquiries would have to wait until they were back in Cambridge. For the moment, the important task was to get the whole book photographed.

So once more the cumbersome photographic apparatus was rigged up, and she set to work. Her companions, though willing to share her enthusiasm up to a point, couldn't help wondering whether the manuscript really merited all this labour. Being unable to read even the upper writing, they were compelled to accept Agnes' assurance of its importance; and Maggie was doubtful whether it was worth the expenditure of three-hundred and seventy-two negatives. 'Are you *quite* sure of what you're saying, Agnes', Maggie kept asking, 'may not the earlier writing simply contain more of these foolish legends?' Suppose they were later to discover something even more interesting, and had no negatives left with which to photograph it? But Agnes was adamant and eventually her sister gave in. She and the Librarian held the heavy volume on the manuscript stand and turned the pages while Agnes struggled with the unwieldy camera. The task – which included copying the top line of each page into a notebook, for subsequent identification of the prints – occupied ten whole mornings of their precious thirty days' stay; and both Agnes' assistants grumbled at regular intervals, for the work involved them in standing for two or three hours at a stretch. Agnes must have been very sure of her judgment to withstand their complaints and expostulations.

On this and other manuscripts the sisters expended over one thousand films. It was an exasperating business, for, apart from the technical trials which have already been recorded, the camera itself was inclined to be temperamental – to break down at critical moments, or to become tangled up in its winding mechanism, so that films either tore or suddenly acquired a deckle-edge. Such eccentricities were later to add considerably to the burden of identifying and classifying the prints, for sometimes the all-important top line would prove to have been sliced off. Today, science has discovered more compact and convenient ways of obtaining copies of such documents. In the first six months of 1950, Professor Kenneth W. Clark of Duke University, North Carolina, microfilmed over 2,700 manuscripts, mostly in St Catherine's. (It is interesting to note that, in this immense undertaking, he and his colleagues made considerable use of the catalogues of Arabic and Syriac books which Agnes and Maggie compiled on their next visit to Sinai, and presented to the Library.)

On Monday March 7th, they tidied up their work, packed their notebooks and their precious films, and prepared for their departure on the morrow. The monks were now in the middle of their Lenten fast, a discipline which involved a suspension of all the pleasant little conversations and occasional fun which had enlivened the long hours the twins had spent in the Library. Their hosts' continued to help them, but, reports Agnes, 'they looked sleepy, useless and miserable.' Galakteon was very distressed to find that the twins took no special notice of Lent, and not even the knowledgeable Euthymios was able satisfactorily to explain this plain neglect of pious duty on their part. Agnes did her best to set his mind at rest when, as she signed the Visitors' Book just before their departure, she wrote after their names: 'There are diversities of administration, but the same spirit:' (a blend of 1 Corinthians xii, verses 4 & 5) but it is doubtful whether the good Father understood this delicate reference. The Visitors' Book, incidentally, was a modern touch which had been introduced in 1860, perhaps as a result of Dr Tischendorf's departure, the previous year, with the Codex Sinaiticus in his trunk. (Posterity has been divided as to the exact meaning to be attached to his declaration that he 'borrowed' it for further study. It was never returned. For this breach of trust, Tischendorf blamed the Tsar who, he declared, declined to part with it after inspecting it and being apprised of its value. It was subsequently bought by the British Government, and is now in the British Museum.)

So they began the long journey home, well satisfied with the fruits of their visit. There is no need to recount in detail the happenings of the return trek, for this was almost a replica of the outward journey, with the added unpleasantness of increasing rows with Hanna. The latter wished to force the pace, by depriving them of their three-hour siesta in the noonday heat, in order that, by compressing nine days riding into seven, he might be available 'for hire' by the next party of travellers a full two days earlier than he would otherwise have been. But the twins were not Scots for nothing: they, too, could be obstinate, especially where money was involved. Hanna was compelled to climb down – a little too swiftly for his liking, since at the evening halt he fell backwards off his camel and was badly shaken. (No doubt the twins regarded it as an act of Divine justice.) He vented his bad temper on the headman; and, in the course of his abuse (believing the twins to be out of earshot) he let fall the information that Agnes had been supplied with an inferior beast. Here at last was the explanation of the fact that her back felt as if it had been broken, as she endlessly jolted on a saddle that would never keep straight. Agnes craftily kept this useful knowledge to herself for the moment; but, next day, innocently suggested to Hanna that she should exchange saddles with him. One up to Agnes who, the exchange having been reluctantly agreed to, absolutely declined to change back again – and so left the dragoman in considerable discomfort for the next nine days. Hanna, however, conducted guerilla warfare to the end: he would fasten the tent ropes insecurely for the night, so that with any luck the tent might blow down (it did, several times), and at each oasis would supply them with the dirtiest drinking water he could find (but their pocket filters rendered it safe, if not very palatable). To add to the pleasures of life, Maggie developed a poisoned foot, immediately after this first battle with Hanna, which gave her constant pain (and which, incidentally, took months to heal). However, they eventually reached Suez, crossed to Marseilles, and took a French boat for home.

Approaching Her Majesty's Customs with a thousand undeveloped negatives stowed between the petticoats in the trunk proved rather an ordeal, even in those relatively casual days. The twins were anxious lest some over-zealous official should mistake the rolls for quids of tobacco, undo them for a closer inspection, and let in a ray of light before he could be restrained. Happily this danger did not materialise; and, as Agnes was fortunately not given to dropping valuable possessions all over the place in the manner of her late husband, they were able to reach Cambridge with their precious freight undisturbed.

It had always been their practice to develop their own negatives. This time, however, well-intentioned friends strongly advised them to send at least one roll to a professional photographer, in order to have a standard to 'work up to'. This counsel proved to be a classic illustration of Wilde's dictum that 'all advice is bad, and good advice is fatal'; for, when the negatives were returned by the professional – they had sent one roll of the palimpsest films, and half a roll of scenery, some three dozen negatives in all – these were found to have come up very much fainter than those they had developed themselves, and it proved quite impossible to obtain prints from them. Thus about twenty-four pages of the palimpsest seemed to be irretrievably lost. The twins, naturally, were much upset; but there was a happy ending to the story. It transpired that one day when Maggie had been turning the pages of the manuscript on the photographic stand, she had momentarily lost her place without realising she had done so, and thirty pages had been photographed twice. By an extraordinary stroke of good fortune, it was this duplicate roll which had been sent to the photographer. Providence, they felt, must surely be strongly in favour of their researches.

When they had made prints of the whole thousand photographs, they set about arranging them in proper order. Work on the Arabic manuscripts, which fell to Maggie, was quite straightforward, and she was soon able to assemble them correctly. But Agnes' task, with the Syriac ones, was much more difficult. Faced (as she was, in the case of the

130

palimpsest) with a hitherto-unknown manuscript, she had nothing to guide her but the top lines of the pages, which (it will be remembered) she had copied into her notebook. In the photographs, however, these top lines were, more often than not, either blurred by the underwriting, or completely missing. Frequently she was compelled to go over the whole three hundred and sixty pages of her notebook in order to place a single photograph correctly, a task which took a lot of time and unlimited patience. She had to be careful, too, not to muddle up already-identified sheets with prints not yet arranged. The twins were working against time, for they wished to exhibit some of their discoveries at the Ninth International Congress of Orientalists (to which Professor Robertson Smith was taking them), which was to meet in London in September. This meant that some preliminary attempt, at least, had to be made to *read* the documents and to assess their value, if the paper they were to give was to be worth delivering at all. Some of their Cambridge friends who were Syriac experts spent long hours poring over the prints with Agnes. 'It is not a little amusing now' (wrote Maggie the following year) 'to look back and think how nearly several eminent Syriac scholars just managed to miss discovering the value of the palimpsest.' Agnes, however, was quite confident that her first snap judgment had been correct, and she now set herself to study both the overwriting and the underwriting in detail.

Looking, today, at those yellowed photographs neatly pasted in a large black exercise book, one can only be astonished that anyone, however erudite, should ever have been able to decipher the underwriting at all. Most of us would make nothing whatever of even the clearest page. Small wonder that the distinguished scholars were baffled – or couldn't even be bothered to attempt a reading. ('Mr X did not trouble to look at them: Mr Y, though present, was equally indifferent,' she later wrote to Rendel Harris.) But one Friday in July Agnes held a large luncheon party and among the guests were Frank Burkitt and his wife. This young man, then in his middle twenties, was a brilliant scholar who had graduated only four years previously, and

who was eventually to become Norrisian Professor of
Divinity in the University, a Chair which he was the first
layman to occupy. It will be recalled that the Burkitts lived
in Harvey Road, and so were old acquaintances of the twins:
Frank had also assisted Kennett in the teaching of Syriac to
Agnes. When the other guests had departed (with the
exception of their special friend Mary Kingsley), Agnes
produced the photographs and spread them out for Burkitt's
inspection on the grand piano. His eyes, she reflected, were
after all younger and keener than those of some of his senior
colleagues, and it was just possible that he might see
something which they had missed. Burkitt was keenly
interested, and begged the loan of the prints for a few days.
On the Sunday, a messenger arrived after breakfast, bearing
a note from Mrs Burkitt which announced that her husband
was 'in a state of great excitement', that he had been to
Professor Bensly (the Professor of Arabic) with a
transcription of part of the underwriting, and that they had
discovered that the palimpsest was nothing less than a copy
of the Curetonian Syriac Version.

Few of us would become wildly excited at these tidings,
never having heard of this document until now. It should
therefore be explained that the Curetonian ('Syr. Cur.' as it
is usually cryptically footnoted by the experts) was a
5th-century fragment of the Gospels, containing almost
nothing of Mark, which had been discovered in 1838 by
Archdeacon Tattam in the Monastery of St. Mary Deipara,
which lies in the Natron Valley west of Cairo. Tattam found
it in a kind of oubliette, into which, lighted candle in hand,
he had been lowered on a rope, in order to burrow like a
rabbit among manuscripts which covered the floor to a
depth of two feet. On his return to England, he sent his
collection to the British Museum, where this particular
fragment had been identified, four years later, by the Revd.
William Cureton. By one of those strange coincidences of
which life is full, one of Cureton's daughters (a Mrs
Howard) lived in a house adjoining the twins' former home
in Harvey Road; and when Agnes, preparing for the trip to
Sinai, had been unable to buy a second-hand copy of the

Cureton Gospels, this lady lent her the copy from her father's library.

The gaps in the Cureton manuscript were now made good by the twins' palimpsest, which came to be known as 'The Lewis Syriac Gospels' (or 'Syr. Sin[aiticus]' as distinct from 'Syr. Cur.'). The excitement in Castlebrae was so great that Agnes and Maggie were even ready to overlook Mrs Burkitt's commission of the unforgivable sin in scholarship: inaccuracy. ('Mrs Burkitt, in her excitement, had not given us a perfectly correct account of the transaction,' writes Maggie tartly: 'we learned later that it was the photographs themselves, and not merely a transcription from them, that Mr Burkitt had taken to Professor Bensly.') Hard on the heels of his wife's note came Burkitt himself, bearing a letter from Bensly begging them to keep the discovery a secret until they could get the whole palimpsest transcribed. To this they agreed – 'at least to the extent of not publishing it, and of telling only a few friends whose advice we were in need of,' says Maggie, her feminine desire to share a secret losing on points to her scholar's wish to make no claims until the supporting evidence had been properly marshalled. The friends 'in the know' had all been told before Bensly's letter arrived: these included Prof. Macalister and Prof. Robertson Smith – and also Canon Cureton's daughter, Agnes considering that it would have been 'treachery' for this lady to have learned of the document from a third party. The twins were not the only ones to be excited: Professor Bensly's head was so much in the clouds that he completely forgot an important dinner engagement.

Agnes and Maggie summoned Rendel Harris, and went into conference with him as to the immediate next steps to be taken; young Burkitt conferred with Bensly and then with the twins. Finally it was agreed that no mention of the discovery should be made at the meetings of the Congress of Orientalists, lest some enterprising scholar should depart hotfoot for Sinai before they were ready to publish a preliminary text. It was further resolved that the three hundred and sixty photographic prints should be divided between Bensly, Burkitt and Harris for transcription and subsequent publication, with Agnes to write the Introduction to the proposed volume. The final decision was that, in the New Year, all five scholars (and the men's wives) should pay a visit to Sinai for the purpose of studying, in the original manuscript, such passages as were doubtful or illegible in the photographs, and to explore further the musty coffers in the Library cupboards. Bensly's new edition of the Cureton text was already advertised, and he was naturally anxious to collate it, at the earliest possible moment, with this new manuscript – one which, as he could already see, had close affinities with that version and yet so many variations on it.

For all the group's common enthusiasm for the project, there were difficulties to be surmounted in connection with the expedition. All the men scholars already had pressing work on hand, and there was some talk of postponing the trip for twelve months. But Agnes argued that Galakteon was in very poor health and, should he die before their visit, their work would be infinitely harder, for no other monk knew much about the Library's contents. Two members of the party also had health problems. Bensly was elderly and delicate, and his friends were all horrified when he announced that he proposed to join the expedition. Under pressure, the Benslys withdrew . . . and then changed their minds again, when Bensly's doctor raised no objection, provided his patient had no attacks of bronchitis or throat trouble while he was in Cairo. Burkitt's wife, too, was not robust: was she fit to travel? Or would it be worse if he left her behind, with no one to take her mind off her 'delicacy'? This consultant thought she should go, that consultant felt she should stay at home; and so on. Eventually she collected sufficient favourable expert opinions to feel justified in joining the party. Friends then objected to Burkitt himself going, on the grounds that he was an only son. This objection was not quite as absurd as it seems: the journey was generally considered to be a most hazardous one. No doubt the protesters were recalling the sad fate of Bensly's predecessor in the Chair of Arabic (Professor Palmer) who had been murdered a few years previously on that very stretch of desert. But Bensly's almost-completed book filled his mind to the exclusion of all else: weak chests and murderous Bedouin were waved aside as irrelevant or of minor concern, and he resolved to go. The only one who absolutely declined to join the party, in spite of all the eloquent coaxings of the twins, was Mrs Rendel Harris: it was not her sort of jaunt, of that she was quite sure. If Rendel wanted to go, he was welcome to do so; but he would go alone.

The composition of the party finally settled, a further argument arose as to the means of arranging it. Should they travel under the benevolent wing of Messrs. Thomas Cook and Son – the view of Bensly and Burkitt, who had never ventured abroad in any other way – or should they go independently, as was the custom of the twins and Harris? The latter pointed out that they had never come to any harm through so doing. Maggie even wished to take the drastic step of dispensing with the services of a dragoman. This extreme proposal had one advantage: it made the 'no Cooks' motion into the compromise resolution, and so managed to pass the assembly. When the final planning meeting broke up, it had been agreed that they would all go east in January.

By a curious combination of circumstances, the twins had found their metier at last. They were to be scholars. The vision had tarried; but they had waited for it, and it had come.

VII

Father Galakteon Overdoes his Welcome

O my son! make thy speech fair and sweeten thy tongue and permit not thy companion to tread on thy foot, lest he tread at the last on thy breast.

– *The Story of Haiqar and Nadan*,
translated from the Arabic by Agnes Smith Lewis

The members of the party travelled to Cairo by different routes: the Benslys from Brindisi, the Burkitts from the Riviera, the twins from Paris, Harris by the last possible boat from Liverpool. Agnes and Maggie, who were the first to arrive in the Egyptian capital, called on the Archbishop of Mount Sinai to present their respects. He was still living in what might be described as the Cairo branch of St Catherine's, a small subsidiary monastery which it had been found prudent to establish as a base of operations whenever pressure needed to be brought to bear upon the Government. The twins' visit, however, was more than simply a courtesy call, for Agnes was anxious to solicit his support for a plan she had formed to open a fund in Europe to finance the construction of extensions to the Library – financially the community was very impoverished – as well as to outline to him the work it was proposed to tackle on this expedition. The second part of her task, which would seem to be the easier, was in fact the harder; for, in view of her promise to Bensly, it was necessary to conceal the fact of their discovery of the palimpsest. Agnes, however, was a gifted diplomat and, fulminating inwardly against the Professor of Arabic, skilfully presented a drastically-edited version of their research programme. The Archbishop was much interested; and, moved by Maggie's protestation that she did not want always to be 'a deaconess to her sister, but to do something herself,' gave her permission to catalogue the Library's collection of Arabic books. He warned her that this task would consume a great deal of time; but she was not discouraged. 'What are we going there for, if not to work?' she retorted. Well, if that was what they had set their hearts upon doing, said His Grace with a smile, they had his blessing. Indeed, they were at liberty to catalogue the Syriac books as well, if they wished; but the check-lists must be in Greek and the originals must be left behind when they quitted the Monastery. He did not add (preferring to embody his third command in a private letter to the Prior, as they were to discover after their arrival at Sinai) that this permission was for the twins alone, and was not transferable.

Gradually the party assembled; and each scholar, as he arrived, was taken along to Archbishop Porphyrios and introduced. The twins were relieved to find that Bensly was looking extremely well, with a healthy tan and a springy step to his gait. Mrs Burkitt, by contrast, arrived in a very indifferent state of health, and her Cairo doctor advised against the trip; but after some days of delay, and changes of mind, and curious experiments with a litter slung between two camels (ending, naturally, in disaster), Mrs Burkitt suddenly decided to chance it and accompany the party, as originally planned. This decision was finally taken after her romantic nature had been stirred by a day-excursion to the Tombs of the Kings, and was attended by only one drawback, namely that the luggage of her companions had already left by camel. Hence it was necessary for the other members of the party to dash madly round Cairo, buying the necessary extra provisions, having them hastily packed, and arranging for them to be dispatched to Suez by train. Eventually, after a few days' delay, the party was able to set off. This time, their dragoman was one Ahmed (whom the twins had tried to engage on their previous expedition, as he had been strongly recommended; but at the time he had been down with influenza).

From the standpoint of scholarship, the second visit to Sinai proved to be as rewarding and successful as the first. Unfortunately, the same cannot be said of the personal relationships between the various members of the party. There were a number of reasons for the tensions which arose, all of them – as is usual in human affairs – perfectly understandable. To begin with, the twins, on their previous trip, had been entirely their own masters: now, they were members of a team – a team, moreover, which included two women (one, Mrs Bensly, elderly; one, Mrs Burkitt, very young) who were not scholars at all, and who must inevitably have regarded the tour as simply an exceptionally-exciting kind of holiday. There was, too, a great diversity of temperaments, exacerbated by a considerable variation in ages: R.L. Bensly was sixty-two, Agnes and Maggie were fifty, Harris was forty-one, Frank Burkitt was twenty-eight. A further complicating factor was that the scholars in the party fell naturally into two groups (which threatened, at times, to become camps): Burkitt was a pupil of Bensly, and therefore, when faced in his study of the palimpsest with an indecipherable word or with some curious usage in syntax, would naturally turn to his teacher rather than to the twins for a second opinion. Rendel Harris, on the other hand, was primarily a friend of Agnes and Maggie and had joined the expedition at their invitation, and so tended to work in the closest collaboration with them, and to take his problems to their table. Further, Bensly was elderly, and a professor; and though of a shy and retiring nature, would be accustomed to a certain amount of deference to his wishes, especially from those whom he considered to be not only junior in age but also less expert in scholarship. And he would have been a very exceptional elderly man if he did not have, at his time of life, fixed notions of the way in which most matters ought to be conducted – the more so as he was noted for his meticulous approach to his work. Burkitt, on the other hand, was very young and probably, at that stage, a little full of himself, as brilliant and recently-graduated young men are apt to be. His knowledge of feminine psychology was doubtless very limited, and his enthusiasm for his work an absorbing passion which left him no time (even if he had possessed the inclination) for tactful and carefully-worded approaches to rather prickly women more than twenty years his senior. In his riper years, Burkitt was a greatly-loved man – more than one person has described him as 'a saint' – but it is likely that he sometimes could be tactless, dogmatic and impatient when young.

The forceful temperaments of Agnes and Maggie did not improve matters. It was only natural that they should feel strong proprietory rights in both the Monastery and the palimpsest, in view of the fact that the discovery of the latter within the walls of the former – that discovery without which there would have been no expedition at all – was theirs, and theirs alone. Further, they had already put in a good deal of preliminary work on the document. Maggie computed that they had devoted an entire fortnight to photographing it, and 'at least two hundred and ten hours at home in developing and arranging the plates.' This fact made them feel that they should be constantly consulted about every problem connected with its text – which they were not. In addition, they knew the monks personally, and the Librarian was already a close friend; they knew, as no one else did, exactly the appropriate technique for coaxing the Monastery authorities into according them the precise facilities that were needed. Bensly and Burkitt could hardly fail to be irritated by the twins' constant air of general knowledgeability; nor would their pique be lessened by the fact that the Prior – now none other than old Galakteon, who had been elevated to this high office since their previous visit – had expressed the wish that all requests should be made to him through Agnes. As the leading scholars in an essentially-male field, Bensly and Burkitt could not be expected to take kindly to female domination, least of all from the stubborn residents of Castlebrae, who always knew exactly what they wanted, and meant to get it.

But there was a deeper and more subtle difference between Bensly and Burkitt on the one hand and Harris, Agnes and Maggie on the other – a difference of attitude towards that scholarship which was their common passion. The academic world is inhabited by scholars of two distinct kinds, whose difference can best be expressed (though only very approximately) by borrowing terms from mathematics: there are 'pure' scholars, and there are 'applied' scholars. The former would insist that scholarship is, and must always remain, an end in itself. The sole objective of all their study and research is to increase the sum of knowledge, to add to what is *known* in their particular subject. Other scholars, however – often no less brilliant and erudite – are always anxious that what they have learned or discovered shall, if possible, be put to some definite practical use, either by themselves or by someone else. For men of this second type, scholarship is always, basically, a tool: a means, ultimately, to some other end. In English studies, for example, there is a wide gulf fixed between the man who unearths, edits and (for no other reason than that they are new material) publishes a number of quite trivial and uninteresting letters written by some major figure in English literature, and the man who uses his scholarship and research to write a book which will enable the same author's major writings to be better understood and better enjoyed. Between these two types of scholar there tends to exist a slight tension, in any field of study, though it usually lurks below the surface until some situation brings it into sight.

In terms of our *dramatis personae*, Bensly and Burkitt were 'pure' scholars, the twins and Harris were 'applied' scholars. To the latter, scholarship was, in the last analysis, the particular means by which they served God. They were delighted to add to existing knowledge; but they would have repudiated any suggestion that research was an end in itself. On a long view, it was simply one of the many means by which men were enabled to feel more sure of the fundamental facts of their religion, and so might be set on the road to becoming better Christians. They would accordingly become more excited over the Lewis palimpsest (since this provided men with a very early version of the Gospels, and so helped them to feel more confident that the actual words of Jesus Christ were in their possession) than over, say, *The Story of Ahikar*, which was simply a pagan legend of no possible moral or spiritual value. This difference in fundamental presuppositions and basic attitudes towards their work would, in itself, make for slight below-the-surface irritation between the two camps: those who formed the opposite group, though excellent folk in their way, would be considered to have very definite limitations.

But the explosive material included in the party has not yet been exhausted. There was, for example, Mrs Burkitt. She, like her husband, was extremely young, and was, in addition, both beautiful and richly endowed with charm. In short, without any deliberate effort on her part, she was only too well equipped in personality and appearance for stealing the limelight in the preliminary stages of the journey. Chatting with acquaintances in the lounge of Shepheard's Hotel, or when the party was consulting the head of the American Mission in Cairo about a suitable dragoman, she would be the centre of attention, unconsciously shifting the focal point of the group away from the twins to herself. She was endowed with all those essentially-feminine airs and graces which the twins were conscious that they lacked. She dressed very well, and looked extremely attractive, and knew it. The Giblews dressed badly, and were aware of the fact; their virtues lay, perhaps, a little below the surface – their lovableness, especially, being revealed only to intimate friends. It is perhaps not unjust to Mrs Burkitt to surmise that she regarded the sisters as two quaint and rather comic figures. She would remember funny old Samuel Lewis from the days when his household lived in Harvey Road; and no doubt her opinion of his wife and sister-in-law had been formed at that time. A further nail in poor Amy Burkitt's coffin was the luckless chance that she, alone of the whole party – she, the very antithesis of blue-stocking erudition – proved to be highly skilled in the debased dialect spoken by the dragoman and the camel-drivers (the legacy of a childhood spent in Beirut): a dialect which even Maggie, whose conversational Arabic was considered to be very good indeed, and Bensly, who was said to be the most distinguished Arabic scholar in Europe, were unable to follow at all closely. To be defeated in one's own field by a fashionable and wholly unscholarly woman, whose interests were essentially those of other fashionable women, was a very bitter pill indeed for the twins to swallow.

But if, from the twins' point of view, Mrs Burkitt was something of a trial, Mrs Bensly was a disaster. This lady came of an aristocratic Prussian family – Bensly had married her during his student days at Halle – and was, to put it mildly, unaccustomed to roughing it. On her own admission, the rate of progress was seriously slowed down and precious time unnecessarily wasted during the first few days in the desert because of her repeated complaints. The whole caravan would be halted while the dragoman was fetched from the head of the procession to adjust her saddle for the fifth time. Also, with that good-but-not-quite-perfect command of the English language which is common to foreigners, she was liable at times to use not only the wrong word, but the downright unfortunate one. In the book which she was later to write, for example, she describes Mrs Lewis' photographs as 'excellent of their kind', and announces that, when some difficulty arose at the Monastery, it was smoothed out 'by the kind interference of Mrs. Lewis.' If these unfortunate phrases are to be taken as characteristic samples of her conversation, it is hardly surprising that she frequently poured troubled waters on the oil of social intercourse. Whatever splendid virtues she may have possessed, tact, it is clear, was not one of them. When, subsequently, she came to write her recollections of this expedition, her phraseology strongly suggests that she regarded the twins simply as experienced travellers and nothing more: two women who had been taken along merely because they would be useful as guides and interpreters.

There is no mention of their academic knowledge; and her choice of words, when alluding to them, is consistently belittling and condescending in tone. When she mentions the palimpsest, there is not so much as a hint that it was Agnes who discovered it; and her references to 'photographs' suggest, in their context, a couple of hasty snapshots rather than a skilled reproduction of each of the manuscript's four hundred pages. Deliberately or unwittingly, Mrs Bensly anticipates the 'selective reporting' of the less scrupulous modern journalists: that is to say, every recorded statement is true (or has a clear basis of fact), but it is so presented as to give the reader, overall, a totally false impression.

No doubt Agnes and Maggie were over-sensitive and inclined to be touchy; but Mrs Bensly must certainly have been very trying, and there is much to excuse the twins' angry irritation. They were, in Ibsen's phrase, 'fighting at the outposts of thought' – fighting for recognition of the fact that some women have as good intellects as any man, and that such individuals have a right to be considered men's equals, if their gifts and their knowledge justify it. This view was winning very slow and reluctant acceptance in the academic world in 1893. Now when one is maintaining an unpopular position, one is always inclined to assume – sometimes too readily and on insufficient evidence – that acquaintances hitherto considered to be 'on one's side' have 'gone over to the enemy' and are deliberately plotting one's overthrow. Trival incidents become magnified when pondered; the molehill-sized thoughtless remark swells into a mountainous insult or snub; fresh facts, viewed from one's own suspicious, defensive angle, are quickly fitted into the new disquieting hypothesis; innocent words or actions come to seem capable of no interpretation but a sinister one. In the present instance, was not Mrs Bensly a German – and therefore (as she was at no pains to conceal) bitterly opposed to women who abandoned their own proper sphere and dared to invade the sacred intellectual precincts of the male? Whether the twins were right or wrong about the Professor's wife it is impossible to tell at this distance; but we can at least sympathise with them in this situation – she was certainly a very difficult woman – and also at those many other points in their lives when they felt (sometimes, but not always, mistakenly) that they were the objects of antagonism, malice and intrigue. Agnes and Maggie were, in their small way, pioneers; and a pioneer, to be successful, needs a streak of fanaticism. If he is to swim vigorously against the tide, he needs a high degree of confidence in his own judgment. Those who would suggest to him (or her) other ways of doing things need to be diplomats of a high order. This, Mrs Bensly plainly was not: indeed, none of the party was, with the exception of Rendel Harris who, perhaps, as a Quaker, possessed a higher innate respect for women, knew how to deal with them as persons, and was accustomed to their taking a full share in all important matters, whether intellectual or spiritual. Mrs Bensly's Prussian blood did not allow her to view her own sex in this light: 'kids, kirk and kitchen', and not Syriac codices, were their province. And, apart from all other considerations, it has always been the Prussian tradition to command, rather than to yield gracefully.

The party, outwardly cordial, had split into two clearly-marked camps long before the travellers reached Sinai. It is possible to feel a strong sympathy for the members of each group: given the conditions, the temperament, the background and the outlook of those on the expedition, friction could scarcely have been avoided. But for the fortunate chance that each 'camp' contained one kindly gentle soul – Bensly on one side ('he was always very kind to us' Agnes wrote to Harris when they were all back in Cambridge) and Rendel Harris on the other, – things might have been very much worse.

Ultimately, of course, the group was held together by the work they had come to do, and by the one attitude which all shared, namely, a total consecration to scholarship. This papered over the cracks, and prevented an open breach. Whatever the tensions and irritations on the personal level, the task in hand was duly accomplished. How exactly did they tackle it? Let Agnes describe the way of working: 'After much discussion' (a euphemism, one suspects), 'the three scholars agreed to the following division of labour: Mr Rendel Harris to read the first hundred and four pages of the palimpsest, Mr Burkitt the second hundred or more (these included thirty which he had already copied from my photographs), and Professor Bensly the remainder, together with revising as much of the others' work as possible.' The day was divided into three watches, so that someone might always be at work from eight to eleven, from eleven to two, and from two to five. In view of the fact that the sun began sinking at half-past three, with consequent bad light, each watch was taken in rotation on successive days. It was agreed that the palimpsest should never be left unattended, the scholar taking the middle watch being required, that day, to postpone his lunch until two. By the Prior's special instruction, the palimpsest – wrapped in 'a pretty silk cover' which Mrs Bensly made out of a treasured handkerchief formerly belonging to her dead son – was to be housed each night in Agnes' tent: a mark of Galakteon's special favour which would perhaps not be too well received by some members of the party. Agnes considered the moment when this order was transmitted to be 'one of the proudest and happiest moments of my life', and was probably at no pains to disguise her satisfaction.

Harris, as the expedition's expert on ancient documents – he had recently been appointed lecturer in palaeography at Cambridge – pronounced the palimpsest to be 'by no means a difficult one, as palimpsests go,' though the pages varied greatly in distinctness. Naturally, the words of the under-writing were much more legible in the original than in Agnes' photographs; but there were many sheets from which the actual ink of the under-writing had faded, leaving only faint indications on the vellum from which words could be traced. Add to this the fact that many of the words were completely covered by the dark upper writing, that others were totally obscured by greasy thumbprints, and that most of them had to be read between the lines of the later script, and the reader will have some appreciation of the difficulty of the task.

While the three men settled down to work on the Lewis Codex, Agnes herself began to tackle a Jerusalem Syriac Lectionary (dated approximately 1120) which she had found on her previous visit. Harris, in his 'watches below', as it were, started cataloguing the Library's many unbound Syriac manuscripts, all of which were stored in open baskets and most of which were in a hopeless muddle – a task with which Agnes helped him whenever she felt the need for a change of occupation. Maggie set about that listing of the Arabic documents which, it will be recalled, the Archbishop had given her as a personal task. These were, for the most part, equally casually stored, and sorting them all out proved to be a much more time-consuming matter than cataloguing the Syriac collection, for they were much more numerous. At first, she was helped by Mrs Bensly, who counted the pages of each musty volume for her, but soon some of the monks had to be pressed into service lest the work be left unfinished. As to the contents of the storeroom where the twins' original discovery had been made, Agnes insisted that each basketful, as it was brought forth, should first be examined by Bensly and Burkitt, lest the twins or Harris should seem to have an unfair advantage over them in the matter of possible 'discoveries'. This arrangement, typical of Agnes' scrupulous sense of justice, proved however to be unnecessary: nothing at all exciting came to light.

On some mornings, as the scholars worked at their various tasks – the palimpsest-decipherers in the open air, the cataloguers in the Library – the desert silence would be suddenly broken by a babble of excited voices coming from beyond the garden, among which could be distinguished occasional Greek, or French, or even Russian words as orders were shouted to camel-drivers: yet another party of pilgrims had arrived. The leader of one such pious expedition, dismounting with relief from his camel and stretching his aching limbs, found himself the spectator of a curious scene. Close by the Monastery gate, that February morning, and in the centre of a little cluster of tents, could be seen what appeared at first sight to be one of those *tableaux vivants* so dear to the Victorian heart. A little knot of Europeans were grouped round a trestle table, at which was seated a dumpy middle-aged woman, wearing a sun hat and extremely dowdy clothes. She is bending over a small grubby manuscript, which is being held open for her by a second woman who seems to be almost a replica of the seated figure. The remarkable characteristic of this scene, as the pilgrim onlooker soon realised, is that everyone in the little group is tense and motionless, caught in 'Anglo-Saxon attitudes' like a fly in amber. It is as though something vitally important is about to happen; as though Sinai, by an act of faith, were about to be removed into the distant sea. As the pilgrim quickens his step and approaches, the dumpy woman suddenly moves – making it unmistakably clear, by her swift gesture that this is, indeed, no *tableau vivant* but rather some gripping drama, at the central moment of which the onlooker has chosen to arrive.

The woman at the table has dipped a watercolour brush into a small bottle of colourless liquid at her elbow: the three ladies and the three gentlemen bend eagerly forward, slightly altering their grouping against the backcloth provided by the white glare of the Monastery wall. 'Now!' she cries exultantly (as though she were in charge of an execution or a bayonet charge), sweeping her brush dramatically across the discoloured page in front of her. As the pilgrim cranes his neck to observe the result, bright green lettering, as if by magic, suddenly appears on the blank and grubby page. A gasp of excitement goes up from the three watching women, a mild cheer from two of the men; indeed, the gentle-faced bearded man – much to the astonishment of the watching pilgrim – goes pirouetting off round the tents, in a little solo dance of ecstasy. The young man holding his wife's hand is smiling broadly, and seems to be no less excited – though perhaps in a more subdued, well-bred English fashion. Alone of the group, the elderly gentleman with the heavy moustache appears quite unmoved. His only contribution to the general chorus of satisfaction is a grunt; nor does he look up as the party's Arab cook, hearing the muffled cheer which greeted the sudden appearance of the green writing, comes running out of his kitchen-tent, soup ladle in hand, to discover the cause of the excitement. The elderly man's face displays no emotion whatever. 'How long will it last, Mrs Lewis?' he enquires with the discouraging practical outlook of the sceptic, pointing at the splash of colour on the page. 'It will last for a hundred years!' replies the dumpy woman ecstatically, leaning back in her chair and waving her paintbrush in triumph. 'Huh – it hasn't yet been tried for a hundred years!' growls the elderly gentleman with a snort.

The occasion merits a somewhat melodramatic presentation, for this moment was Agnes' second great triumph at St Catherine's. The background to this scene may be quickly sketched in. Before leaving England, she had made enquiries in the Manuscript Room of the British Museum as to the best means of reviving ancient writing, where this had become faded, without risk of injury to script or vellum. As a result, she had come to Sinai armed with four bottles of an evil-smelling composition, together with a respirator to protect her from the fumes when the mixture required to be used indoors. This brew she was determined to use; but with womanly guile she bided her time, waiting for a suitable opportunity to broach the subject tactfully to Galakteon. She waited ten days. On the eleventh, she came upon an old volume whose pages were so faded as to be totally illegible, and which was plainly valueless in its existing condition. When Galakteon looked in to see how the twins were progressing, she casually asked his permission to work on this document with her 'scent-bottle'. He readily gave his consent; and when the writing came up in a brilliant hue of green, he was so astonished that he urged her to paint up the entire volume – and thereafter to use the magic mixture on several loose fragments in which he was especially interested. This was exactly what Agnes had been waiting for. In no time, she obtained permission to use it on the palimpsest itself – 'though only in places where it cannot be read otherwise, Kyria [Madame] Agnes,' Galakteon took the precaution of adding. Bensly at first disapproved strongly of the whole proceeding. He had seen, in Paris, a valuable codex which had been utterly ruined in this way (by a quite different reagent, it transpired). But eventually he was talked into agreement by Burkitt and Harris. With this treatment, much that it had hitherto been impossible to read became available to the scholars: in respect of Harris' allocation, as much as one-sixth of the whole. Which explains the Quaker scholar's little dance in the open air on the occasion of the first application of the 'scent' to the palimpsest.

So, day after day, the work went forward: the three men working at a washstand table in the open air, Agnes in her tent, Maggie and Mrs Bensly in the little draughty room with the glassless windows which adjoined the Library. The immense enthusiasm of the scholars can be gauged by the fact that Bensly often rose at six, in order to get in two hours' work before the first official 'watch' began at eight (whereupon Harris took to rising at dawn, in order to have access to it before the Professor!), and Agnes sat up with the codex far into the night, toiling away by the light of a flickering candle. Mrs Bensly, in her free time, tried to teach knitting to the Bedouin women in the neighbouring encampments. They declined to learn, but their menfolk took up the new craft with such enthusiasm that she soon had more pupils than her limited materials warranted. What did Amy Burkitt do? Neither Agnes nor Mrs Bensly mentions her at all in their subsequent books, nor does she figure in the former's unpublished journal. Perhaps she helped her husband as Mrs Bensly helped Maggie, doing those routine tasks for which no knowledge of the language was necessary; or perhaps she just yawned and counted the days till they could leave. There can have been little at Sinai to interest her, once she had explored the place, wandered round the monastery garden, watched the earnest class of apprentice knitters, and overtaken her arrears of correspondence.

There was little to break the ordered routine of each day, beyond the arrival and departure of parties of pilgrims. Sometimes these pious expeditions would be led by some noted continental scholar, with whom 'shop' could be talked after the day's work was done; and on one occasion, a lighter note was introduced by a woman member of a Russian party who, espying a cauliflower outside the cook's tent, rushed towards this somewhat prosaic symbol of home and clasped it to her bosom, her eyes filling with tears. From time to time, working hours would be enlivened by a discussion between the Greek-speaking scholars and the monks, 'a frequent topic being the authority of Synods.' When this subject came up, the twins were once more in a strong position, since under Presbyterianism Synods have definite authority; and their prestige would rise a few more degrees in the status barometer, at the expense of the Anglicans Bensly and Burkitt, whose Church was of the opinion that danger, rather than safety, was to be found in numbers. But now and then in these spirited exchanges between guests and hosts, argument would veer dangerously towards some thorny subject. At such moments, the twins found it a safe plan to make some casual reference to the Pope, for (says Agnes) 'this at once caused a diversion of the monks' energies to an antagonist worth hitting.' The Greek Orthodox Church, to which the monks belonged, is of course organised quite separately from the Roman Catholic Church, and regards the Pope in much the same light as would an Ulster Protestant.

Agnes, whose thirst for knowledge was unquenchable and wide-ranging, repeatedly tried to learn some bad language, but never succeeded. Whenever an interminable parley arose between some pilgrim party and the Bedouin over the precise route to be taken on the homeward journey, and when, in spite of the patient moderatorship of Father Nicodemus – who always presided over such wrangles – tempers became frayed and rude words flew about like arrows at Agincourt, Agnes would edge cautiously towards the angry group, in hopes of, (as she put it,) 'studying this department of Semitic science.' But, always, her attempts to eavesdrop were frustrated: 'the loud voices dropped and uplifted hands fell', she reports, 'whenever I tried to make my way into the centre of the throng; so I was baffled in my laudable effort.' It was, perhaps, the one male enclave into which she never succeeded in penetrating.

On the last evening of their stay, the Prior came to dine with them. They killed their fattest turkey in his honour and, though he would eat nothing, he was in a very jovial mood, teasing Harris unmercifully about his vegetarian principles. Some of the party had originally planned to visit the Holy Land on their way home; but there was too much work to be done on the palimpsest, and the project had to be abandoned.

Instead, they stayed till the last possible day consistent with being back in Cambridge for the beginning of term. Even on the morning of their departure, when the tables and inkstands had been packed, the three men continued to work on the codex with pencil and paper, for forty-two pages still remained unstudied (the twins were to tackle these on their next visit.) Father Galakteon put on his full Prior's robes to see them off; they signed the Visitors' Book, exchanged gifts, and struck camp. Galakteon insisted that the rest of the party should go on ahead, that he might have a last brief talk with the twins. He accompanied them a short distance towards the desert, leaning heavily on his gold-topped staff and walking very slowly. It was plain to his companions that he was now very ill and failing fast. They parted from him with scarcely a word, their hearts too full to speak, only too well aware that they would never see him again.

It had been decided that the party should travel at a leisurely pace, taking a full ten days over the journey and riding no more than twenty miles a day. But in the event they suffered repeated delays – now because of sandstorms, now because the Bedouin repeatedly spotted good camping sites early in the afternoon and insisted that the tents be pitched for the night. They began to grow anxious about the steamer, which sailed fortnightly for Marseilles, usually on a Thursday. It was essential that they should catch it; and they needed time at Suez to cash cheques, settle with the dragoman, repack their boxes, and secure passages at a time of year when the boats were invariably crowded. The twins and Harris, who had made the journey before and so knew the problems, were most insistent upon an increase of pace. They knew from experience that to miss the fortnightly boat at Suez meant, not only waste of time, but a hot and uncomfortable journey to Alexandria, where steamer berths would be much more difficult to obtain. But they were unable to convince the others that speed was imperative. Eventually, after a tiresome argument, they announced their intention of pushing ahead on the last evening, for by a few hours' ride in the moonlight they could catch up on their disrupted timetable. The indignation of the rest of the party at this decision was increased by the fact that Ahmed, the dragoman, insisted at the last moment on accompanying the advance guard, though the twins had given him strict orders to remain with their friends. Such disobedience was most uncharacteristic of this particular man: Agnes, with a touch of asperity, was not slow to attribute it to 'the excessive deference paid to him by *some* members of our party,' who had unwisely treated him as a father-figure (as the phrase would go, today) instead of as a senior servant, similar in rank to, say, a butler at home. She had several times rebuked him for quietly adding himself to the fireside circle in the evenings. Angry though she was at his flouting of her instructions, it was with a certain malicious satisfaction that she noted that her policy of keeping her distance and speaking with authority had paid the better dividends: he obviously respected her (and, we might guess, was genuinely attached to her: she inspired great affection in everyone who worked for her), since his determination to look after her safety and comfort took precedence over obedience to her orders. Anyway, nothing would induce the dragoman to return to the others; he waved a vague hand and insisted that the rearguard would be well looked after – had he not left them the cook, the waiter, the sheikh, the kitchen tent with all its equipment, and even the dining tent? ('Even', because this tent served as Harris' bedroom: he had to sleep that night in a wattle hut.)

This parting of the ways, trifling in itself, proved to be the last straw as far as personal relationships were concerned. It was to cause trouble later, for Mrs Bensly, in her book, was to attribute their departure to nothing more important than a desire to catch the mail with their letters for England, and to comment (yet another of her unfortunate phrases) 'we fared none the worse for this desertion.' The rearguard party was still further incensed to discover, next morning, that the oasis of 'Ayin Mousa was not four hours ride away (as the twins had insisted) but a mere hour and a half distant (Ahmed had misled Agnes); which meant that they could easily have reached it that evening without separating at all, and could still have ridden into Suez by noon the next day, their private deadline. It was all very unfortunate; and, viewed from the Bensly camp, the behaviour of the advance guard seemed wholly selfish, unreasonable and inexcusable.

The twins and Harris managed to catch the steamer, though the only double cabin available for the two women had been used for the storage of bananas from China to Suez; it smelled vilely musty, and was overrun with cockroaches and spiders. However, the fifty-two copies of *The Times* which had awaited them at Suez soon took their minds off the study of entomology. The Benslys had caught up with them in Suez, and there was a slightly strained and embarrassed meeting in the bank, – eased by the fact that there was no money for anyone, the bank agent having gone bankrupt: fortunately Harris banked elsewhere, and was able to finance everyone for the moment – and thereafter the Professor and his wife departed for Alexandria by the night train. Agnes advised strongly against this enterprise, knowing it to be an exhausting and uncomfortable journey, especially for a delicate man; but by this time relations were so strained that the Benslys felt it to be almost a matter of principle to reject her counsel. They travelled from Alexandria to Rome, where they were to meet their daughter; and while in that city, the elderly professor was rash enough to climb the Palatine Hill at dusk without an overcoat, and caught a severe chill. He could not wait to nurse it, for term was only a few days away. Three days after his arrival back in Cambridge, he was dead.

This sudden tragedy made final the breach between the two groups. Mrs Bensly would have been less than human had she not felt, in her grief and generally overwrought condition, that it was the fault of the twins that she had lost her husband. If they had not shown him the photographs of their silly palimpsest, he would never have gone dashing across deserts at his time of life, and after long years of very indifferent health. This view, apparently, she did not scruple to express to sympathetic friends and callers. It was equally natural that Agnes and Maggie, deeply as they felt for her in her bereavement – for had they not both lost their husbands as suddenly and swiftly? – should feel intense irritation and indignation when they learned that they were being blamed for the whole tragic affair. History, in the person of the Fellow of Bensly's college who was commissioned to write his memoir, seems to side with the twins in this unhappy controversy. The expedition, he writes, 'was a rather venturesome one for a man of his habits and time of life. But he seems thoroughly to have enjoyed the camel-riding which he had dreaded, and other experiences of his desert life, and to have been in such excellent health during his sojourn there that it is difficult to connect his death directly with this journey.' Was this, perhaps, a delicate way of hinting to his widow that she was being grossly unfair in thus blaming the Giblews? Poor Mrs Bensly, however, had further troubles with which to grapple. Her sight, always poor, began rapidly to fail, perhaps as a result of shock; and within a comparatively short period she became totally blind. Agnes tried not to be angry, and did her best to make allowances for her, especially when she learned of this new burden. She called upon her, and they had a long talk, mostly about her husband and children. 'She is very much broken down,' she wrote to Harris' wife, 'but if she could find a fresh interest, she may recover.'

Alas, she did 'find a fresh interest', and it only added fuel to the flame. Some kind friend suggested to her that she should learn Braille and thereafter write a short account of the expedition for the entertainment of the sightless. *Our Journey to Sinai* was published in ordinary type in 1896. It is a charming and interesting book, on the whole more enjoyable than Maggie's *How the Codex was Found*, which had been published at the end of the year of the second expedition, i.e. three years earlier. The latter volume, of course, deals mainly with the first expedition, and only very sketchily with the second; whereas Mrs Bensly's describes only the second trip and is written from the standpoint of a traveller, not a scholar. She has a vivid pen, and her failing sight at the time of the trip may account for the wealth of interesting detail. (Many critics have felt that there is a direct connection between Tennyson's intense particularity and his shortsightedness.) Knowing the circumstances under which it was written, one can visualise Mrs Bensly re-living those last days with her husband, as she sits at her Braille machine – can feel, indeed, the poignancy of each remembered detail. But as she goes *à la recherche du temps perdu*, she has eyes only for her husband: 'we' means she and him, and hardly anyone else comes into the picture – not even Burkitt, much less the twins, the references to whom, as we have seen, tend to be both slight and slighting. Any reader who simply skimmed the book, and who forgot the first few pages as soon as he had read them, might well be left with the impression that it had been a journey *à deux*. Under the circumstances, it would be foolish to expect any other kind of book; but there is no denying that, from other points of view, the total effect was unfortunate. The falling barometer of the twins' esteem, already lowered by the storms occasioned by her company in recent months, sank still further after reading Mrs Bensly's account, say, of the journey home, with its long list of inaccuracies and misrepresentations, and its harsh indignant references to 'forced marches' and 'desertion'. Agnes and Maggie were, at this stage, only beginning to establish themselves as scholars; but they had already acquired the scholar's approach to work in general, and to published work in particular. You must, above all else, be exact and accurate, even under circumstances where indisputable facts inconveniently destroy one's own preconceived theories. Yet here was a deliberately falsified picture being put about. One can scarcely blame them for being extremely angry. To do them justice, their anger was not prompted by personal vanity, though no doubt they were human enough to be more than a little mortified in that direction. What enraged them was this irresponsible and malicious attitude towards *facts* – as sacred to them as to the famous editor of the *Manchester Guardian*. Here was plain fiction, no less, which those who had no means of checking would accept as the exact truth. As they read on, all their irritation, damped down by the tragedy, began to return.

But there was worse to come. They had looked first at the final chapters, suspecting that Mrs Bensly might well provide the public with a different version of the last days of the ride home. Now, they began to read the book right through, from the beginning. In the chapter describing the welcome accorded to the travellers on arrival at the Monastery, the author launched forth on a 'purple passage' describing the hallowed associations of this sanctuary down the centuries. Here, she set the scene for the appearance of the Prior by dwelling solemnly on his holy office as 'the highest dignitary of the Catholic Church in this wide Mohammedan district. Had the rules of the Monastery required it,' she continues, 'we would willingly have knelt on the threshold, or kissed the hem of his garment.' So far so good – if a trifle emotional. The next paragraph, however, was shattering:

'. . . but our pious exaltation was doomed to disappointment. A stout redfaced monk, in the plain black garb of the Greek priesthood (rather greasy in this case), rushed forth with loud shouts of merriment, and fell on the neck of Mrs Lewis, with whom he had made friends during the previous winter. He patted her affectionately, he felt her garments, he made her sit by his side with his arm around her shoulders. A lively conversation then followed in modern Greek, of which we understood nothing, but frequent bursts of laughter showed it to be of a very pleasant nature . . . Several young monks watched this unecclesiastical mode of reception with unmoved faces. We tried to do the same . . . The good old man had to be propitiated, yet we did not relish the thought that we might have to submit, in our turn, to similar familiarities. However, we were dismissed with a gracious shake of the hand . . .'

Agnes' feelings, when her horrified eyes fell upon this passage, can be imagined. 'Fell on the neck of Mrs Lewis . . . patted her affectionately . . . felt her garments . . . sit by his side with his arm around her shoulders . . . might have to submit, in our turn, to similar familiarities . . .' – Castlebrae rocked to its very foundations. To be accused, and in print, and in a book which all Cambridge was buying, of flirting outrageously with a monk . . . and for That Woman deliberately to suggest, maliciously and in cold blood, that dear

Father Galakteon was no more than a satyr in a cassock –
really, it was too much. This offensive, and wholly untrue,
picture of herself would, she knew, be seized upon eagerly by
her enemies ('a shameless flirt, my dear chap – and at her age!
Must be fifty if she's a day! Disgusting! All that poppycock
about wanting to be a scholar – women are all the same, my
dear fellow!'), for it was exactly what they wanted to believe
about bluestockings. But far worse was the cruel libel on
poor Galakteon, hardly cold in his grave, poor man – they
had learned that he had died a fortnight after Bensly – and,
even if he had been still alive, too far away to defend his
reputation against the shameful accusations of this dreadful
woman! To see his warm-hearted, friendly nature given such
a disgusting twist!

She strode to her desk, seized a pen and a sheet of
notepaper, and sat down to pen a strong letter to the editor of
the *Cambridge Chronicle* – a letter which subsequently filled a
column and a half of small print in that journal, and which
ran to some two thousand six hundred words. When, a few
days later, the *Cambridge Independent Press* printed a short
notice of the book, in the course of which the reviewer
innocently commended the writer for 'that special freshness
and a confidential frankness which makes the charm of
private letters,' its editor, also, received a two-thousand-
word rejoinder. So did the editor of the *Leeds Mercury*, whose
reviewer, in the course of a long write-up, unfortunately
singled out (and quoted in full) the account of Galakteon's
welcome, as 'giving the reader a lively idea of the Abbot who
ruled this religious fraternity.' Agnes was on the warpath. In
each case, she expresses the hope that the publishers will
suppress the book, containing as it does such an 'absolute
travesty' of the facts. The truth was – she goes on to explain –
that Galakteon, who was already dying at the time (though
he had concealed the seriousness of his illness from his
friends) was merely overjoyed at seeing once more three
people (the third, of course, was Harris) whom he never
expected to see again in this world; but he had *never* 'fallen on
her neck' or 'embraced her'. Writing temperately but very
firmly, Agnes disposes of one misrepresentation after

another, setting forth the true facts, not only of the welcome at St Catherine's but also of the parting of the ways at the end of the return journey. Dates, times, names and places (down to the most inconspicuous oasis) are all listed; the evidence marshalled; the facts supported by cross-references. These letters are some of her most painstaking works of scholarship. She had no intention of allowing the good Prior's reputation to be smeared, neither was she willing to go down to posterity as an unfeeling ogre who would lightheartedly slave-drive an elderly, delicate Professor to a premature death (for Mrs Bensly had broadly hinted that his vitality was so depleted by the forced marches that he could offer no successful resistence to a germ). She generously attributes all the major blunders to misprints, and is at pains to refer to the Professor's widow as 'someone we all love and respect' – surely the only time on record when Agnes told a deliberate lie? – but, in the manner of a cross-examining counsel, she makes the witness discredit herself by every means in her power.

Did she take the whole affair far too seriously? Who, in Cambridge, *really* believed that she had flirted with Galakteon, apart from the usual handful of village gossips who will believe anything? No doubt we can appreciate that it would be painful to see an old and dear friend maligned in print, especially by someone who had received much kindness at his hand; and anyone would wish to clear themselves of an implied charge that they had been directly responsible for the death of a much-respected man. But to dismiss the whole affair as a storm in a teacup would surely be wrong: Agnes realised that, behind the actual happenings, much was at stake. She was fighting, not for herself, but for her sex – and in particular, for those of her sex who aspired to intellectual activity. The position of such daring women, in those days, was a precarious one, and their role difficult. On the one hand, it was essential that they should not give the impression of having become unsexed. They needed to retain, and to display, all the essentially feminine virtues and graces (sweetness, gentleness, womanly sympathy – not to mention skill at needlework and cookery) in order to show that, in spite of being 'clever', they were just *typical* women, and not freaks. Brains must not become associated with pseudo-maleness in other directions, if the trail were to be blazed. On the other hand, it was equally vital that they should never put themselves in a position where they could be accused of trading on their sex in realms where it should not operate: they must not be 'feminine' in more sinister directions, using womanly wiles to entrap aged but susceptible scholars into divulging academic secrets or (worse still) luring them into unsuitable marriages. Much more than Agnes' personal reputation, then, was involved in this situation. Once let the idea gain currency that that Castlebrae woman was so heartless that she could display all lack of consideration for a delicate elderly man, or that she would make sheeps' eyes at any male (even one dedicated to poverty, chastity and obedience), and her work, however good, would henceforth be written off with scorn. Damned in the dons' Combination Rooms – those centres of gossip akin to the village pub – she would henceforth be coldly excluded from the academic circles which she was struggling to enter, and any work she might henceforth produce would be assumed to have been filched, by feminine guile, from some male scholar. It took courage to write those letters, to set Cambridge buzzing like a beehive, to become involved in much unpleasantness and malicious tittle-tattle; but such considerations had never deterred Agnes from doing what she saw to be her plain duty, and they did not deter her now. Posterity should respect her for the vigour with which she flung herself into this battle. In time, the nine days wonder faded from the public memory; but a blow had been struck on behalf of those women scholars of a later generation, who were one day to enter upon the inheritance she left them.

One of the sadder repercussions of this row was that it naturally worsened the twins' relationship with the Burkitts. The latter, as was only to be expected, sided with Mrs Bensly out of loyalty to her dead husband – though no doubt they were fully aware of her weaknesses. Outwardly, the friendship remained cordial, but it was never the same again. Agnes, from this time forward, was always inclined to be suspicious, often feeling that the Burkitts were 'getting at her'; even that Burkitt was making use of her scholarship for his own ends, quietly helping himself to her work in order to further his own career. That she was totally unjust in this suspicion is agreed by all her intimate friends who are still living. Burkitt was a man of absolute integrity, and of such brilliance and erudition that he had no need to make use of anyone else's knowledge, least of all hers. From time to time, he certainly disagreed with some of Agnes' conclusions on various Semitic matters, as he did with the opinions of other experts in the same field; but his disagreement was always on the academic, never on the personal, level. He could always support his dissent with sound arguments. Sometimes he felt – no doubt with justification – that Agnes had not ranged widely enough before coming to her conclusions. If he stood his ground, it was not because he despised the twins' scholarship, but because his own was greater or more exact. Burkitt was a fine type of man, and no doubt this subsequent tension gave him pain. But if we have sympathy for him, we can feel a like sympathy for Agnes. She had, no doubt, something of the defensiveness of the person who has reached distinction by other than the conventional route. The twins were made of tough fibre. They sprang from a respectable, middle-class professional background in which intellectual strenuousness was taken for granted; they came from a country of broad culture, in which it was not enough simply to be 'clever' – one was expected also to value the things of the mind and the spirit. In their circle, character was prized as much as culture, and – thanks to Dr Robertson – culture as much as mere knowledge, and it was taken for granted that one's knowledge would not be confined to the subject by which one earned one's daily bread. They were also, by nature, sociable women who enjoyed the company of other people and could adapt themselves skilfully to different environments – whether of a Master's Lodge or the slums of Romsey Town. Through Samuel Lewis and the Scots dons at St Columba's Church, they possessed the entrée into the right circles; and they were rich – rich without being parvenu. Hence, in spite of the obstacles, they were able to make a place for themselves in Cambridge, and ultimately to be accepted by all but the most old-fashioned and starchy among its residents.

But beneath all their self-assurance there always lurked vestiges of unsureness, based, not on background (in which they found nothing of which to be ashamed) but on their sex: that faint undercurrent of defensiveness which, even today, can still sometimes be discerned in women who have invaded such traditionally-male spheres as medicine. These qualities did sometimes rise to the surface, causing their over-sensitive nostrils to scent impending trouble where, in fact, Cambridge lay in unruffled calm. In after years, as they pursued their studies, it did seem to them that, from the Burkitt's spacious house on the corner of West Road, wisps of smoke were occasionally emerging which their over-sharp eyes alone could perceive: wisps of smoke which others would ignore, but which seemed to the twins to be shaping themselves into a cloud, no bigger than a man's hand, heralding the faint rumblings of yet another approaching storm. Viewed from the higher ground of ninety years later, we may be convinced that they were mistaken and must regret this ready assumption of theirs as unfortunate. But a biographer must, above all else, be honest: and the fact remains, and must be duly recorded, if only to be sympathetically deplored.

VIII

The Ladies of Castlebrae

Many of the noblest characters, those who refuse to conform to the common pattern, are not only many-sided, but many-hued. Like the opal, they must be contemplated under various aspects before their rich significance is thoroughly comprehended. We are sometimes mysteries to ourselves – can we wonder that we are often mysteries to others?

– Agnes Smith: *Effie Maxwell*

'A good book might be written (and a bad book could very easily be written) on Great Widowhoods,' writes Dr G.M. Trevelyan in his introduction to the memoirs of one such woman, Mary Paley Marshall. Looking back on a lifetime spent in Cambridge, the historian no doubt could recollect a dozen or more women whose portraits might fittingly adorn such a gallery; for within the ancient universities there are always to be found a number of remarkable widows – women who are seen at their true 'Greatness' only after death has removed the overshadowing brilliance of their husbands.

The marked individuality of Agnes and Maggie had never, at any time, been obscured or even dimmed by the existence of their respective husbands. Nevertheless, they would merit a place in such a book as Dr Trevelyan envisages – should anyone, in the face of his warning, be courageous enough to write it. The quarter of a century stretching from Samuel's death in 1891 to the outbreak of war in 1914 is the period of their Great Widowhood, and it can conveniently be studied as a unity, though technically it could be extended several years in both directions.

Over this span of time, Castlebrae became the centre of a social, intellectual and religious circle. There were other constellations more brilliant, of course, and more adorned with Famous Names; but few more interesting and entertaining. In their home, between their travels, the twins entertained widely, worked assiduously at their scholarship, prepared lectures for learned societies, wrote books, and sallied forth to receive honorary doctorates from various universities. It is this period of their life which is today recalled most distinctly by those who still remember them; for no one can remember either Mr Lewis or Mr Gibson, or could tell an enquirer who they were or what they did. The Ladies of Castlebrae became, in their lifetime, almost legendary figures: clever and somewhat eccentric hostesses in a world already peopled by such full-bodied 'characters' as Montagu Butler and Oscar Browning. 'Mrs Lewis and Mrs Gibson,' (writes Aelfrida Tillyard) 'were not in the least like any other learned ladies whom you have ever seen or heard of. They were not like Hypatia or Corinna or Les Femmes Savantes or Hannah More or any of the Newnham and Girton dons. They were like each other and like no one else.'

In their forty-ninth year, they were becoming distinguished; but physically they still remained almost indistinguishable from one another. Possibly the truth about them can only be expressed in an Irish way, by saying that one could only tell them apart when they were together: confronted with one of them on her own, most people would hastily try to work out which one this was. But even when they were in the same room, not everyone could remember which was which. Dining for the first time at the home of Sir Robert Ball, a gentleman quietly drew his host to one side and murmured, 'I am to take Mrs Lewis in to dinner: which of the two is she?' Sir Robert (so the story goes) replied,

'Frankly, I can't tell you; but so-and-so is taking in Mrs Gibson – watch whom he takes, and then approach the other one.' Five minutes later, Sir Robert's sleeve was anxiously plucked by Mrs Gibson's dinner partner, with a similar question. But the Astronomer-Royal was equal to the occasion, and astutely replied, 'Well, so-and-so is taking in Mrs Lewis: wait till he has collected his partner, and then take her sister.' The Presbyterian minister's Highland maid once entered her master's study with the remark, 'Excuse me, sir, but there's a lady to see you: she *says* she's Mrs Lewis – but it's Mrs Gibson!' Had they learnt of such incidents, our heroines would have been delighted, for they were immensely proud of being identical twins. Their intimate friends, however, always maintained that once you had observed the difference between them, it was impossible ever again to confuse them. Agnes' features were more definite – 'a little crumpled up, somehow,' as one expressed it: her cheeks more red, her voice more loud, her manner more assertive. Aelfrida Tillyard makes use of an entertaining analogy. 'When we were children,' she writes, 'we liked our bacon "puzzled" – that is, steeped in hot water until most of its colour, taste and salt had been removed and it had become mild and benign. If you had taken Mrs Lewis and "puzzled" her and then smoothed her out, the result would have been Mrs Gibson.'

They shopped at Worth for their clothes – on the way home from the Middle East – but *haute couture* was the very last thing their appearance suggested, somehow: it may have been the fault of the sombre colours they invariably chose – or of the bunchy figures upon which the elegant gowns were perforce displayed. Though they did not dress alike, the general effect was always the same: black or dark grey dresses trimmed with lace, topped by squashy black hats with limp brims (and more lace) which, when combined, gave them the general appearance of College bedmakers. And white stockings – always worn, and their best-remembered article of apparel; indeed, on occasion, they were positively thrust upon the notice of friends, as on the day when the twins insisted upon demonstrating to a slightly shocked Professor

Macalister 'how we ride our camels'. This exercise involved sitting astride on the arm of the sofa and disclosing, in the process, an alarming amount of white-sheathed leg. More than one Magdalene Street shopkeeper was sternly rebuked for carelessly swilling down his front step in a way that spattered these precious objects with mud.

Agnes rather fancied her taste in dress, and enjoyed, in her leisure moments, the thoroughly feminine occupation of improving upon the creations of M. Worth by adding inconsequential jet panels here and there to make her gowns 'more sparkling'. Such adjustments were sometimes slightly *outré*. Once, when she was going out to dine, she was unable to find the modesty vest which was a quite indispensable adjunct to her favourite evening dress which possessed an alarming décolletage. She could not possibly appear in public without it, and all the other modesty vests which her maid produced were quite the wrong colour. Her resourceful mind, faced with the need to leave in five minutes, was, however, equal to the occasion: she pinned a large bunch of daffodils across her too-visible bosom, and departed in triumph. Unfortunately for her, however, her host's drawing-room was extremely hot, and before the end of the evening the daffodils had wilted considerably, with disastrous results.

Castlebrae was a considerable mansion of more than twenty rooms, very Gothic Revival in appearance – their enemies declared that they had attempted to make it look as much like a Master's Lodge as possible – and with a room projecting over the porch. From a practical point of view, this last feature enabled visitors to enter or alight from their carriages without getting wet; but from the visual point of view, it made the whole building look twice as impressive and considerably larger. Within, the corridors formed a squat 'T', with a short upright for the entrance hall, and a long crosspiece leading to the various public rooms. At the extreme end of the left side of the crosspiece was the drawing-room, occupying most of the west side of the house, with the twins' bedroom above; between the drawing-room and the hall was located a small room called 'the boudoir' (but in reality Maggie's study), wherein hung the photograph of the Gibsons playing chess (see epigraph to Chapter IV) and the oak mantelpiece of which bore, beneath the shelf, a melancholy inscription in Arabic testifying to the brevity of man's enjoyment in the present world. The corresponding small room on the right-hand side of the hall housed the twins' library . . . until Agnes' unwearying use of the pungent reagent on palimpsests exercised such a deterrent effect upon everyone's appetite that the books had to be moved to the most isolated possible location, namely the tower room over the porch. Adjoining the library, and balancing the drawing-room on the opposite side of the house, was the dining-room. This contained one of those huge rectangular Victorian tables, running the whole length of the room and enlarged by several 'leaves'. It was here that Agnes and Maggie usually worked, since such a table could accommodate innumerable pages of manuscript and still leave room for lunch to be set at one end. This room had a further advantage: it commanded a view of the drive, and so enabled the scholars to have a preview of prospective callers, and to issue appropriate instructions.

Their days followed a set pattern. Each morning, after family prayers with the servants, the twins would sit in opposite corners of the bay windows and read the Bible devotionally in the original tongues, preparatory to drawing up their chairs to the dining-room table and tackling the morning's work, or visiting the University Library to check some reference. After lunch – often no more than a poached egg and a milk pudding, for like so many intellectual people they were absolutely indifferent to food and never noticed what they ate – the afternoon would be filled with social calls of the formal kind which convention then prescribed. (Like most wise rebels, they knew the importance of careful conformity in the matter of non-essentials: any other behaviour merely means that you will be written off as a crank, and your valuable new ideas discounted.) In the evening, or on such evenings as they were neither lecturing nor entertaining, their studies would be resumed, or they would peruse scholarly journals – of which a large pile, in innumerable languages, was arranged on a little table at the foot of the stairs – or write those long interesting letters to friends which no one today seems to have the time to compose.

There were always people coming to stay, or being entertained to meals while on a visit to Cambridge: continental scholars anxious to learn more about the palimpsest, learned priests of all branches of the Church – Belgian Catholic fathers, French Protestant pastors, Waldensian ministers, an occasional Orthodox Archimandrite, and even – years later – the Archbishop of Mount Sinai himself (they took him up the river to watch the May Races); friends they had met abroad, such as Whitelaw Reid, the American Ambassador, met at Sinai in 1895 (they had acted as his interpreter); women who, like their friend Mary Kingsley, had 'done interesting things'; dons from Girton and Newnham; and, in due course, pioneer suffragettes – all these and many more would flit in and out of Castlebrae, sometimes in ones and twos, sometimes in droves.

Of the scholars who came to stay, one man in particular had good reason to remember his visit. He was attending a College Feast, and over lunch explained to the twins that he would probably not return until the small hours. Agnes declared her intention of sitting up for him. The usual polite argument followed, which ended in her agreeing to provide him with a doorkey, so that the household could retire at its usual hour. It was about two o'clock when he walked, yawning, up the drive, more than ready for bed. As he approached the lawn before the front door, he was startled to hear an alarming bounding noise. Over the kitchen wall there suddenly appeared a veritable Hound of the Baskervilles, dragging his kennel behind him at the end of a chain with a series of menacing bounces. The huge animal rushed up to the unfortunate reveller, leapt at him, knocked him flat and stood on his chest, uttering menacing growls. Any slight movement or faint gasp for help on the scholar's part resulted in snarling fangs snapping at his throat. So he had no alternative but to remain silent and stay put. He was still there, with the dog mounted like a sentinel on his chest, when the maid came down at six o'clock and was able to release him – chilled and bedewed and stiff and in a very bad temper – from his undignified position. It transpired that, only a few days before his visit, the twins had bought a dog, having been alarmed by the number of burglaries in the neighbourhood; and an obliging friend had procured for them (in all innocence) a Cuban bloodhound. This animal had been specially trained to pursue runaway workers on his master's plantation and to imprison them, in the manner described, until the arrival of the overseer.

But the occasions by which the twins are best remembered are not the times when they accorded hospitality to occasional visitors, but their full-dress dinners, receptions, and garden-parties. They dearly loved a crowd; and on these formal occasions would often entertain more than twenty people to a ten-course dinner, when the table would be decorated with a bowl of dusty shrivelled fruits from Sinai, and the repast would end with the handing round of chocolates which, for some unaccountable reason, invariably tasted strongly of mothballs. Somehow, there was always something slightly off-key about these affairs. For example, the guests would perhaps include two clergymen, and each would be asked by one of the sisters to say grace – so that, at the appropriate moment, both divines would rise simultaneously and begin different graces at the same moment, in a sort of choric speech. Or, if it were a lunch party for undergraduates, there was sure to be some student present who had received an invitation really intended for another man of the same name in his College, so that a youth whose sole interest was horseracing would find himself in a company where conversation was confined to Presbyterian affairs, to the great bewilderment of himself and his neighbours. Sometimes it was the invitation itself which, through infelicitous wording, caused the trouble, as on the day when the Vice-Chancellor received a printed card bidding him to lunch 'to meet the students of Westminster College.' And sometimes the inflexible protocol of hospitality was startlingly varied in the interests of what seemed to them to be justice. For example, there was a day when one of the guests, a young Scottish nobleman, arrived for lunch nearly three-quarters of an hour late. The twins did not delay the meal for his benefit; and by the time that he turned up, stammering his embarrassed apologies (his watch, it appeared, had suddenly gone wrong), the rest of the party had reached the dessert. He was not forgiven. On the contrary, the unhappy man was served with the full meal – five courses – and had to gulp it down, as best he could, under the uncomfortable eyes of the rest of the company, who waited with ill-concealed restlessness for him to finish. Agnes' view was that he had been inexcusably rude, and must be punished: God might think twice before damning a man of such quality, but she herself did not share the Divine hesitation. If insistence upon the requirements of good manners meant that some 'important' or 'influential' person would be offended, that was a matter of indifference to her. Had she been in his place, she would have accepted the rebuke meekly, and she expected him to do the same.

It is hardly surprising that she sometimes made enemies in this way. There was another occasion that is remembered. The guests of honour at one of her dinner parties were Dr Alexander Wood – Fellow of Emmanuel and University lecturer in Physics – and his young bride, then newly returned from their honeymoon. Mrs Wood, attired as was the custom of those days in her wedding dress minus the train, was given the place of honour on Agnes' right, the young physicist (who looked exactly like Sherlock Holmes) on her left. Shy and nervous, Mrs Wood was dismayed to observe, at the far end of the table and seated next to Mrs Gibson, the wife of the Master of one of the Colleges. As a matter of course, this important lady assumed priority rights as 'leader of the lady guests'; and, after dessert, began to collect her bag, gloves and wrap in readiness for the first sign from her hostess that the meal was ended and the time had come for her to lead the withdrawal to the drawing-room. Agnes observed these preparations with a cold eye, and called out, 'Mistress Wood firrrst, if you please!' The young don's bride wished that the floor might open and engulf her; but, avoiding the furious looks of the Master's wife, she obediently led the company into the other room – and thereafter was on tenterhooks for the rest of the evening lest she should select the wrong moment (a shade too soon, perhaps, or a shade too late) for giving the signal for the party to break up. The photographs of the Lewis Codex, which were passed round by way of entertainment, did not, on that occasion, receive the interested study which they merited from at least two of the guests. This incident may not seem to be of much importance; but Agnes would not be forgiven for it in the various Masters' Lodges of Cambridge.

Whenever there was an 'at home' in Castlebrae, the house was invariably jammed to suffocation. The long narrow corridor from drawing-room to dining-room would be packed with guests – for the sisters usually presided over different rooms – and frightful congestion would result as the visitors sought to worm their way from one room to the other through the chattering groups. Professor H.H. Farmer, who was an undergraduate at the time, once witnessed an entertaining happening from the drawing-room window, where he had become firmly wedged. Glancing down the drive, he suddenly saw a distraught figure come hurrying towards the house, and recognised the visitor as Islay Burns, an elderly scholar of an extremely highly-strung and nervous disposition who, whenever agitated or upset, always jingled his money frantically in his pockets. Such symptoms were now distinctly visible – and no wonder, for he was half an hour late, and Agnes' views on unpunctuality have already been made plain. Young Farmer, anticipating some fun, thrust his way through the guests and took up his position within earshot of Mrs Lewis. In due course the flustered scholar appeared and approached The Presence, holding out his hand and prepared to murmur profuse apologies. Agnes, however, seeing the outstretched hand, instantly jumped to the wrong conclusion. 'Oh Mr Burns,' she exclaimed, 'must you really go so soon?' The nervous guest's confusion redoubled. 'Ye-yes, I'm afraid I must,' he stammered, shook her warmly by the hand, and fled. The undergraduate returned to his post in the window in time to see the don retreating at top speed down the drive, still in the same condition of agitation. He had been in the house less than five minutes.

In the summer, there were always garden parties – for their friends in the University, for the members of the women's meetings in the various missions where they taught (such as York Street and Hope Hall, in Romsey Town) or in support of various 'good causes'. There were two permanent features of all such functions. First, a Scottish piper in full dress, who marched up and down the front lawn, playing throughout the afternoon (on one occasion, he was discovered fast asleep behind some bushes, having drunk too much whisky off-stage; on another, the same cause led to the reverse effect, and he became too lively, dancing destructively among the geraniums); and secondly, a model of the Jewish tabernacle of the Mosaic period, which had been made in Jerusalem to their specifications, and was a somewhat elaborate affair featuring innumerable gold-headed pins and brocaded hangings. It was alleged to be accurate to the tiniest detail, even to the exact place where young Samuel slept - though the University Reader in Talmudic had been known to express his private doubts on one or two points. Agnes would point out to any children present that the horns of the altar were made out of crab's claws, covered with gold paint: she kept a spare set in a matchbox, in case of damage. After tea, guests would be encouraged to climb Castle Hill by the private path which the twins had persuaded the Town Council to allow them to lay down, and which wound through the Scotch firs which had been planted to remind them of Ayrshire.

From time to time, Agnes and Maggie would even give a party for children, an undertaking which says much for their high sense of duty, for children were scarcely their *metier*, except when seated in decorous rows in St Columba's Sunday School, and perhaps not always even then ('Can any boy or girl spell Ur?' Agnes once asked her class). Those who can still recall those occasions do so with mixed feelings: if 'the ladies' did not approve of a child's frock, she would be sent home, even if mother had made it specially for the party. On the credit side, many remember being taken to see a tiny fragment of radium – then newly-discovered – which the

The Ladies of Castlebrae

sisters had purchased, and which glowed, surprisingly, from the innermost recesses of the linen cupboard. Agnes would lecture them on the significance of this strange object, and would explain how its discovery had been the work of a woman.

Sundays in Castlebrae had a routine of their own. The time between family prayers and morning Church was always spent in mending the white stockings. Their strict sabbatarianism which, as we have seen, obtained even in the desert, condemned them to the long journey to Church on foot, though their kind hearts prompted them to send round the carriage for the minister of St Columba's, who was inclined to be delicate. Dr Perowne, the Master of Corpus, who was a strict Evangelical, was one of many Cambridge residents who misinterpreted the presence of their carriage outside St Columba's, and who muttered angrily to their womenfolk as they passed it. In Church, the twins always followed the lessons in Hebrew and Greek, and more than one minister became accustomed to his Monday mail containing a long letter which criticised his scholarship or his theology. But the great day in St Columba's was the third Sunday in October on which, whatever the temperature, the twins appeared in their fur coats for the first time that year: this day was irreverently known among the congregation as 'Mothball Sunday', on account of the all-pervading fragrance.

After lunch, they would travel the considerable distance to York Street Mission, which Agnes and Maggie had bought in 1905 from its founders and presented to St Columba's – a somewhat Greek gift, since the Church thereafter became responsible for the considerable expense involved in its upkeep and staffing. This centre of sweetness and light was situated on the side of the town farthest from Castlebrae and served a densly-populated working-class area inhabited by railwaymen, manual workers and shop assistants, many of whom lived in squalid and overcrowded conditions. At the time when the twins took over, Alex Wood had already been teaching a class of some eighty boys for over a year, and had started clubs for both sexes on weekday evenings. The twins arranged for additional rooms to be built on, and saw to it

172

that the premises were comfortably furnished (even to tip-up chairs and curtains) so that the place might be as comfortable as St Columba's halls, instead of resembling a station waiting-room, as did most 'missions to the poor' at that time. As we have seen from *Glenmavis*, the Giblews had little patience with the remote and patronising role of a Lady Bountiful: the giving of personal time and energy was an inescapable concomitant of their creed. So they at once began to take classes themselves – of married women for Agnes, of rowdy male urchins for Maggie. The latter proved to be a tough assignment, and it says much for her persistence and sense of duty that she persevered with it; for the lads were addicted to throwing hassocks at one another while she vainly tried to interest them in the more respectable activities of the patriarchs.

During Samuel's lifetime, Agnes considered it to be her duty to attend Evensong in St Bene't's, but after his death she returned with relief to the metrical psalms and austere simplicities of the Church of her fathers.

As the years passed, more and more of the twins' time was taken up with lecturing up and down the country, mostly about their discovery of the Lewis Codex. The audience might be composed of eminent semitics scholars from all over the world (as at the Congress of Orientalists), or it might be one of schoolgirls (as when the famous Miss Beale brought them to Cheltenham Ladies' College, where their young friend Olga Sturge, who subsequently married Sir Robert Ball's son, was a pupil); but frequently the visit was to some local congregation of Presbyterians, perhaps as far afield as Newcastle or Dundee, or to a local literary society (such as the vigorous one at Ealing, where they spoke the week after a young war correspondent named Winston Churchill).

Whenever they delivered a lecture, it was invariably Agnes who did the talking, while Maggie worked the magic lantern and coped with the slides. On such evenings, sooner or later, there would be an argument between the sisters, conducted *à haut voix* from opposite ends of the hall, as to the precise subject of some slide:

Agnes: '. . . and this slide shows Mrs Gibson on her camel.'

Maggie: 'No, it's yerself, Agnes.'

Agnes: 'It is NOT, Maggie – it's you!'

Maggie (firmly): 'It's yerself, Agnes – it's the next one that is of me.' (Quickly changes slide.)

Agnes (grudgingly): 'Och aye, ye're right – so it is.'

Sometimes they would divide the lecturing time between them, leaving a friend to manipulate the lantern. Whenever this happened, Maggie would take good care that Agnes did not overrun her allotted time: if she did so, her sister would pluck at her skirts and say urgently in a stage whisper, 'Agnes, Agnes! It's my turn now,' and continue her attack until her sister sat down. Sometimes even this reminder failed to take effect, and Agnes would go on and on, losing all sense of time, until the audience grew restive. Once, at York Street, she concluded an interminable lecture with the words, 'Well, I think I'm done' – a statement which received enthusiastic endorsement from an old man in the front row. 'Well, it's time you were done,' he remarked grimly in a voice of remarkable carrying-power.

The tiffs between the twins sometimes took on a more highly coloured character, even in the presence of visitors. 'Maggie, ye're interrupting – ye know it's verra rude to interrupt,' Agnes would say when some slightly inaccurate statement had been pounced upon by her sister. One morning, the maid went into the dining-room to lay the table for breakfast, and saw a note on the table. Thinking it was some special instruction, she picked it up and was astonished to read 'I promise not to disturb Agnes between the hours of 9 a.m. and 12 noon. Margaret D. Gibson.' This solemn document bore a twopenny stamp.

But these little disagreements served only to cement them more closely together; indeed, some of their friends maintained that squabbling with each other was their chief recreation – even their chief joy: it was a form of mental exercise akin to dialectics among undergraduates, the intellectual equivalent of a swing on the ropes which hung from hooks fastened to the head of the tower-room stairs (their odd notion of bodily exercise: the hooks are still there).

In common with many people who give themselves with intense concentration to a narrow field of study, the twins were apt to be very naïve and uniformed about matters which lay outside their province. Sherlock Holmes is said to have affected ignorance as to the workings of the solar system: Agnes once remarked to an undergraduate when the snow lay deep on the ground outside, 'Ye'll be playing cricket, I expect, – or is it football just now?'; and a don's wife had to explain to them the use of coathangers in connection with the storage of clothes – a wildly improbable story, but one for which an eyewitness vouches.

From all that has been said, it can be imagined that the domestic staff had quite a lively time. The pivot of the household, for twenty-three years, was Emily Free. An unusually beautiful young girl, she came to them as housemaid, was promoted to table maid and later to personal maid, and ended almost an intimate friend. In her early days, she had to cope with all the massive furniture of a Victorian home – vast immoveable wardrobes, huge carpets, heavy brass bedsteads – but towards the end of her service, she slept in Agnes' room and nursed her like a daughter. Emily was capable, reliable, intensely loyal and not in the least disconcerted by the twins' eccentricities. She went everywhere with them – on their holidays in Scotland, to the University Library, to the 'Messiah' in the Guildhall, to concerts at which Melba sang, and on all such recreational jaunts. She was a 'treasure', the 'brisk fond lackey to fetch and carry, The true warm-hearted slave', in the words of a Cambridge poet: member of a now-extinct race.

A less indispensable but more colourful character was Rayfield, their first coachman. Both he and his wife were heavy drinkers, and had been in a succession of situations, none of which they managed to keep for very long. When drunk, they became quarrelsome and threw things at each other, Mrs Rayfield being definitely the superior marksman. This couple provided Agnes with an opportunity to put into practice all those theories about 'the duties of the rich towards their servants' which she had expressed at such length in *Glenmavis*. It must have been a severe test of her principles, for Mrs Rayfield became steadily more inebriate and took to pawning everything, even her wedding ring, for drink. But eventually the mistress had to confess herself defeated and, furnishing the couple with an excellent reference, found them another situation. The new employer, presumably, did not share Agnes' sense of responsibility towards the frail, for he wrote her a very offensive letter, abusing her for misleading him with lies and threatening prosecution. Agnes was compelled to admit that it was not always easy to 'regard one's employees as one's family'.

Rayfield was succeeded by Frederick Eastwell, a temperate man who was in no danger of imagining their mare Saleem to be two horses when it came to stabling her late at night. He outlived his charge, for Saleem eventually died and was replaced by another elderly mare – they stuck to mares, being a keenly feminist household – which they hired from a local undertaker. When the age of the motorcar dawned, and the twins – progressive as ever – bought the first car to be seen in Cambridge, the mare returned to her original profession and thereafter was often to be seen lugubriously pulling a hearse and dreaming of the days when her passengers took a more lively interest in their drive. Eastwell's services were retained as chauffeur; an automobile engineer was imported from Scotland to instruct him how to control the movements and more complex digestion of his new steed. Thus was the transition from the old to the new effected painlessly – literally painlessly, for the twins had chosen their car by the simple method of sitting in all the models displayed, and selecting the one with the most comfortable seats.

But to return to the guests. Let us (to some extent anachronistically) imagine an evening when all their favourite visitors were present at the same time. The minister with the masterful face, whose vast gales of laughter rise above the hum of conversation, is the Revd. Dr John Watson, minister of Sefton Park Church Liverpool, better known to Scots as Ian Maclaren, the author of *Beside the Bonnie Brier Bush* and other best-selling stories of what was to become known as 'the Kailyard School'. He is having an argument with Maggie about politics, and maintaining that the secret of Mr Gladstone's success is that he is totally devoid of any sense of humour: 'Had he possessed the faintest sense of the ridiculous amid the multitude of his talents,' he is insisting, 'he would not have been able to address a crowd from the window of his railway-carriage, and to receive the gift (if my memory does not fail me) of a case of marmalade. It's just because he can do such things, and is always in the most deadly earnest about everything, from the Bulgarian atrocities to the making of jam, that the British trust him. The conditions of tangible success in British life, my dear Mrs Gibson, are these: to be well built, with a moderate stoutness; to have a solemn expression of face suggesting the possession of more wisdom than has been given to any single person; to be able to hold one's tongue till some incautious talker has afforded an idea; and to have the gift of oracular commonplace. If to such valuable talents can be added an impressive clearance of the throat, there are few positions short of the highest to which their owner may not climb in Church or State. Young men should congratulate themselves that by the will of Providence they have been cleansed from this dangerous quality of humour – or, if this be not their fortunate case, they should hide it behind a mask of sustained and impenetrable solemnity until they have made their fortunes, and then give it play as the foolish freak of a rich man.'*

Maggie is laughing too much to be able to reply to this oration; she can only reflect that it is scarcely surprising that the more pompous and self-important Aldermen of the city of Liverpool fear the preaching of this notable deflater of egos, who had helped to shape the life of the city by awakening in his congregation such a hatred of shams and cant, such an impulse to serve, and such a civic conscience that practically all his people had become involved in doing some useful work for the community, and no fewer than six of his flock had become Lord Mayor. Matthew Arnold, on

---

* These remarks are not invented. They are taken, verbatim, from one of Watson's public lectures, and are highly characteristic of the man.

the day he died, attended Watson's service and subsequently remarked to his sister that he had 'rarely been so affected by a preacher.' The fan mail which reached the Doctor daily from nostalgic exiled Scots (for his Kailyard stories) and from old ladies in Cheltenham (for his religious books) was usually more than counterbalanced by a pile of anonymous letters, often couched in soldierly language, which (where possible) he read aloud to his family over the porridge, whooping joyously over each blistering phrase. When he died, worn out, in the course of a lecture tour of America, a white-faced Liverpool tramdriver leaned from his cab to hail a passing clergyman with the words, 'Have you heard the news, sir? John Watson is dead. It's a bad day for us.'

Seated on the sofa opposite the fireplace are a man and a woman. Let us look at the woman first: thin, pale, dressed rather frumpily in black and with a soft musical voice, she looks misleadingly nondescript. This is Mary Kingsley, niece of the novelist, who, depressed by the successive deaths of her father and mother and by the departure of her brother to the East, had, a few years previously, 'gone down to West Africa to die.' The phrase was not melodramatic, for West Africa, in those days, was still the 'white man's grave', and definitely no place for a woman – least of all for a woman whose sole trip abroad had been to Paris (for a week) and who was too timid to ride on the top deck of an omnibus. But women (as Mary wrote to a friend) have always gone where they have no business to go – witness her friends Mrs Lewis and Mrs Gibson, who 'stroll to and fro in the Sinai desert as though it were Sauchiehall Street.' So to Africa she went, became interested in anthropology, wrote outspoken books which deplored the natives' 'secondhand rubbishy white culture,' denounced the missionaries for failing to understand the sound logic behind customs such as polygamy, and was rude about Government administration. Instead of dying as planned, she became quite famous: eventually consulted, indeed, by the Colonial Office itself. Mary had courage, and she had humour; and she exercised both to as deadly effect in the Congo and along the Gold Coast as John Watson did on Merseyside. Nor was her courage limited to jungle pioneering, the braving of swamp fevers, fraternising happily with cannibals, and the writing of outspoken books pervaded by an immense gusto: on one occasion she released a hungry leopard from a trap in which he had languished for some hours and, when he advanced menacingly towards her, said sternly 'Go home, you fool!' He did. Agnes and Maggie were devoted to Mary, in spite of her inherited agnosticism, for she was just the kind of unconventional individualist who most appealed to them. When the Boer War broke out, this 'reckless fool boddie' (as the Scots engineer of a West Coast ship once called her to her face) offered her services as a nurse to the Boer prisoners, then dying in scores in their typhus-ridden camps. While engaged on this highly unpopular errand of mercy, she caught West Coast fever and died within two days, aged only thirty eight. Agnes did not exaggerate when she wrote to *The Times*, after news of her death was received, 'Her mind was like a finely-tempered sword which was forever wearing out its scabbard.'

This remarkable woman who, in the words of her biographer, 'made people think and feel by making them laugh', is, at the moment, complaining to Professor John Stuart Blackie that the *Glasgow Herald* has just described her as one of the 'New Women'. 'It's nonsense, professor – I'm only a case of atavism: my father was a great traveller, and in more remote times my ancestors were Robin Hood and Erik Rosder, who is taxed with having discovered Ireland.'* Blackie, who is responding with his high cackling laughter and doing his best, in his peculiar cawing voice, to defend the *Glasgow Herald*, holds the Chair of Greek at Edinburgh, and is the author of that lively pamphlet on its proper pronunciation which converted the twins and may be said to be indirectly responsible for Agnes' acquisition of a husband. The intimate friend of Coleridge, Lockhart and Monkton Milnes, Blackie often stayed at Castlebrae, and, after his first visit, wrote to his wife that his hostesses 'are as familiar with spoken Greek and spoken Arabic as the best-travelled English ladies are with French. They form in themselves a

---

* The remark is taken from a letter to Agnes.

phenomenon as interesting as it is singular, and here, in the academic atmosphere of Cambridge, it acts as an attractive centre round which are congregated notabilities of various types, rarely to be met with either in aristocratic Oxford or West-Endy Edinburgh.'* He was in many ways the professor of the popular imagination – craggy, unconventional, eccentric, and *outré* in dress (he always wore a Highland plaid when he walked the streets of Edinburgh). Today he is little more than a minor name, remembered perhaps by the pious for his hymn 'Angels holy, high and lowly' (which he wrote on his honeymoon), and by the frivolous as the only begetter of a joke which has since been attributed to many succeeding dons. Unable to deliver a lecture on the scheduled day, he wrote on the blackboard 'The Professor is unable to meet his classes today.' A student wag rubbed out the 'c'. The next day, Blackie swept into the classroom, gazed at the amended notice, and promptly deleted the 'l'. Like Oscar Wilde, whom he almost equalled as a poseur, he could invariably turn the tables on anyone who tried to score off him.

We will move away from the mane of white hair, bobbing vigorously in Mary Kingsley's direction as its owner pours out his immense vitality, and cross to the corner by the grand piano, where Agnes is talking to another contrasting pair: the two Macalisters, who complicated life for their acquaintances by spelling their surnames differently, in spite of the fact that they were cousins. The contrast is both in build and in temperament, the kinship in brilliance no less than in blood. Alexander, the Professor of Anatomy, thin-faced and gentle with faraway Highland eyes, was the friend to whom Agnes turned most frequently when in need of advice on business or personal matters: his imaginative Celtic temperament, with its swift understanding and unusual sensitivity, frequently restrained her hastiness when deciding upon the next move in the Burkitt-Bensly-Giblew tension, as his business acumen proved invaluable when she sought to do battle with publishers over royalties. His knowledge was encyclopaedic;

* Letter of 27th May 1889.

180

and Sir Humphry Rolleston (who had been his pupil) always maintained that when one was in search of some obscure reference, it was quicker to consult Macalister – who would instantly supply the title of the book and direct the enquirer to the relevant chapter – than to visit the University Library. The Professor and his wife were among the oldest of the twins' friends, for the association, it will be recalled, dated from Harvey Road days.

To Donald, the other McAlister (spelled thus in his case), Agnes turned when she wanted the stimulus of a fierce argument, preferably one which (to the immense satisfaction of both parties) bordered on a row. The Senior Tutor of St John's College was a huge blunderbuss of a man, whose bristling bushy beard was perfectly in character with his tempestuous and somewhat domineering temperament. The son of a publisher's struggling agent in Liverpool, he had begun his career as a mathematician, becoming Senior Wrangler in the days when (as T.R. Glover once remarked) the holders of this coveted honour were, in Cambridge, as renowned as Derby winners, and their names used no less for dating a particular year. After teaching at Harrow, he had returned to Cambridge and studied medicine; and in a remarkably short time was appointed Deputy to the Regius Professor of Physic, and a member of the General Medical Council, over which august body he was subsequently to preside for twenty-seven years. From Cambridge, he went to Glasgow as Principal of the University, and controlled its destinies for twenty-two years. There, the students nicknamed him 'The Bloody Judge', a reference both to his impartiality and to his scarlet-robed formidable appearance in a famous portrait. Donald was a remarkable linguist, being fluent in no fewer than twenty-three languages (which ranged from Japanese and Arabic to Basque and Romany), and in an idle half hour, he could often be seen amusing himself by turning a German poem into Greek verse, or a Russian one into German. He had also read the *Encyclopaedia Britannica* from beginning to end; so it was not surprising that James Ward dubbed him 'the polyhedron, because he has so many sides.' When he retired from the Glasgow Principalship, he received a knighthood and returned to live within the bounds of that University which had launched him upon his career. Hence his presence in Castlebrae this evening.

But Agnes must break off her conversation at this point, for the maid has just entered to say that the (undergraduate) secretary of the University Presbyterian Association has called to see her, and that although the young man had declared that he would return later when informed that Mrs Lewis was engaged with guests, she has ventured to detain him. 'Quite right,' says Agnes, 'bring him in here.' A moment later, a tall, rangy, fair-haired youth enters, whose natural shyness and reticence increase a hundredfold when he catches sight of the distinguished company, whose eyes switch in unison to the doorway. This young man, a law student at Christ's College, has called to make the final arrangements for Mrs Lewis' forthcoming lecture in St Columba's Hall. He is a youth for whom a great future is already being prophesied by the discerning among his teachers. His name is Jan Christian Smuts.

Young Smuts having been interrogated and dismissed, Agnes makes for the corner where Rendel Harris is sitting with a curious little man of semitic appearance. This is one Alphonse Mingana, who has a strange history in which Harris had played a significant part. A Syrian monk of some brilliance – he held a doctorate from Louvain, and occupied the Chair of Semitic Languages in the Syro-Chaldean seminary at Mosul – Mingana had begun to collect material for a thesis on the infallibility of the Pope. His researches, however, had led him (so to speak) in quite the wrong direction; and he became convinced that the whole doctrine was nothing less than a fallacy. With this discovery, his faith in Roman Catholicism rapidly evaporated and, as a monk of that communion, he found himself in an intellectually untenable position. Pacing his cell in the Bagdad monastery where he was stationed, he realised that he must abandon his vocation and return to the world. Monasteries, however, are not designed to be easy to escape from: one needs outside help. It so happened that he had entered into considerable correspondence with Rendel Harris (at that time Director of Studies at the Woodbrooke Settlement in Birmingham), so he conceived the idea of writing to the Quaker scholar, explaining his dilemma and invoking his aid. Harris acted promptly: through certain contacts he had in the vicinity, he arranged for the monk to be met by a dragoman on the outskirts of the city on a certain night. Mingana borrowed the monastery key, made his way to the rendezvous, changed his clothes, mounted the waiting horse and rode to Aleppo. When he eventually reached England, Harris took him to Birmingham, and subsequently secured an appointment for him under the War Office. Later, at the Selly Oak Quaker Meeting to which Harris took him, Alphonse met, and fell in love with, a Norwegian girl student, and the two married, though neither understood a word of the other's language – both courtship and marital conversation had to be carried on in very broken English.

Harris has brought Mingana down to Castlebrae for Christmas, for the refugee has only recently arrived in England: the invitation from Agnes followed Harris' first mention of the ex-monk in one of his letters. Agnes is now busy hushing the company, for Rendel has whispered to her that the cheerful little man could, he is sure, be persuaded to sing one or two Kurdish songs. Mingana takes up his stance on the lionskin rug before the fireplace, and begins with a pleased smile. The guests lean forward with that keen simulation of absolute absorption which is the essence of drawing-room politeness . . .

After the dutiful applause, conversation resumes with slightly altered groupings. Ten minutes later, Watson lays his hand on Macalister's arm and jerks his head towards the centre of the room. The Professor of Anatomy glances round, and nods understandingly: Agnes and Maggie have left their armchairs by the fire, and have gone to sit by themselves on the *chaise-longue* which is set in the centre of the broad expanse of carpet. It is the recognised signal that the twins have had enough, and will not actively press their guests to stay any longer.

IX

The Honoured Scholars

Their labours have created a new era in the criticism of the New Testament . . . and the spirit of enterprise and the rare scholarship which they have shown have produced for their age a higher idea of what woman can accomplish.

> – Lord Balfour of Burleigh, Chancellor of St Andrews' University: from his speech when he conferred doctorates on the twins, April 1901

Mrs Lewis and her sister made a real and valuable contribution to biblical scholarship. They spared no money or effort to provide the fullest and most exact information possible about the readings of the manuscript . . . and for that alone they would deserve the gratitude of all New Testament scholars.

> – Professor T.W. Manson: letter, January 1956

To Samuel Butler, learning was no more than 'the cobweb of the brain.' Some may be inclined to share his opinion; nevertheless, the mental picture of the twins which, up to this point, has been evoked, now needs supplementing by a few random glimpses of their actual scholastic achievement. If Butler's metaphor be pursued (without his sentiments being necessarily endorsed), it may be said that our two industrious spiders have now been studied in their habitat; and that the time has now come for a somewhat closer scrutiny of those webs of their creating which, as the years passed, increasingly adorned corners of learned libraries all over the world. Obviously, such an account will need to be highly selective, if it is to be even mildly interesting: those who are curious as to the full range of the twins' output may refer at this point to the Appendix. Anyone whose taste is only for anecdotes and personal eccentricities is free to indulge in judicious skipping at this point; but it is only fair to warn him that, if he does so, he will be left with a very partial picture of the twins. Their work meant everything to them, and it is as scholars, and as women scholars, that they would wish primarily to be remembered.

1893 saw the publication of *How The Codex Was Found*, a popular account of their first journey, written up by Maggie from Agnes' journals and notes. An uncompleted manuscript in Westminster College Library suggests that Agnes originally embarked on this book herself, but passed the task over to her sister when it became clear that her hands would be full with work on the Codex itself, if publication were not to be unduly delayed. It is interesting to notice, by the way, that both in Agnes' first draft and in Maggie's published account, the incident of the *ersatz* butterdish is not mentioned: the discovery begins in the cubbyhole. The twins' affection for Galakteon, and their gratitude to the monks, obviously constrained them to suppress the more sensational details of bachelor housekeeping – though Agnes told the full story to one or two trusted friends, who passed it on.

In October 1894, some eighteen months after the second Sinai expedition, appeared an edition of the underwriting of the palimpsest. This large tome, published by the Cambridge University Press, was edited by the three men who had done the work on the Lewis Codex – Bensly, Burkitt and Rendel Harris – and the responsibility was carefully shared between them on the title page, though presumably Burkitt had done almost a double stint: it would no doubt have been he who would have transcribed and collated Bensly's work after the latter's death. Agnes' share in this volume was to contribute the introduction, which described the discovery, condition and decipherment of the manuscript, explained the nature of the upper writing and, with lengthy quotations in Syriac and Greek, sought to relate the Codex to other versions such as the fragmentary Curetonian.

In the same year, she published her own translation of the entire Codex, the fruit of long hours of study during and after the two expeditions to St Catherine's; two years later, after a further visit to Sinai, she issued *Some Pages of the Four Gospels Re-transcribed from the Sinaitic Palimpsest, with a translation of the whole text*: this she arranged to have printed on blue paper, so that scholars might interleave it with the earlier work. As her knowledge accumulated, the books grew larger – and their titles longer; the final definitive work, which she published in 1910, boasted a front page which perhaps might be said to win the Scholars' Logorrhoea Prize: *The Old Syriac Gospels or Evangelion da-Mepharreshe: being the text of the Sinai or Syro-Antiochene Palimpsest, including the latest additions and emendations, with the variants of the Curetonian text, corroborations from many other manuscripts, and a list of quotations from ancient authors: with four facsimiles*. This forty-gun salute was doubtless prompted by the appearance, some six years earlier (in 1904), of Burkitt's two-volume *Evangelion da-Mepharreshe* (observe how she incorporates his title in hers!). Though this latter work was characterised by her rival's usual painstaking scholarship, and showed the fruits of his immensely wide reading, Agnes was disgusted to find that it was essentially an edition of the Curetonian, with the Lewis Codex considered only where it provided alternative readings. Surely the proper thing to do would have been to issue an edition of her palimpsest, with the reader's attention drawn to the Curetonian variants thereon? Accordingly, in the preface to her book, after praising Burkitt's 'fine work', Agnes adds tartly: 'The Sinai text deserves a better fate than to remain for all time in a position of subordination to the Curetonian which, however interesting, is neverthless inferior both in antiquity and purity.' She further accuses Burkitt of preferring, on occasion, his own conjectures to the actual readings of the document . . . and gives examples. Agnes wrote her volume after her sixth visit to Sinai in 1906, and she does not omit to point out that Burkitt had not seen the actual codex since 1893, when he had transcribed 'about one-third' of the text. The satisfaction with which she penned those words was not, perhaps, entirely a scholarly one; but a decisive victory must nevertheless be allowed her on academic grounds alone. Her enemies, and some of her friendly critics, have on occasion maintained that her knowledge of Syriac was relatively superficial, and that she was in no position to criticise Burkitt or to challenge his textual judgments. But a sidelight on this duel is provided by some extant letters (in the Angus collection) which R.H. Kennett wrote to her, in which he deals with queries arising from obscure or puzzling readings of the text. In every single instance, he either supports her judgment, or agrees with her that the problems raised are insoluble. Kennett was a Syriac scholar of the front rank, and, as her former teacher, would certainly not have hesitated to correct her firmly if her judgments had been, in his view, amateurish or stupid.

Finally, in 1917 (if we may anticipate in order to view as a unity her total output on the Codex) she reduced this vast corpus of knowledge to a small compass and issued a popular book for the parish minister and the intelligent layman. This volume, which aimed at summarising her conclusions in non-technical language, she called *Light on the Four Gospels from the Sinai Palimpsest*. Here we may glimpse a further facet of her character. As we have seen, Agnes was above all else an 'applied scholar': she was not one to be satisfied with a series of books, each more scholarly, detailed and recondite than the last, which would moulder in some dusty corner of the University Library: she wished those who were keenly interested in the Bible to have before them the fruits of all this exhaustive research which had occupied her, off and on, for twenty-four years.

But why were these particular documents, written in an obscure tongue, of such importance for Biblical studies? This question must be briefly answered at this point. Most of the versions of the gospels which are used in England today – the

Authorised, the Revised, the New English and the earlier modern renderings of Weymouth and Moffatt* – are translations of *Greek* manuscripts. Where variant readings are to be found in versions written in other languages, the latter have, of course, been carefully weighed by scholars and taken into account – their relative importance varying according to the antiquity and source of the version concerned; but the manuscripts from which scholars principally work are in Greek. These are either uncials (manuscripts written in capital letters, like the Codex Sinaiticus), or cursives (those written in ordinary lower case Greek letters), mostly not earlier than ninth century. The three Syriac versions, of which the Lewis Codex is one, are generally agreed to be older translations of the Greek gospels – older, that is, than any Greek manuscript which has survived. They therefore bear witness to originals which have been lost, and so are of great value for confirming the accuracy of such documents as are still extant – for they are closer in time to Jesus Christ and to the events which they record. Other things being equal, their readings will often be preferred to those of the Greek uncials and cursives which have come down to us. Secondly, Syriac is the literary form of Aramaic, which was the dialect actually spoken in Palestine at the time of Christ. Syriac versions can therefore give us (as it were) the authentic accents of Christ, in a way that Greek ones, being a translation, can not – though there are fragments of Aramaic scattered here and there in the Greek versions (and preserved in the English ones), such as *talitha cumi* (Mark v.41), *ephphatha* (Mark vii.34), and *eloi eloi lama sabacthani* (Matt. xxvii.46) – in each instance the actual words used by Jesus. The Syriac versions emanated from Edessa, which had become the established centre of Syriac-speaking Christians by the middle of the second century. Of these Syriac translations, Agnes' palimpsest (usually cryptically referred to by scholars as 'Syr. Sin', to distinguish it from the Curetonian 'Syr. Cur.') is generally considered to be the

---

* But not, of course, Knox, whose translation is (officially, at least) of the Latin Vulgate, the version approved by the Roman Catholic Church.

most important. Rendel Harris, in a letter to Eberhard Nestle, a leading continental New Testament scholar who revised much of Agnes' work for her, described it as 'the most important find since Tischendorf's discovery [of the Codex Sinaiticus].' Even the careful and cautious Burkitt, by temperament and training averse to making exaggerated claims, referred to it (in a paper read to the Church Congress in 1895) as 'a very faithful representative of the earliest Syriac translation of the gospels . . . written in the fourth, or early part of the fifth century; but the version of which it is a copy is very much more ancient, certainly older than the Peshitto, probably older than the Diatesseron which is not earlier than A.D. 170.' Modern scholars are inclined to date it even earlier: Professor T.W. Manson, for example, considers it to be early third century at least, and thinks it may have been made as early as A.D.150. 'It therefore bears witness to the type of Greek text used in Antioch probably in the second century, and that is something very important indeed.' Contemporary reviewers of Agnes' volumes were – as is the habit of scholarly reviewers – cautious and non-commital, though one went so far as to claim that her work had 'doubled our source of knowledge in the darkest corner of New Testament criticism.'

These assessments are quoted in order to demonstrate that Agnes' discovery, and her scholarship, were taken very seriously indeed: she was in no way regarded as a light-hearted dilettante, incautiously rushing into areas of knowledge that were far beyond her understanding or competence.

The publication of the Lewis Codex caused considerable flutterings in ecclesiastical dovecotes – infinitely more than that occasioned by the discovery of the Dead Sea Scrolls in our time. The variations on existing manuscripts were few, but one difference was startling. In the genealogy at the beginning of St Matthew's Gospel, the Lewis Codex reads: 'Jacob begat Joseph; Joseph, to whom was betrothed Mary the Virgin, begat Jesus who is called the Christ.' As early as July 1893, Mrs Humphrey Ward, the popular Victorian novelist and niece of Matthew Arnold, had heard disquieting rumours of this verse, and had besought G.W. Prothero to write to Agnes and enquire if they were true. When the Bensly-Burkitt-Harris edition was published a year later, agnostics smiled triumphant and satisfied smiles, while elderly clergymen in their country rectories and devout bishops in their remote palaces trembled for the ark of God. The version was heretical! To find, in such an early manuscript, the Virgin Birth disposed of – why, this struck at the very foundations of the faith! Agnes did not think so at all and, in her introduction to the English translation, set herself with her accustomed vigour to dispose of the charge. No one (she maintained) would have called Mary 'the Virgin' if she had not, in fact, been one; it was 'simply inexplicable' that Joseph should be troubled about Mary's condition if he were in fact the father of Jesus; why should he, explicitly described as 'a just man', wish to 'put her away' if the truth were as the verse suggested? There is no genealogy of Mary, quite naturally; for Jesus' social position and civil rights were determined by the relation in which He stood to one who was both his reputed father and his foster-father. Elsewhere she quotes Robertson Smith's *Kinship and Marriage in Early Arabia* to the effect that 'if a child is born in the tribe of a woman brought in by contract of marriage, it was reckoned to the tribal stock as a matter of course, without enquiry as to its natural procreator', adducing, as a parallel, the statement in the Bible that the childless Jeconiah begat his grandson Ozias. The debate raged for some time, in both scholarly and unscholarly journals: the *Manchester Guardian* and the *Cambridge Review* were unimpressed by Agnes' 'explanation', while in the more learned *Academy* she was attacked by F.C. Coneybeare who claimed that in the early church women who had been widowed young and did not remarry were 'entitled to the rank and title of Virgin', while R.H. Charles defended her. And so on. But in time the dust died down, leaving the contestants – as is usual in such circumstances – pretty much as they were before: the devout relieved, the sceptical more sceptical than ever.

Returning in 1894, text and translation were both in print, and most scholars would have turned to other tasks. But Agnes, as we have seen, was not content to leave the matter there. Gaps still remained in the published editions. Accordingly, she and Maggie returned to St Catherine's for the third time in 1895.

They had hoped that they might be able to persuade the monks to bring the precious document to Cairo, a procedure which would save them the fatiguing desert journey and enable them to fill in the remaining *lacunae* in the comfort of their hotel. This course, however, the monastery authorities declined to sanction in view of the palimpsest's value. The twins were not really surprised by this decision: what did surprise them was to learn, when they reached Cairo, that visitors to St Catherine's the previous year had been refused permission even to inspect it in the monastery library, much less to work upon it. Was it still worthwhile to continue their journey, then? Galakteon was dead; his successor, Nicodemus, might well have quite different ideas. Needless to say, they decided to go on, but were fully prepared for the journey to be a fruitless one. From the gossip which they had picked up in Cairo, it seemed likely that this sudden stiffening of the official attitude might well be connected with the known fact of several thefts from the monastery library. In this surmise they were correct. On reflection, they remembered that, on the 1893 expedition, Rendel Harris had remarked on the total disappearance of several important manuscripts which he had studied on his previous visit four years earlier. That he had not been mistaken in his suspicions of thievery was proved to them while they were still in Cairo on this 1895 trip: for part of one of these missing documents – several pages of a beautiful sixteenth-century manuscript of II Maccabees – was actually offered to them by a dealer in antiquities.

It was only by the luckiest chance in the world that they succeeded in identifying this document for what it was. When Harris had first seen the book, he had photographed a few pages for future reference. Agnes had borrowed one of these prints to serve as the frontispiece to her catalogue of the monastery's Syriac books, hoping that some scholar would recognise it and arrange for it to be returned to its lawful owners. By a coincidence, Agnes' own copy of this catalogue happened to be lying on the sofa in their hotel room, open at the frontispiece, at the very moment when the dealer entered with his 'bargains'. The moment Agnes' eyes fell upon his wares, she whispered to Maggie, 'It's stolen!' – and, walking across to the sofa, laid original and photograph side by side.

The question was: What was to be done? The easy course was to buy the manuscript and say nothing: this would keep happy their future relations with the Cairo dealers, and would ensure that the document went back to Sinai. But Agnes' astute mind saw that such a course of action would not only offend her conscience: it would be imprudent – for might not the monks assume that the twins themselves had stolen it and, having made use of it, were now returning it with a cock-and-bull story? So they decided to take the hard course, and to denounce the theft. On pretence of examining the manuscript further, they persuaded the dealer to allow them to retain it for a few days, sent a telegram to the monastery, and paid a visit to the British Consul. Having convinced this gentleman of the identity of the document, and armed with a wire from the monastery Librarian confirming the theft, they instituted proceedings in the courts against the dealer in the name of the Archbishop of Mount Sinai (who, as ill luck would have it, was not in residence in Cairo at the time, as was his custom, but away on a visit to St Catherine's.) The monastery's *skeuophulax* (the monk responsible for the safety of manuscripts), who happened to be in Cairo that week, appeared twice in one day at their hotel, imploring them with agitation to conceal the matter from the Librarian; but they declined to save his, or anyone else's, face. The affair was too important. In due course, they attended the court, with the manuscript 'tied up in a cambric handkerchief with a bit of white ribbon, and looking like a bridal present' (as Maggie put it); but, to their dismay, judgment was given against them. The judge, no doubt, was more concerned with protecting one of the principal local industries than with maintaining the rights of a distant ecclesiastic. (The actual thief was never finally identified, but they had good reason to suspect a German who, posing as a missionary, had spent a protracted visit at

Sinai, and who was, at the time of the trial, serving a prison sentence in Cairo for other thefts. His dragoman had already fled to America.)

Their bold move seemed to have failed, but the incident had pleasant repercussions: it determined the reception accorded to them when they finally arrived at St Catherine's. The twins were given a royal welcome, and every possible arrangement was made for their comfort. When they began work, coffee and sweets were brought to them several times a day, and the Archbishop (who was still in residence) frequently looked in to see how they were progressing, and told them to call for such refreshments whenever they wanted them. They would have been less than human had they not wished that Bensly and Burkitt could have been there, to see who had been the *really* important members of the 1893 expedition.

There had been great changes in the monastery since their previous visit. The replacement of lovable, scholarly, easygoing Galakteon by the efficient businesslike Nicodemus was reflected even in the condition of the buildings. The library had been reconstructed (partly with money which Agnes had sent), and a new whitewashed building erected for the convenience of visiting foreign scholars. The sisters were amused to notice that this study-room could only be reached by a staircase which was in constant use by the monks on their way from their cells to the church or refectory: thus, visitors working on the manuscripts were under as effectual surveillance as any reader in the British Museum. From now on, the authorities were taking no chances. The interior of the old buildings had been whitewashed, and the doors and banisters painted blue ('this would grieve an artist or even an antiquary, but from a sanitary point of view it is most commendable,' Agnes wrote to Rendel Harris). But the greatest transformation was in the Library itself. The poky little airless closets had been swept away, the partitions removed, and the whole converted into two airy rooms, shelved all round, with the books arranged in proper order. The labels on the Semitic books (in the twins' handwriting) had been 'gummed on more securely', and the Greek ones similarly identified. There was even glass in the windows, now. The place of honour in the Library had now been given to the Lewis Codex, which had been housed in a special wooden box, ornamented with Catherine wheels, and provided with an inner glass lid, which permitted the contents to be examined without being handled. A new rule forbade the taking of books into the monastery garden – a procedure which Galakteon had always allowed (to the twins, anyway): foreign scholars who wished to study manuscripts must henceforth do so in the room provided – a room which, incidentally, was furnished with divans all round the walls in addition to the necessary chairs, tables and carpets: so that facilities were even provided for scholarly forty winks, or for those who preferred to ponder problems lying down.

It was pleasant to be able to work in this room with its glazed windows, after being exposed to the icy desert winds, or having to toil at a washstand under the olive trees, or being compelled to grope about in the dark, grimy closets. But there was one drawback: now, the pungent fumes of the reagent were highly concentrated and extremely overpowering. However, there was a bright side even to this: the monks who dropped in for a chat were compelled to curtail their visits, which saved the twins much valuable time. . . .

So they set themselves to fill in the gaps which existed in their copy of the palimpsest. It was slow work, for these *lacunae* were scattered throughout its pages. Though Agnes worked seven hours a day, by the end of twelve days she had only managed to fill in eight hundred words. But it was worth the labour, for it was like mending a broken chain: each restored link made the other links of greater usefulness. By March 14th, they had done all they could, and they set off for home with all possible information in their possession. What was still obscure would have to remain so.

On the journey back to Cairo, Agnes developed a large and extremely painful carbuncle – presumably, from Maggie's delicate references in her letters, on her posterior. But she was never one to give in; and on the last day (when the pain was so agonising that she ought by rights to have been carried), she walked fifteen miles and rode her camel for four hours. Back in Cairo, she spent a week in bed, unable even to walk across the room; they were fortunate, however, in discovering one of Professor Macalister's medical pupils in the city, and this gentleman dealt successfully with the unfortunate addition to Agnes' anatomy. This enforced rest gave them the leisure to revise their work, and to write a 'progress report' to Harris. The Quaker scholar, Maggie wrote, had made only three serious mistakes in his conjectures, whereas Burkitt had made several that were 'really grotesque', and Bensly several that were 'the reverse of accurate'. Agnes amplified this pungent judgment in a later letter: 'Those mistakes in Mr Burkitt's pages proceed from a lack of imagination. He has written correctly what he saw, but where he had only a few letters, he has conjectured something recondite and complex, instead of something simple and correct' (a common fault, alas, with experts in all fields!). The worst blunder, as it happened, was by the great Bensly, whose guess was refuted by the reagent which brought up a totally different word. Agnes maintains a prudent silence about her own mistakes (of which doubtless there were several), but produces these misshapen rabbits out of her scholarly hat with an obvious relish which is not necessarily malicious or personal. Nothing gives a scholar greater satisfaction than to find that some rival Homer has nodded: it's part of the fun of the game.

It was a fortnight before the doctor allowed Agnes to take a little walk – and even then he forbade her to ride any sort of animal during the rest of their stay. 'Perhaps it is just as well that I have broken down,' Agnes wrote to Harris, 'for we have quite enough work on hand for the present.' 'Breaking down,' however, was for Agnes a relative expression: four days after her first walk they took a Russian steamer for Port Said, whence they travelled to Beirut and spent a fortnight visiting local monasteries. At one of these, the twins were hauled up the side of the wall at the end of a rope, suspended in a kind of cargo net: it was the only means of entry. After this experience, they sailed for Marseilles and home.

During the remaining months of 1895, in such odd moments as they were able to snatch from their preparation of the corrected edition of the palimpsest, the twins began work on another manuscript which, it will be recalled, they had come across on their first visit to Sinai. This was the 'Palestinian Syriac Lectionary' which Galakteon had shown them, remarking that only one visitor to the monastery had hitherto been able to read it. The lectionary, which was written in a dialect quite distinct from literary Syriac – one which 'bore the same relation to literary Syriac as the broad Doric of Scotland does to the more polished but less forceful English tongue' – was only the second book in existence in that particular patois, the other being the *Evangeliarium Hierosolymitanum* in the Vatican Library. Agnes had taken four specimen photographs of this work in 1892, and these she had shown to Harris, who had pronounced the volume to be a second copy of the Vatican document. He himself had discovered a third copy at Sinai in 1893. Collating and editing these two volumes occupied the twins – apart from a visit to the Congress of Orientalists, at which they both read papers – during 1894 and 1895. The spring of 1896 they had planned to devote to seeing their edition through the press; but the Rendel Harrises (who were in the Mesopotamian valley helping survivors of the recent Armenian massacres) wrote to say that they had seen manuscripts of special interest on sale in Cairo, and would the twins please come out at once? So they set out once more on their travels, though this time with some reluctance.

It seemed foolish to go so far merely to haggle with a few dealers, so they used the opportunity to revisit Jerusalem. With their penchant for encountering misfortunes, they succeeded in making a normally dull journey into an adventure. Travelling by camel down to Jaffa, they allowed their caravan to go on ahead while they inspected some hillside caves; and they were still searching for their entourage – enquiring fruitlessly of every passing traveller – when the sun went down and it began to rain heavily. Neither they nor their drivers were sure of the way; and when, after stumbling on foot for two miles over the rocks and mudpools which

formed the track, and squelching in the wet sticky clay of the
olive gardens, they eventually came to the village of Allar-el-
Foca, it was only to discover that the convoy with the tents
had gone still farther on ahead. All they had with them was
the luncheon tent, a flimsy three-sided shelter against the sun,
such as Englishmen erected in the garden in the summertime;
and in this they had to doss down for the night, as best they
could. One of the men roasted them some coffee on a shovel;
they spread the quilts from the camel saddles in the lee of the
tent, and tried to sleep in their clothes. But the coffee had
been too strong, their skirts were still sodden from the rain
earlier in the evening, the fire attracted a vast swarm of
insects with excellent biting capabilities, the damp on the
ground soon soaked the flimsy quilts, and the wind was
bitterly cold. In the morning, after a most uncomfortable
night, they washed as best they could in a biscuit tin, drank
some milk (there was no more coffee) and continued their
journey. It was not until they were on the outskirts of Jaffa,
and the shadows of the olive trees were long on the ground,
that they finally caught up with their caravan. However, the
thought of a decent sleep in a proper tent revived them; but
once more they were over-optimistic. No sooner had they
retired for the night than a furious storm arose: the rain beat
in torrents on the tents, penetrated the canvas and drenched
Maggie's bed. The floor, indeed, became literally a pond, 'on
whose surface our boots and shoes were swimming leisurely
about.' To strike camp in the middle of the night was
obviously impossible, so they had no alternative but to stick
it out. 'Very curious objects we were when we arrived
eventually at our hotel,' Agnes wrote to a friend. No wonder
she subsequently suffered from rheumatism: such experiences are not recommended for women in their fifty-fourth
year.

However, this was only 'pleasure': with 'business', they
were more successful. They bought a large number of
Hebrew manuscripts, some in Sharon, some from the Cairo
dealers to whom Harris had directed their attention, and one
– under somewhat odd circumstances – from an Oxford
scholar named Saffrin. This gentleman, who was staying in

the same hotel in Jerusalem, had just bought a fifteenth-century copy of the Pentateuch from a Jewish Yemenite family who were down on their luck and reduced to selling the family treasures. He had intended taking this back to the Bodleian, but, on the very day he and Agnes met in the hotel lounge, he had happened to see a still older volume, a commentary on the Talmud, never published and with illuminations of an exceptionally interesting kind. But having bought the Hebrew Pentateuch, he had no money left with which to buy the second volume. The astute Agnes at once made him an offer for the Yemenite Bible, which he accepted gratefully. Thus she acquired one more 'prize' to take home: a stoutly-bound volume with metal clasps, the first two pages of which contained the 119th Psalm 'in the form of an ornament', followed by an introduction, the text, and a number of family records relating to the pedigree of a Yemenite Jew who had been born in 1501 and who traced his descent back to Judah.

When Agnes' first excitement had worn off a little, however, she realised she had landed herself with a problem. A recent law had expressly forbidden antiquities of any kind being taken out of the country. One might be able to smuggle a few loose sheets, sandwiched between dresses, especially with the aid of a little baksheesh discreetly distributed among underpaid Customs officials; but what in the world could one do with this huge volume, the size of an English family Bible? She consulted the Consul, but he was unable to help her, remarking that for some reason his baggage was more closely scrutinised than that of any tourist. However, he was able to make a helpful suggestion: Cook's 'inspector', a certain Mr Sheen, who was staying in Agnes' hotel, was about to leave for England and might be persuaded to take it with him and deliver it to some friend of hers in London. Cooks, it seems, had some special arrangement with the Government, under which all their couriers were exempted from Customs search. Mr Sheen proved agreeable, bore it away, and in due course deposited it with the Principal of the Presbyterian Theological College in London. (The volume can be seen today in one of the showcases in the library of Westminster College, Cambridge, to which institution Agnes subsequently presented it. The curious will find, tucked in the endpapers, her letter to Dr Dykes explaining how it was smuggled back to England.)

The twins succeeded in smuggling through the tattered fragments of manuscript which they had bought themselves, but only with some difficulty. The Cairo Customs officers viewed these objects with deep suspicion; and it was only after Agnes had indignantly thrust under their noses an important-looking letter on Foreign Office notepaper (contents quite irrelevant to the matter in hand) that they finally agreed to allow her to keep her trophies.

Sorting out these bits and pieces, back in Cambridge, was such a pleasure, that the anxieties of getting them home were soon forgotten. Maggie, to whom fell this task (for Agnes was fully occupied with the proofs of her Syriac Lectionary), was soon able to report a 'find'. Solomon Schechter, the University's Reader in Talmudic, identified some grubby scraps as part of the original Hebrew manuscript of Ecclesiasticus, a book which had hitherto existed only in Greek and Syriac translations, and which was believed to be totally lost. St Jerome had mentioned a copy in the fourth century, but since that date there had been no trace of one. Agnes wrote to several learned journals announcing this discovery, as a result of which nine more leaves were unearthed in the Bodleian at Oxford. The twins were particularly delighted with this find, not least because the author of this second century book, Jesus Ben-Sirach, was a woman-hater: had he not deliberately omitted Deborah and Ruth from his list of national heroes? And did he not so far forget himself as to write 'Better is the wickedness of a man than the goodness of a woman'? It was with some malicious satisfaction that they reflected on the fact that it had been left to two women to recover part of his book, after a lapse of fifteen centuries, in the language in which he actually wrote it.

But on the very day on which the Ecclesiasticus leaves were identified, Agnes caught a violent chill, and retired to bed for three months with fever and severe rheumatism (so perhaps Ben-Sirach was revenged on them after all) and it was October before she began to regain the full use of her legs. Maggie was therefore rather taken aback when her sister proposed a fourth visit to Sinai in the following spring; but Agnes cunningly suggested that her rheumatism would assuredly vanish the moment her feet were once more set on the warm sand – an opinion in which she contrived to get Professor Macalister to support her. Why did she wish to go? Well, she wanted her text of the Lectionary to be absolutely correct in every detail: if the proofs were to be held up for a few months longer, they could make a final check against the originals.

So January 1897 found them once more loading their trunks on to a cab. Maggie's opposition was finally overcome by the news that their friend Dr Schechter had succeeded in obtaining access to the Genizah* of the Cairo synagogue, and, having dived into a great hole filled with fragmented Hebrew manuscripts, had decided that this was undoubtedly the place from which that Ecclesiasticus fragment had originated, whence it had probably been stolen by some enterprising thief who acted as wholesaler to the curio-dealers. Confronted with this news, the scholar in Maggie triumphed over the sister and the nurse, and she withdrew her opposition to the trip.

Schechter met them in Cairo, and conducted them to the synagogue which was situated in one of the most densely-populated quarters of the city. Agnes describes the scene thus: 'A very broad gallery runs round three sides of the building, and above one of these there is a door high up in the whitewashed wall, to which the roughest of rude ladders gave access. As its rungs were very wide apart, I dared not attempt to mount it'[because of her rheumatism, of course.

---

* The authorities of Jewish synagogues had always felt that it would be disrespectful to destroy such rolls of Holy Writ as had become hopelessly frayed and damaged through incessant use. It was their custom, therefore, to build a small room on to the synagogue, in which these superseded rolls could be placed and left to rot. Such a room was called a *genizah*. In a warm, dry country, scrolls made of vellum would scarcely deteriorate at all, even after the lapse of many centuries.

Ladylike modesty would not have weighed with her in such a situation]; 'but the servant of the synagogue did so, and as he jumped down on the other side we could hear the crackling of vellum leaves under his feet.' Maggie went next, followed by Dr Schechter and by a young Girton student, a Miss de Witt, whom the doctor brought with him. The mess within – for as such it can only be described – was appalling. Upon the discarded manuscripts, whitewash from the walls had tumbled in the course of centuries, augmented by dust from the street and sand from the desert, and some liquid had also seeped through ('whence it were perhaps better not to enquire' comments Agnes delicately), with the result that the fragments were all absolutely filthy and glued together. By comparison, the Sinai cubbyholes had been models of loving care.

The whole of this unappetising hotchpotch had been presented to Dr Schechter by the Grand Rabbi of Egypt, no doubt because the former happened to be a Jew as well as a scholar. Arrangements were made for the whole contents of the genizah to be packed into sacks; but as Schechter was unable to supervise the packing personally, various light-fingered gentlemen were able to indulge in extensive pilfering, and subsequently disposed of their haul to the local curio-dealers. Many of these fragments Agnes and Maggie succeeded in rounding up, to the delight of their Jewish friend.

Agnes, with her insistence upon tidiness and hygiene, saw no point in carrying home large quantities of Cairo dirt, so she cleaned up the manuscripts as best she could in her hotel bedroom. Most of them were so wet and odoriferous that she had to spread them out on tables and trunks to dry in the sunlight, 'removing a quantity of sticky treacle-like stuff with bits of paper.' To the disappointment of the party, no further leaves of Ecclesiasticus were found; but various valuable scraps came to light, one of which was of considerable scientific interest by reason of the composition of the paper. Under microscopic examination and chemical analysis, it proved to be made of flax which had not passed through the intermediate state of rags.

Under the combined influence of the warm Cairo air and the services of a German masseuse, Agnes' knees recovered sufficiently to enable the sisters to continue their journey to Sinai, which they reached on February 13th. The almond trees in the garden were a mass of blossom, and fresh young cypresses had replaced the old trees which had been cut down. The old mosque had collapsed for want of attention, and only the tower remained standing. The Archbishop was in residence, and received them 'with his usual affability', and – so closely were the twins and the Codex linked in the mind of the authorities – the palimpsest was automatically produced for them. Agnes spent a few days trying to extract a few more words from it, to avoid hurting the old man's feelings; but thereafter she concentrated upon checking the proofs of the Lectionary. Maggie busied herself with photographing a little eighth-century Arabic manuscript which had taken her fancy on her first visit, and with examining a Codex of the Arabic Gospels which they had photographed at the same time. Everything had gone wrong with their Cambridge work on the latter document. As usual, they had transcribed the text from their photographs, leaving illegible words blank until they could be filled in on the next visit to St Catherine's; but, pressed for time in the weeks before departure, they had decided to transcribe only the Epistles themselves, leaving the Gospels to be copied by another hand. The 'other hand' in this case had been an Arab whom they had found in London who, for ten pounds, had agreed to the task, leaving blanks for whatever he could not read. As Agnes was packing his work in readiness for the 1893 visit, she happened to notice that one of the photographs was perfectly white from the effects of an intrusive sunbeam, and yet there was no blank to correspond with it on the Arab's written page. When she drew her scribe's attention to this discrepancy, he had blandly replied that he had filled up all blanks and all indecipherable words from the version published by the British and Foreign Bible Society!

So, on this visit, every single photograph, and the whole of the Arab's work, had to be done all over again, and compared with the original. As a result, fifty defective pages had to be re-photographed. At this point, more trouble arose. When, the photographing done, they were taking the rolls of exposed film out of the camera in their tent, with the aid of a red lamp, a brilliant white light was suddenly flashed around. Their dragoman, forgetful of their strict instructions that no lights were to be shown in camp during the next half-hour, had suddenly lit a magnesium flare, 'simply to gratify his Arab love of display.' Fifty-four negatives – a whole morning's work – were ruined. After this, the twins were too disheartened to attempt any further study of those unlucky Arabic gospels.

Then their cameras broke down. In the haste of their departure, they had omitted to take their usual precaution of returning them to the makers for a check-up. One machine jammed, and in the other the roller declined to stay in position. The twins had seven hundred films they were waiting to use, and no camera expert nearer than Cairo. The manuscripts they wished to photograph were already sorted into heaps, but the two women, in spite of energetic fiddling, were helpless. Agnes tossed sleepless on her camp bed, and even dreamed about the problem. After a delay of several days, however, she managed to improvise what seamen would call a jury-rig, which proved marginally satisfactory. Taken all in all, it had proved a nervously-exhausting trip.

The journey home was uneventful, and they were back in Castlebrae by the middle of April. Macalister had been correct in his prognosis: Agnes' knees were once more in proper working order.

In the month after their return, Agnes and Maggie had a pleasing duty to perform, namely that of laying the foundation stone of the English Presbyterians' new Theological College in Cambridge. For many years, this seminary had been housed in London, in the building in Queen Square where George III had been confined after he had lost his reason – a coincidence which was naturally the subject of many jokes in Presbyterian circles. As far back as 1873, it had been proposed to move the College to Cambridge, but the General Assembly had been divided as to the wisdom of this step. Cambridge was subjected, by the 'London party', to a number of highly uncomplimentary epithets – it was secluded, cloistered, superannuated, remote from life. Worse, it was predominantly Anglican: the students would almost certainly become infected by horrid Erastian and episcopalian heresies. And who would foot the bill for what was bound to be a highly expensive move? Year after year the matter was raised in Assembly, debated, and the proposal defeated by a narrow majority. At this point, enter our heroines – in a new role: *eminences grises*. They had noticed a vacant plot of land in the Castle Hill area of Cambridge – at the foot of Mount Pleasant, five minutes walk from Castlebrae – and discreet enquiries elicited the fact that the owner would be willing to sell this site for £5,000: a very reasonable price for a location which faced down the famous 'Backs'. They allowed it to be known, through their friend Dr John Watson (who happened at the time to be Convener of the College Committee) that they were willing to buy this site and present it to the Church, to give a further £5,000 towards the erection of the buildings, and to bequeath £15,000 to the College in due course. Fortified with this generous offer, the 'Cambridge party' carried the day in the 1895 Assembly by the narrow margin of thirteen votes. The twins laid the foundation stone of the new college on 25 May 1897.

During the summer of the same year, Agnes wrote a popular account of their various visits to Sinai, which was published under the title of *In the Shadow of Sinai: a story of travel and research from 1895 to 1897*, while on the more scholarly level she was working, with Rendel Harris, on *The Story of Ahikar*, a tale which forms part of the *Arabian Nights*, but which Harris considered to be the original of the Parable of the Wicked Servant (Matt. xxiv.48). This edition, when finally printed, included versions in four languages and translations from seven: Agnes' share was the Arabic version. It is the usual story of the wicked nephew who comes to a sticky end, but whose uncle revenges himself by adding to the lad's sufferings in prison by giving him improving counsel to the tune of one hundred and twenty-four axioms.

These include the inappropriate advice to go always to church on holiday and to avoid the company of shameless women. This avuncular prosing proves too much for the nephew who, in Harris' words, 'simplifies the action of the play by swelling up and bursting asunder in a melodramatic way which satisfies all the instincts of justice.'

Cynical critics of university honours, basing their views upon their observation of recently-capped over-knowledgeable young men, have been known to murmur that all degrees corrupt and Ph.D's corrupt absolutely. Such sardonic observers would probably attribute the simple unspoilt natures of Agnes and Maggie to the fact that they possessed no academic honours whatsoever. This state of affairs was, however, about to be remedied. In July 1899, Agnes received her first degree: the University of Halle conferred upon her an honorary Doctorate of Philosophy, together with the title of Master of the Liberal Arts. This was in recognition of her discovery of, and work on, the palimpsest. She herself was very indignant that no award was made to Maggie; but the logical Germans no doubt argued that the Official Photographer to the expedition, however valuable her labours, could not quite be placed in the same class as the actual discoverer of the Codex. That the conservative, intensely anti-feminist Teutons should confer this degree at all upon a woman – and that its bestowal should result from a wholly unanimous vote from the entire Faculty of Philosophy – is an indication of the remarkable esteem in which Agnes' scholarship was coming to be held on the continent. The citation, indeed, uses quite extravagant language about her: she is 'eminent amongst all women, not only in her own country, but in the whole world for her learning.'

In passing, it is interesting to note that a correspondent in the *Cambridge Review* subsequently waxed indignant because the University within whose precincts the twins lived had taken no steps in this direction. Many men who have received honorary Cambridge degrees, the writer argued, were far less distinguished than the sisters, and had contributed much less to the sum of human knowledge.

'Many men as well as women here,' he concluded, 'are loudly pleading for honour to whom honour is due.'* But he might have saved his ink: Cambridge never gave them so much as an honorary M.A. The day was far distant when the august Senate was to honour, in this way, a local tailor who had made a special study of academic robes.

In the autumn of that year, Westminster College was formally opened, the keys of the building being delivered to the Moderator of the General Assembly by Dr John Watson, who had worn himself out touring congregations and collecting money to ensure that the seminary opened free of debt. With typical quaintness, Agnes and Maggie handed out artificial roses to the guests in honour of the author of *Beside the Bonnie Brier Bush*, and the former wrote a special hymn for the occasion, about which the less said the better. The wittiest speech of the day was made by the Vice-Chancellor, Dr Chawner, Master of Emmanuel College, who replied to Watson's toast to the University. Struck by the fact that the Roman Catholics had recently opened a seminary close to the new Westminster College, he remarked: 'My ideal university would welcome every form of college. I would gladly receive Roman Catholics at the top of Mount Pleasant, and Presbyterians at the bottom. I can imagine that some persons would say that the same Providence which had created poison and its antidote, and the dock in close proximity to the nettle, had also established these two colleges, so that one of them – I will not say which – might serve to heal the mischief wrought by the other.' Those more conservative clerics, lately members of the 'London party', no doubt looked darkly at the twins, holding them responsible for their defeat, and shook dubious heads over the new venture.

---

* He signs himself 'Pertilote'. Was it Harris, perhaps, or one of the Macalisters? The use of a nom-de-plume suggests either someone who feared that his known friendship with the twins would cause his sound arguments to be discounted, or someone fairly highly-placed (a professorial member of Senate, say) who thought it imprudent to support such an 'irregular' claim with his own name, for fear his words might later be cited as a precedent, should some 'unsuitable' female be nominated. The former argument points to Harris, the latter to one of the Macalisters.

They certainly did not envisage a day when Westminster would give to the University one of its Professors of Divinity in the person of H.H. Farmer, Norris–Hulse Professor from 1949 to 1960.

Two years later, Agnes received her second doctorate, and Maggie her first. They travelled north to St Andrews, where the newly-installed Chancellor, Lord Balfour of Burleigh, conferred upon them the honorary degree of Doctor of Laws. In 1904 they received Doctorates of Divinity from Heidelberg – the first theological doctorates to be conferred upon women by any university in the world. Finally, in 1911, Trinity College, Dublin, conferred a Litt.D. upon the twins. Part of the fun of these occasions was that the local newspapers invariably became confused about the distinguished visitors who came to be 'capped', and the sisters were more than once described as 'two Cambridge women dons'. Fortunately any Cambridge academics present would be on the train for home before the gaffe appeared in print, so no sensitive feelings would be ruffled.

These awards set the seal on the twins' labours. Universities have always been extremely sparing in the administration of their honours, and are careful not to cheapen their value by indiscriminate conferment. Now, not only had justice been done: it had been seen to be done. The place that they had sought for so long to win for themselves in this essentially male field of semitic scholarship had, at last, been accorded to them by bodies whose imprimatur carried weight.

In 1914, Agnes and her ex-monk friend Mingana collaborated in editing a work with the unexciting title of *Leaves from Three Ancient Qurans, possibly pre-Othmanic*. It is not a title-page to set the pulses beating, but it nevertheless created a stir in Islamic circles comparable to that occasioned in Christian ones by the 'heretical' verse of the Lewis Codex. For the Quran (or Koran, as it is usually spelled) is absolutely binding upon all Muslims as a rule of faith and conduct, and they claim for it final textual accuracy, alleging that it was personally dictated by God to Mohammed. There is, in fact, only one version of the Quran in existence, for in the seventh century the caliph Othman – irritated by the differing versions in existence – pronounced one to be the official version and destroyed all the others. The leaves which Agnes and Mingana edited were among some eighty-odd which the former had acquired in Suez in 1895. These fragments were found to contain six sheets with no fewer than three underwritings (superimposed and cross-hatched, as in a Victorian letter), one of which she and Mingana believed to be a leaf of the Quran dating from *before* the official destruction. If this could be proved, it would undermine the basic tenet of the Mohammedan religion: the claim of the Divine dictation of every single word of the Quran would at once become untenable. Agnes and Dr Mingana considered that they had made out a strong case – though they did not finally commit themselves. Most subsequent Islamic scholars, however, have decided that the fragments are of a later date; and the Islamic world has consequently continued to spin upon its axis, as hitherto. But it was this work, coupled with Maggie's edition of the *Commentaries on Ishodad of Merv*, which led, in June 1915, to the bestowal upon the twins of the coveted Triennial Gold Medal of the Royal Asiatic Society – the blue ribbon of oriental research. The presentation was made by Austen Chamberlain, at that time Secretary of State for India, in a speech which is almost a comprehensive anthology of platitudes. Maggie's acknowledgment contained one revealing remark: 'I came into this world as a supplement to my sister,' she said, 'and I have always recognised that it was mine to take a second place. But you will agree with me that it is better to be second in a good cause than first in a bad one.'

The twins were now beginning to grow old. They were nearing seventy, and constant exposure to the desert suns had begun to take its toll of their complexions. A photograph of Agnes, taken in the robes of her final doctorate, reveals a face that is now heavy-featured, and from which the former sprightliness has departed. Strength is still there, and the touch of humour still lurks in her more heavily-lidded left eye; but there is a double chin, now, and head and shoulders have drawn closer together, giving her a curiously dumpy look which is reinforced by the too-large gown which has been placed upon her. The mortarboard is no longer put on at an engagingly rakish angle, but is set levelly on the head, as befitting one who has put away feminine vanities. Her hair has become fluffy and untidy, and sprouts from the bull neck like the spray of a wave breaking against a rock. Agnes is growing old. Maggie, too, is changing: a photograph of her, taken at a Commemoration Day at Westminster College, shows her with a face still full of character, but now verging on the gaunt. Her features have sharpened, with the skin drawn tightly over the high prominent cheekbones, the chin thrust out determinedly, and the eyes full of a certain grim humour. Agnes, it seems, belongs to the type of old lady who becomes steadily dumpier and more podgy: Maggie to the type that shrinks, somehow, with each succeeding year. It is clear that they no longer look like identical twins: there is now no possible doubt as to which is which.

But if their bodies altered, as bodies will, the mind and the spirit remained the same. They worked on, as before; but they began to tire more easily, to feel a sense of strain in the eyes after an hour spent poring over faded Arabic or Syriac writing, to be increasingly troubled by rheumaticky hands when they began to write. 'Whether a screw has been taken off my mind when I finished my last book, or my constitution has been relieved by the haemorrhage in August,' Agnes writes to Rendel Harris in 1911, 'I always find something rattling in my head at night, which does not agree with palimpsests.' But she has no intention of giving in: 'I think a change of work will do me good,' she concludes. There must be no more dashing across deserts now – their sixth and final visit to Sinai was in 1906, when they were sixty-three – but in the same letter she outlines her next four tasks, which she considers will keep her occupied for the next three years. One of these was rather odd: to edit and translate an inscription, in Arabic and Persian, which had just been found in a mosque in (of all places) Hangchow in China, and which dated from the fifteenth century. 'Man must live as though he were immortal,' Principal John Oman once retorted to a friend who, discovering him busily engaged in planting rose trees when he was in his seventy-ninth year, had ventured to tease him about it. A similar philosophy guided the twins. Ahead of them lay the Great War; but they were to outlast that dark time and to work energetically, while it raged, at many tasks besides their scholarship. 'The present moment is God's ambassador, to declare His mandates', wrote de Caussade a hundred years before Agnes and Maggie were born. For the twins, the present moment contained, always, more than enough of challenge and inspiration to keep them fully occupied. The future was in the hands of God.

_____ X _____

The Old Age of the Eagle

_____

The old age of the eagle is better than the youth of the crow.
       – *The story of Haiqar and Nadan,*
translated from the Arabic by Agnes Smith Lewis

When the War came, the twins shared in the successive emotions of utter incredulity and misplaced optimism which characterised most British people at the time: incredulity that war should break out at all in a world which, like M. Coué's patients, had manifestly been growing, every day and in every way, better and better; over-optimism as to its speedy conclusion. As early as November 1914, Agnes was confident that final victory was imminent, and telegraphed to her friend Mrs Turner (Grace Blyth's niece, who was with her colonel husband on his Indian Army station) an invitation that embraced even the domestic animals: 'COME TO CAMBRIDGE YOU KITTY PUPPY GERMANS FLEEING SEA SAFE.' Soon, however, the twins, in common with most of their fellow-countrymen, began to realise that the conflict was likely to take slightly longer to settle than had been anticipated. Whereupon, with their usual energy, they set themselves to tackle 'war work' and 'do their bit' as bidden by Lord Kitchener (and incidentally to learn their fourteenth language: Russian).

They expressed their willingness to give hospitality to Belgian refugees, who were then beginning to appear in Cambridge – a forlorn group, usually excitable, and possessing nothing but the clothes on their backs. The committee responsible for billetting these unfortunates did its best to 'send someone suitable', and eventually allocated to Castlebrae a certain Dr and Mrs de France and their two children – André, a boy of four, and Paul, two years his junior.

Agnes and Maggie had tasted many experiences denied to their contemporaries, but small children in the house was definitely not one of them, and it is not surprising that this invasion caused something of a revolution. Two small, noisy, spoilt boys, whose chief aim in life was to escape from adult vigilance long enough to hammer the dinner-gong as deafeningly as possible, scarcely fitted easily into a household dedicated to the high ends of study in an atmosphere of uninterrupted quiet and orderly routine. To make matters worse, the Belgians (who had been rich, smart, sophisticated and altogether godless all their lives) were totally unappreciative of the sacrifices which the elderly scholars were making, accepted the hospitality as their right, and made no effort to be even minimally considerate. They grumbled endlessly, and their conversation consisted mainly of lamentations bewailing their lost jewels, which they had not had time to seize in the course of their hurried flight from Antwerp. Mrs Turner, when she arrived in response to that telegraphed invitation, did her best to smooth over the various contretemps which arose, and to assuage the ruffled feelings of the two householders; and their next-door neighbour, Mrs Janetta Sorley,* gave them some toys for the Belgian children to play with – toys formerly belonging to her son, Charles Hamilton Sorley, a poet of great promise who was soon to die on the Somme in his late teens. But there was no denying that the experiment was a failure: the

* Wife of the Knightsbridge Professor of Moral Philosophy. She was noted for her sharp tongue. Once, at some college reception, she was asked if she would like an ice. 'No, thank you,' she replied – 'I've just been talking to Professor Sandys.'

Belgians took everything and gave nothing, not even thanks. Whenever the air raid alarm sounded, and the lights automatically dimmed down, Madame de France would rush panick-stricken down to the cellar, shrieking 'Oh ze Kaiser ze devil – eef 'e come I pull 'is nose off', which may have been an admirable patriotic sentiment, but was one which hardly soothed Agnes, still thinking in Syriac from the evening's work, and with little interest in the Kaiser's physiognomy or in the perils to which it might one day be exposed. For the de Frances, understandably enough, the war was everything, and they could scarcely conceive how any other interests could be maintained while it lasted. Agnes had only to begin knitting a pair of socks for Madame to enquire excitedly, 'Pour les soldats? Pour les soldats?' – a question which was not at all satisfactorily answered by Agnes' laconic reply, 'No: for meself.'

Happily, however, they did not stay long. The doctor was offered some medical appointment, and they departed amid general feelings of relief. Less resolute women would have been embittered by such an experience, and would have looked for some less exhausting form of war work; but the twins considered it to be their duty to try again. This time, though, they would have women – single women, unencumbered by the complicating appendages of husbands or children. The billetting officer listened sympathetically, and sent them two milliners, also from Antwerp, Lenaerts by name. This arrangement proved more happy. In normal times, these two women conducted a smart millinery establishment in Antwerp called 'Maison Flore-Louise' (a compound of their two Christian names), and Agnes and Maggie encouraged them to resume their occupation during their exile. The twins scrounged the necessary materials for hat-making from some unspecified quarter and, when their guests were ready to begin work, called in their carriage on those of their acquaintances who 'dress well and go to London for their clothes' (as Agnes put it), soliciting their patronage and inviting them to a kind of fashion show in Castlebrae at which the refugees' work would be displayed.

All these friends loyally turned up on the appointed day, to find the dining-room transformed from its usual austere and dedicated purposes into a *salon*. On borrowed hat-stands (and even on empty whisky-bottles) hats were displayed in various stages of manufacture, ribbons and trimmings of every kind were in readiness, and the two millinery artists hovered uncertainly in the background. Agnes and Maggie tactfully kept out of the way, no doubt with the object of sparing both sides of the counter any embarrassment, but in reality increasing it, for Flore-Louise knew no English at all, and most of their prospective clients were rusty in French and ignorant of Flemish. After an agonisingly long period during which creators and prospective buyers stared uneasily at each other, devoid of any means of communication, Mrs Sorley and Queenie Butler (the daughter of the Master of Trinity) held a whispered conference and took charge of the proceedings: each seized a hat, put it on, and transformed herself into a mannequin and, pirouetting one on either side of the table, began to take orders. Later, when the business grew, the twins took a flat in Rose Crescent for Flore-Louise, turning it into a combined workroom and showroom – thereby giving the Belgians a pleasant sense of independence and, at the same time, allowing Castlebrae to return to its academic calm during the daytime.

The scholars' next venture was to begin breeding rabbits – or rather, to attempt to do so – in order to augment the family diet and to 'increase the amount of food in the country', as Agnes somewhat ambitiously expressed it. They bought, naturally, the most expensive ones on the market, spent a great deal of money having hutches erected to house them, and aroused among their friends pleasant expectations of a steady diet of rabbit pie. There were seven rabbits in all, a buck and six does who were called after the wives of Henry VIII (Mrs Sorley recalls a tearful Agnes calling on her one morning with the news that Anne Boleyn had run away). Much to his disgust, Eastwell, their chauffeur, was put in charge of these additions to the household: he detested rabbits. His irritation increased to cold fury when some friend told Agnes that the creatures were more likely to breed if they heard soothing music: whereupon she bought a gramophone and insisted upon adding the regular playing of this instrument to Eastwell's duties. Music might be the food of love, but, if this were so, Eastwell determined to 'give them excess of it, that so the appetite might sicken and so die.' Learning from one of his cronies that loud, sudden noises were always fatal to conception or to the does' unborn progeny, he thereafter never went near the hutches without supplementing the music by violent percussion action cn the roof, augmented by such other disturbing noises as his ingenuity suggested to him. He had no intention of adding to the number of his charges, if he could avoid it. This policy was attended with conspicuous success: the animals remained obstinately barren. Flore and Louise who, as continental ladies, were naturally better versed in such delicate affairs of the heart, always maintained privately that the rabbits' wholly uncharacteristic infertility had another, and more obvious cause: the Giblews, they insisted, had been cheated by the vendor, who had sold them seven animals of the same sex. Be that as it may, the experiment certainly proved highly disappointing. It is recorded that, at one of the twins' smart dinner parties, during the brief and unaccountable silence which always descends at some point upon every company, Agnes was heard to reply to some polite enquiry as to the rabbits' health: 'Aye, they're all right – but they havena been verra intimate yet.'

The twins' care for refugees, however, extended far beyond hospitality and professional rehabilitation, and embraced, also, their spiritual welfare. In a very short space of time, Cambridgeshire was teeming with Belgians, all soi-disant Roman Catholics, in whom, it appeared, the local British priests did not take a great deal of interest – either because they were seriously overworked, or because they did not speak Flemish. Agnes felt a sense of responsibility for these poor foreigners, left without much in the way of spiritual food. She therefore wrote to the British and Foreign Bible Society and ordered a large crate of French and Flemish Bibles. Thereafter, as the sisters drove round the county on their outings, they would stop the car every time they sighted a Belgian, and present him or her with a Bible. But here, as in other matters, charity began at home. They discovered to their dismay that Flore-Louise not only possessed no Bible of their own: they had never even seen one. Agnes presented them with a copy, and urged them to begin reading it without delay. Unfortunately (but not unnaturally) they began at page one; and, having waded dutifully but with growing consternation through the more sensational chapters of Genesis, exclaimed in answer to Agnes' anxious enquiry: 'Mais madame, – c'est une vraie chronique scandaleuse!' The vocation of a missionary, it appeared, was not without its attendant problems.

In 1917, when the war was at its height, Grace Blyth died. It is some time since she was mentioned in this chronicle, for though she was often in Castlebrae – she had followed the twins to Cambridge, and lived at Douglas House in Trumpington Street – little is known about her between the early travels and her last days. All we know is that she 'never took to' Samuel Lewis, as Agnes revealed to Mrs Turner (Grace's niece) in a letter shortly after their friend's death. 'She looked on him as having separated her dearest friends; any unfriendliness on my part might have caused a serious quarrel, which would have meant misery to her and to me. He was quite as touchy as she was, if not more so.' As the years passed, poor Grace became increasingly eccentric. Her whole life revolved round her little dog Lappie. This animal was supplied with a chop every day for lunch, and was subsequently knighted (the gardener was instructed always to address him as 'Sir Lappie'). Wishing to provide him with added comfort as he grew older, Grace wrote to Heal's of Tottenham Court Road and asked them to make a bed for him, to her specifications – a commission which they declined with some indignation. However, a local craftsman proved less stubborn and proud, and soon Lappie had his own tiny bedstead, complete with sheets and blankets. Grace and Lappie always went to Castlebrae for their Christmas dinner, and every year there was a row at table because Agnes absolutely declined to serve the dog before the human beings, as was Grace's invariable custom in her own home. Another eccentricity was that she never slept two nights in succession in the same bedroom, alleging that this custom sprang from the gipsy blood in her veins. The Romany, however, can scarcely be blamed for other peculiar habits, such as scrubbing all the furniture (including the piano) with soda-water, and having even unused chimneys swept regularly 'to clear out the foul air'.

When Sir Lappie eventually died, general mourning was prescribed for the whole staff of Douglas House. His body was wrapped in an expensive Persian rug and lovingly interred in the middle of the lawn. A marble memorial was erected on his grave, bearing the inscription 'His pure soul has gone straight to his Maker', and an expensive wreath laid at its foot, in a sort of Remembrance Day ceremony, by his prostrated mistress.

Grace's death was a tragic one. Standing by the mantelpiece one day, her long dress was swept into the gas fire, and she was taken to hospital suffering from extensive burns and shock. The twins, greatly concerned, visited her and tried to turn her mind to higher things. 'Are you thinking of Jesus, dear?' asked Maggie anxiously. 'I'm much too ill to be thinking of any such person,' was the disconcerting reply. A few days later she died. There was an inquest, at which Agnes made an impassioned attack upon the Gas Company for failing to provide a proper fireguard with the dangerous objects they sold; but the Company retorted, reasonably enough, that such safeguards were surely the responsibility of the purchaser. Agnes argued and argued – to the great delight of the reporters from the local papers, who took down her remarks verbatim and made columns of copy out of them – but the coroner was unsympathetic. 'Accidental death' remained the verdict, instead of 'Died as a result of the Gas Company's carelessness' which Agnes demanded. On Grace's death, the twins recovered the £10,000 which they had settled on her, and the money was later used to endow a Chair at Westminster College.

'Life is a tragedy,' wrote Swift long ago, 'wherein we sit as spectators awhile, and then act our own part in it.' As the war dragged to a close, the sky began to darken for Agnes and Maggie: the health of both began to fail. It would perhaps be uncharitable to suggest that the first ominous symptoms of Agnes' failing powers was the publication, in 1917, of that volume of her collected poems to which reference has already been made, and about which the kindest thing that can be said is that it adds little to the meagre output of Scottish poetry. Apart from an occasional vivid line, it is poor stuff; and Agnes, had she been still in full possession of her powers, could scarcely have failed to realise the fact. But about this time she, too, began to grow steadily more eccentric, and Maggie in consequence became increasingly worried about her. At the outset, the change was manifested by nothing more serious than a slight forgetfulness over detail, a weakness by no means confined to the elderly or the mentally impaired. But soon more alarming symptoms began to display themselves. When Professor Macalister died, Agnes called on the widow six evenings in succession in order to express her sympathy; at morning family prayers, she would read aloud the same Bible passage that she had selected the previous day, or would choose some wildly unsuitable chapter (of the kind usually passed hurriedly over in silence by the readers of Lessons), to Maggie's obvious confusion. Maggie, however, was intensely loyal: mistakenly loyal, in the opinion of her friends. She refused to face the situation that was arising, and could not be persuaded to discuss Agnes' palpable decline. She would drag Agnes round visiting, long after she was fit to appear in public, and would talk with animation on a number of subjects, while her elder sister sat silent, gazing with vacant eyes into space. 'I know Agnes doesn't add much to the conversation,' Maggie once confided in an undertone to Mrs Turner as they exchanged goodbyes on the doorstep, 'but it's very good for her to go out.' It wasn't; and everyone but Maggie, determined to preserve the brave pretence that nothing was wrong, could see it. It was embarrassing to their friends, and heartrending to their intimates, to see Agnes' steady decline – her massive mind, which had been such a wonderful tool, slipping and failing to engage, like the worn over-driven gears of an old car, which hold for a few minutes and then slip, whirring to no purpose.

One day, as she sat writing at the dining-room table, Agnes suddenly found that the pen had slipped from her hand: her arm had lost its power. She was put to bed and the doctor sent for: he was vague in his diagnosis, and simply prescribed massage, though the attack was obviously a stroke. Gradually, the paralysis wore off and physically Agnes seemed to recover. But though the body, with its iron constitution which no desert rigours could impair, fought its way back to health, the mind slipped still further.

By this time, Maggie herself was beginning to feel the strain. She grew absent-minded through perpetually grappling with her insoluble, unshared problem, often running round to the Turners in Storeys Way without an overcoat on freezing winter days. In January 1920, she was attacked by a cerebral thrombosis, which carried her off within twenty-four hours. All their friends were intensely anxious as to the repercussions of her death upon Agnes' clouded mind, and the nurse drugged the latter heavily on the day of the funeral. But they need not have been concerned: Agnes was past taking in the fact of her loss. When the sad news was broken to her, her only comment was 'How very inconsiderate of Maggie!' – no doubt an allusion to the long-standing arrangement between them that Agnes should die first, a plan which Maggie had now thoughtlessly upset. But it is doubtful if the realities of the situation ever really sank into her consciousness or, if they did, they were forgotten five minutes after being grasped; for, long afterwards, she would suddenly rise from her chair and exclaiming 'I'll go and see Maggie!' would wander, bewildered, round the vast empty house calling her name.

Until Agnes became too ill, Maggie had always shared a bedroom with her, as she had done from childhood except for the brief interlude of their respective marriages. After Samuel's death, they had even shared a bed – a huge, heavy double one, with a tape tied down the middle from the brass rail at the head to that at the foot, marking out thus (in their characteristically exact fashion) the frontier of each sister's 'sphere of influence'. But when Agnes began to fail, this was exchanged for twin beds. After Maggie's death, the faithful Emily moved into the vacant one; but the ordeal proved too much for her. Agnes would go to bed at eight, but by midnight her vigorous constitution had had all that it needed of rest, and she would rise and dress in preparation for the day's 'work'. Poor Emily became so exhausted by endless broken nights of this kind that the experiment had to be abandoned, and a nurse installed who could catch up on lost sleep during the day as Emily, with her household duties, could not.

Agnes lived for six long weary years after Maggie's death – years in which one day differed little from the preceding one, in which one week was essentially similar to the last, and all, as far as Agnes was concerned, equally devoid of significance. Human beings possess one characteristic in common with the botanical world: even the most highly cultivated among them tends to revert to type in old age. Failing health, too, is a searching test of character. When these two afflictions converge simultaneously, the naked self begins to show through the crumbling casing, and the person is seen as he or she really is. The polite civilised veneer flakes off; all those gracious dissimulations which form, as it were, a high polish upon the surface of the personality dissolve before the advancing acid, and one can perceive, perhaps for the first time, the quality and texture and grain of the wood beneath. Under such a test, those who have always evinced a tendency to be self-centred and petty become stridently so; those who have been inclined, all their lives, to be demanding and exacting and self-pitying begin to display those qualities nakedly and in an exaggerated form – too weary, now, to act a part any longer; those who have been firm and gracious and lovable characters become, when death begins to grin at them over the bed end, more gracious and lovable still. Agnes, who, beneath her brusque exterior and forceful, plainspoken manner, was fundamentally a good and lovable person, reacted to this new and testing situation with characteristic dignity. Her character did not collapse, nor was the soul that occasionally peered through the surface foolishness anything but the firm and controlled and thoughtful director it had always been. She who, in Dryden's words, had always united

> a female softness with a manly mind,

who had been

> a daughter duteous, and a sister kind,

was, at the last,

> in sickness patient, and in death resigned.

220

The Old Age of the Eagle

She retired into herself, and, like Swift in his last tragic years, took refuge in silence. Whole days sometimes went by without her speaking a word; yet this sphinx-like posture seemed rather to enhance her dignity than to underline the spectator's awareness of her decay. The old age of the eagle was indeed better than the youth of the crow, as the Arabic storyteller had maintained.

If the weather was fine, she would be taken for a little drive in the car, or in a bath chair, staring stonily before her, recognising no one, not even her oldest friends. Almost every day she would be brought to call at the Turners, be helped inside, would sit silent for an hour, and then leave without a word. But every now and then, the slipping cogs would engage for a second or two, and she would flash out some remark which recalled the old Agnes. One such day, when her companion Miss Ford was sitting by her, Agnes suddenly laid a hand upon her arm and said, 'My dear, this life must be very dull for you.' The old care for people, the old sense of profound responsibility for those whom one employs, which, over sixty years earlier, had moved her to write *Glenmavis*, had risen suddenly to the surface and, for a fleeting instant, had resumed control. Those who had most to do with her were never wholly sure how much she understood of what was said to her. Sometimes it seemed as though, like the hard of hearing, she could grasp the remark with the personal reference, while missing much else: our awareness of ourselves is perhaps the last thing we lose when all else finally slips from our grasp. One such occasion has been remembered. Her companion had come in from a walk, and drew up a chair to the bed. 'Mrs Lewis! Mrs Lewis!' No flicker of recognition crossed the impassive face. 'Mrs Lewis! – I met Dr Burkitt along the Backs this morning.' Still no response, no transient glimmer of understanding. 'And he said to me: "Mrs Lewis is the most learned lady in Cambridge".' The living statue suddenly spoke. 'And so I am,' it said. Praise, as Sydney Smith observed, is the best diet for us, after all: long after the appetite for life has gone, we can apparently subsist on a crumb or two from that dish.

221

There were few for whom her eyes lit up, in a transient flicker of recognition: Emily was one. Her faithful maid was compelled in these final six years to leave her service in order to nurse a sick mother; but she called frequently at Castlebrae, and was always rewarded by a sudden softening of the stony eyes, though never by a single word – not even her name. When Emily departed, Agnes' cousin Jean Connell came to live, and took over control of the household. In September 1922, this lady wrote to Rendel Harris (who was researching in the Sinai monastery at the time): 'She has certainly failed much in the last year. Your sister, Mrs Whibley, offered her carrying chair (which she does not use now) to help Mrs Lewis downstairs, and it is a great boon to her as her knees are weak. She still walks up, though. I am sorry I cannot say she has improved mentally, though at times she has flashes of intellect. We shall look forward to seeing you after your return and I am sure Mrs Lewis would be glad. She often speaks of you and sometimes says that she had your company driving.' Harris shook his head sadly when he received this letter, and carefully preserved it among his papers, where it was found after his death. Five months later, Miss Connell wrote again, to give him the latest news (he was still abroad): 'I was telling Mrs Lewis that you are living in the Convent of St Catherine, and she was very much interested. She speaks very little now, though, and is much failed since you saw her. Last month I was very anxious about her, as on the 11th [the anniversary of Maggie's death, and also her birthday] she got very low and weak, and I feared she was going too. I had told her nurse and maids to say nothing about the date to her, but it is curious how she changed that day, and more than a fortnight passed before she recovered.' The old, deep link with Maggie was as strong as ever: deep down in her subconscious mind, that sad date had been entered in the log-book of memory and, when the anniversary came round, the book fell open at the unforgettable page. The muddled mind felt for the raw nerve, like a blind man groping for some precious mislaid object, and the tender place throbbed painfully for a fort-night. 'She is very contented and sweet,' (continued Jean in her letter) 'and always likes to be told anything about you; and when I said you would perhaps come to see her when you return, she said "I will be very pleased to see him." I always think of you as her best friend now, the most understanding and sympathetic, and I would have been writing to consult you long ago about her manuscripts, had you been at home.'

Those manuscripts! There was by now a vast accumulation of them, and anxiety about them had been the principal reason for Miss Connell's letter. At the time of her writing, the library in the tower room (as it was always called: it was the room over the porch) had not been used for three years, and the documents housed there were becoming very damp. When Maggie died, the Irvine solicitors had sent down their junior partner to lock up all the most valuable ones in the strong-room (which was located in the pantry); but Miss Connell had discovered, to her dismay, that this place was even more damp than the library. 'I took all the boxes upstairs,' she continues in her report to Harris 'and after I got the manuscripts separated – but that took weeks, they were so stuck together, and had to be very carefully handled, being in such a fragile condition, – I spread them all out on floor, tables and chairs to dry. It was a slow process, and though many were in fragments when taken out of the boxes, I knew they were valuable, and got worried at the thought that they might go wrong, after all the ladies' work with them. As you were not available, I decided to write to the University Librarian for advice, and told him about their condition. He very kindly came himself to see them, and I was thankful I had preserved every little broken scrap, as he pieced them together and simply gloried over them, exclaiming every now and then, 'Oh, this *is* beautiful!' His (Dr Jenkinson's) advice was that they should be given away *now* to the Universities they are destined for, as there were far too many of them (he did not see nearly all of them) to be possibly taken care of in any private house, and that they ought to be repaired. He said that to have them repaired here would cost Mrs Lewis a fortune, but that each College would bear the expense of their own.'

It seemed the obvious and sensible solution; but the solicitors – who were also Agnes' trustees – sternly forbad anything to be removed from the house while she remained alive. In vain did Miss Connell protest that, while this was a perfectly right and proper decision as far as Agnes' other effects were concerned, manuscripts were surely in a different category. But as a result of her representations, the lawyers were persuaded to write to Principal Oman, asking if the documents could be temporarily housed at Westminster College. Oman and the College Librarian hurried round to Castlebrae to assess the extent of the responsibility involved. He was anxious to help, but 'thought it would be rather an undertaking' to have the manuscripts at the College 'in their present condition'. Miss Connell hinted that Dr Rendel Harris would be the man to advise them, knowing, as he did, far more about the documents than anyone else; but unfortunately he was still abroad. Finally, it was agreed between Oman and the solicitors that the collection should remain where it was until Harris returned and they could discuss the matter with him. Miss Connell wrote Harris a full account of the endless deliberations: letters which were preserved by Harris, and are in the Angus collection.

The upshot was that the manuscripts remained at Castlebrae until after Agnes' death, with one exception. This was a valuable palimpsest which had been sent to the Leipzig Exhibition in 1914 under solemn scholarly guarantees that it would be properly safeguarded and duly returned. But the war broke out before it could be sent back to Cambridge. After the war was over, neither Agnes nor Maggie was in a fit condition to follow the matter up; but Oman remembered the loan, and made strenuous efforts to track down the palimpsest and recover it. He approached two or three leading German scholars in this field, who promised to assist in the search and to ensure the return of the precious manuscript. But, after some months' delay, each in turn wrote abruptly withdrawing his offer of help – as though, in the course of his investigations, he had suddenly come up against a blank wall of officialdom which he dared not attempt to penetrate. Oman expostulated, but in vain; and

224

eventually he was compelled to abandon his pressure on his foreign colleagues. The manuscript was never returned.

In the course of time, Agnes became no longer strong enough to go out for her drives and bath-chair outings: too weak, even, to wander forlornly around the huge, empty house. The clouded mind did not worsen but, inch by inch, the sturdy vigorous body began to give ground, as though sensing the uselessness of a continued single-handed struggle against the advance of the Last Enemy. So Agnes took to her bed and lay there, day after day, staring vacantly into space, watching the evening sun slanting through the bedroom window as it sank behind the airy cages of the garden trees. Her brass bedstead, set against the inside wall of the room, faced the bay window; and through it, she could just glimpse, from her pillow, the corner of Castle Mound. Not much of a hill, in all conscience, towards which to lift up one's eyes: the Psalmist, in all probability, would not have considered it to be a hill at all. But it was the best that the flat fen-country round Cambridge could offer. Castle Mound is, as its name implies, simply a large bump – the Red Queen would have said that she could have shown you hills compared with which you would call it a valley – but, glimpsed fragmentarily through the western window of Castlebrae, with the sturdy fir trees which Agnes had planted upon its slopes, it seemed to her confused mind that it must be a fragment of the Ayrshire countryside. The wheel had come full circle and she was back, surely, among the wooded prospects of her childhood – expecting, at any moment, to hear her father's voice summoning her to get up and go for a country ramble with him and Maggie. As day succeeded day, and she gradually sank into a coma, this was the final picture which was registered upon her clouded brain. She had, at the last, lifted her eyes unto the hills: but no help had come. And, from that prospect, she slipped effortlessly and with relief into the valley of the shadow.

The end came on 23 March 1926, when the daffodils were in flower along the Backs, and an empty Cambridge, devoid of its students, rested quietly before the beginning of the May Term. Peacefully, on that spring day, Agnes' spirit stole quietly away to join her old favourite Moses in the heavenly places, where, no doubt, she at once began to discuss with him (in his own language) the exact location of that rock which he struck in the wilderness, or the precise authorship of the composite Pentateuch. Jean Connell, sitting by the motionless figure in the darkened bedroom while the watery sunlight filtered in through the chinks in the drawn curtains, must have thought of the verse which Agnes had composed for her New Year greeting-card nearly twenty-five years earlier:

Dull souls that are moping in gloom or in sorrow,
Look, look to the Saviour! Uprise to His call!
Then the glow and the light of an endless Tomorrow
Shall gild with their splendour the shadows that fall.

Rendel Harris came down from Birmingham for the funeral, and stayed on to superintend the sorting and disposal of the precious manuscripts in accordance with the will – a document of enormous length and unbelievable complexity, which had been drawn up only a few weeks before Maggie's death. After legacies to Eastwell, Emily Free and the gardener, the residue of the twins' estate was left to the English Presbyterian Church, mainly for Westminster College.

It was on a warm afternoon in early June that I paid a visit to Castlebrae. The old lodge at the gates had been converted into a tiny bungalow, and two large lodging-houses for students had been erected in different corners of the grounds. The house itself, with its Victorian Gothic castellated tower and overhanging porch, has been for many years now a hostel for the undergraduates of Clare College, to which Rendel Harris once belonged: but within, it has changed surprisingly little since the twins' day, for the College bought much of their furniture at the sale. On the afternoon of my visit, a battered jalopy stood at the top of the drive, where once the Highland piper marched up and down at garden parties. Term had ended, and the members of a touring repertory company were finishing a late lunch round the huge table which had accommodated so many distinguished guests and rare manuscripts. Amusement and curiosity were visible on their faces as the housekeeper ushered me into the dining-room, indicated the twins' sideboard and pointed to the carved initials on the solid oak mantelpiece. I wandered from room to room. The Greek mottoes over the doorways of the ground-floor rooms – faded, now, within their brown-edged scrolls – were still legible, emphasising the necessity for purity of conversation in the lounge, for perpetually-boiling kettles in the kitchen, and for vigorous friendships in the dining-room (an unimaginative Bursar has since had these painted over in the course of redecoration). The boudoir mantelpiece still bore its melancholy Arabic quotation from the Koran, black against the smooth grain of the light oak, but now almost invisible beneath a coating of thick dark varnish. Through the bay windows of the old drawing-room, I looked out on to what remains of the tree-shaded lawn, where once the model of the Tabernacle had been set out for the admiration and edification of guests in tight trousers and side-whiskers, or long bombazine dresses and flower-garden hats. The sharp outlines of the panorama of the past had blurred and smudged; yet here and there could still be discerned the scattered details of a recognisable pattern which recalled, even yet, the bright splendour of bygone days – as a pavement artist's vivid sketch, after a heavy shower, will retain, here and there, faint patches of colour or an occasional firm line.

I wandered out of the front door into the hard June sunshine and, passing round the side of the ugly building, climbed by the special private path to the top of Castle Mound – a path now overgrown and almost invisible beneath the long, rank grass – to gaze across the weathered lichened roof of the sprawling house at the College towers which lay spread below me in the clear summer air. As the theatrical party emerged, laughing and noisy, and began to pile into the old jalopy, it was as though the present life of the old house had, as in one of Agnes' palimpsests, overlaid and almost obliterated the life of a forgotten generation which had once lived and studied and prayed within those walls: the underwriting, recording in faded characters the lives of the twins, had for a moment been sharpened and made clearly visible by the powerful reagent of memory; but now it slowly faded again before my eyes and became, once more, faint and illegible. The story of a later generation of students was being superimposed, page by page and chapter by chapter, upon that chronicle of a bygone age, and

> What was near them grows remote,
> Happy silence falls like dew.

So, as the battered car sputtered into life and, comically overloaded, chugged with a grinding of gears down the drive and out into the busy world, leaving only a whirl of dust behind, we may take our leave of Agnes and Maggie:

> By still water they would rest
> In the shadow of a tree:
> After battle sleep is best,
> After noise, tranquillity.

Lampada Tradam

'We are servants,' wrote Agnes in her spidery Italian hand opposite her signature in Mrs Robert Ball's Visitors' Book. She was probably quoting from her beloved palimpsest, which reads thus at Luke xvii.10, where the Authorised and Revised Versions have the more familiar 'We are unprofitable servants.' But she meant what she wrote – it was not simply the sort of thing people put in visitors' books in Victorian days, after the pen had hovered uncertainly and despairingly over the column oddly labelled 'Remarks'. Rather, it was a characteristic comment from one whose ego had been firmly subdued by long years of austere Presbyterian discipline: almost an article of faith, or a summary of the law and the prophets – and, as such, a phrase worth more than a casual passing glance. For no one knew better than Agnes the precise 'station and duties' of a servant. Had she not employed an enormous number of them, in the course of a long life? Certezza, Hanna, Armanous and Ahmed the dragomen; innumerable camel-drivers and cooks; and the large Castlebrae staff – changing, now and again, in the lower ranks, but with the faithful Emily bridging almost the whole span of years in the old house? With Agnes, the phrase was no facile slogan of the advertising agency, no slick Rotarian motto: when it came to servants, she knew what she was talking about.

Looking back from our servantless age to a period in which every middle-class home had one or more domestics, and every well-to-do household a whole retinue, it is not easy for us to think Agnes' thoughts after her as she wrote those words; but the effort must nevertheless be made, for it is in these terms that she chose to epitomise her own, and her sister's, *weltanschauung*. What precisely did the best of her generation expect from their servants? Perhaps this: a devotion and a loyalty to one's employer, under all hazards, and ideally for a lifetime; an extreme conscientiousness and care in all work undertaken (rooms must be swept, not only to the satisfaction of the mistress, but to the glory of God, in the best George Herbert tradition); and, last but not least, a constant and lively awareness of one's 'place'. This 'knowing one's place', indeed, was fundamental to the whole relationship. However warm the affection a servant might come to entertain for his employer, and his master for him, and however much formality might therefore be relaxed and intimacy flower between them in virtue of their long association, such things must never be presumed upon, nor must the slightest advantage ever be taken of them. To be a servant at all, one must live out one's life, as a matter of course, within this framework of accepted ideas.

It was in precisely such terms that Agnes defined her own position in the universe: her duty to the God she served, her status in the Father's house. She was ever conscious that she, no less than Emily Free, was 'under authority'; and to her day's laborious work on the grubby and odoriferous fragments of some mouldering manuscript, she applied the same conscientiousness as was devoted by Emily to the task of turning out the drawing-room. In the background of her mind, as in Emily's, there lurked always the recollection that she, too, had a taskmaster to satisfy – and one whose standards were exacting. In spite of the marked difference in the nature of their duties, she and Emily were both servants; and it was incumbent upon both alike to 'know their place'. Among other results of this attitude was a kind of scrupulous objectivity about her own work, an habitual cast of mind which shunned insincere modesty no less than the tedious egotism of conceit. 'I think it can do no good for you to depreciate your own work,' Agnes wrote firmly to Rendel Harris on one occasion (apropos of an excessively modest letter he had just written to a periodical which had credited him with the discovery of the Lewis Codex), 'for my part, I think the interests of truth are best secured when we take frankly any credit that is due to ourselves, and give other people their due also, neither more nor less.' She would have said as much to the cook, had that worthy stubbornly declined to accept praise for an original and appetising pudding. The labourer was worthy of his hire, even when the wage was paid partly in appreciation. A good servant was, as of right, entitled to a proper respect from his employer; and he should not forfeit it by foolishly pretending that his excellent work was valueless – an attitude as blameworthy and reprehensible as 'getting above himself' and 'taking liberties'. 'We do not really need to talk of ourselves as "unprofitable",' Agnes observed – no doubt still with that text from St Luke in mind – when she acknowledged receipt of the Royal Asiatic Society's Gold Medal, 'I really believe there is nothing in our Lord's teaching contrary to the view that even very humble work may be very profitable indeed.' One had to 'know one's place' – that was fundamental; and the same devoted loyalty, the same profoundly affectionate (but always respectful) service that Ahmed or Emily gave to herself, was given by Agnes to her Great Taskmaster, under whose all-seeing eye she laboured so diligently.

If this attitude preserved her from that spurious humility which prompts beautiful women to pretend they are plain and clever men to pretend they are fools, it also protected her from the no less unpleasing vanity and conceit of the egotist. To use one's scholarship as a ladder by which to scramble up to some pedestal of worldly esteem, to make a wonderful window-display of one's very moderate stores of knowledge (and to press every passer-by to admire it) – what was this but to 'take liberties' in the way abhorrent to every good servant: it was to behave as though servant and master were on one footing of equality. She would not have allowed any of her servants to behave thus towards her, and she never dreamed of behaving thus towards God. There is a certain fitness in the fact that the twins' portraits, in Westminster College Hall, hang on either side of a stained-glass window depicting Jesus setting a child in the midst of His hearers, and bidding them learn the hard lessons of simplicity of heart, true humility of mind, and a glad and willing obedience of spirit. When Agnes wrote 'We are servants', she made it quite clear that she had learnt these lessons; and in this, as in so many other matters, she spoke for Maggie, too. She was not boasting – but neither was she apologising: she was simply stating a fact.

Alongside that faded entry in the Visitors' book may be set another phrase, no less illuminating: the motto which the twins arranged to have carved in stone over the front door of their home, when Castlebrae was built, – and which was engraved, no less, upon the fleshly tables of their hearts: LAMPADA TRADAM [Let me hand on the torch]. Obviously, it is the torch of learning that is meant – though it is interesting to remember that this motto was selected several years prior to the discovery of the palimpsest: indeed, before they had begun to take Semitics very seriously, and while it was still no more than an entertaining hobby. The twins possessed all that Scottish love of learning, that innate respect for knowledge. The Giblews, as essentially 'applied schol-ars', had little use for the attitude which views knowledge as a private possession, and the 'knower' as someone to whom application must be made for information before it will be divulged. The purpose of all knowledge was that it should enrich the spirit of man, that – ideally at least – it should provide him with a useful tool for carving a rich and satisfying and useful life. Whatever facts they had laboriously discovered, these could not be kept to themselves. Knowl-edge must be passed on.

But there were, perhaps, more torches than one. The results of their painstaking researches have long since passed to those who are qualified to profit by them; and it is hardly necessary to dwell on this aspect of their achievement. To us, other aspects of the Giblew phenomenon are more worth stressing here. It is easy for a later generation, who cannot hope to converse with those solid figures and listen to those high-pitched, minor-key voices, to forget that, at the time, it was of enormous importance that these brilliant minds were contained within a woman's body. The torch that burned so brightly was not only one of intellectual brilliance: it was of feminine intellectual brilliance. And in the shadow of that cheerful bulk many members of the acknowledged superior sex were compelled to sit. Nor were they women who, though clever, were uninteresting as persons. Their gifts of mind were enhanced by an intense vitality of personality. Their concern was not with mere existence, but with life: with *zoë*, not *bios*. And the infectiousness of this quality is an important factor in any assessment of the worth of their lives.

Many young members of Girton and Newnham found it an intensely stimulating and liberating experience to be brought into close contact with Agnes and Maggie. Just at the point when – perhaps gauche, adolescent, unsure of oneself – one wanted so desperately to spread one's wings, it was reassuring, somehow, to be confronted with women who had mounted up as eagles, who, in the course of a long life, had run without weariness and walked without fainting. In the twins' drawing-room, one's doubts and hesitancies vanished, and self-confidence returned: before one's very eyes, all the feminist theories that one had so passionately and defiantly preached to amused uncles were triumphantly vindicated. The old ladies extended the torch, and one seized it with exultation and relief.

It is easy to object that the twins were not the only erudite women in their age: in Cambridge itself, there were the dons of the women's colleges – though not all of these possessed the same enormous zest for life, the same infectious vitality; it is easy to point out that anyone as well cushioned with ample money and a large domestic staff could, without difficulty, live a full and adventurous life – though not all who possessed these things did so live, and fewer still were as exciting to talk to. It is easy to point out that there have always been eccentric and scholarly women travellers, from Lady Hester Stanhope onwards. But when every precaution has been taken against over-painting the picture and against making exaggerated claims, the fact of their uniqueness remains: to quote Aelfrieda Tillyard once more, 'they were like each other and like no one else.' The Victorians insisted that character influenced environment more than environment influenced character. The twentieth century, on the whole, has been of the opinion that they were wrong – though perhaps our society is less confident about this than it once was, as it gloomily views a section of the new housing estate or tower block taking on some of the worst features of the old slum. But it is important to be fair to the Victorians: if they handed out tracts to 'the poor', instead of caring for their stunted, tuberculous bodies and pulling down their rat-infested dwellings, it was because they believed that character was, in the last resort, the determining factor in any situation. And character, they insisted, was a by-product of religion.

Such, at least, was the Giblews' conviction and whether or not we are sympathetic to such an attitude, at least it cannot be ignored in any assessment of their lives. The third torch was that of religious faith. Within this flambeau glowed the flame which gave both light and warmth to Castlebrae, and which burned steadily in York Street Mission and Hope Hall, with their women's meetings and Bible Classes and Sunday Schools. The twins' warmth and vitality were kindled at this torch, as their high seriousness – their enormous investment of energy in unremitting personal service – was the oil cast upon it. It was the flame of Pentecost, no less, which they sheltered with their rheumaticky hands, and which they sought to keep alight amid the chill winds of scepticism which were beginning to sweep across England and even to blow in fitful gusts up College staircases. An inward religious experience – that divine spark struck by Robertson of Irvine in their youth – had been, always, the driving force in their own lives: this it was which lit up the road ahead, which indicated the ends after which they must strive and prescribed, no less, the means they should use to achieve them. This torch, too, they must hand on: the next generation – slum-waif and undergraduate alike – must be shown that it was worth possessing.

Such were Agnes and Maggie. Masterful women, who yet saw themselves essentially as servants; stubborn egotists, who nevertheless possessed a remarkable humility of spirit; unconventional adventurers in body and mind, yet decorous stay-at-homes in faith; tenacious graspers of the torch, yet insistent that their prime duty was to hand it on. It is part of the paradox of human nature. The wise will not attempt to explain it.

APPENDIX

Chronological List of works by Mrs Lewis and Mrs Gibson (including volumes they edited or to which they wrote an introduction, but excluding articles for scholarly or popular periodicals).

1870   *Eastern Pilgrims*, by Agnes Smith (London: Hurst & Blackett).

1876   *Effie Maxwell:* a novel by Agnes Smith (3 vols. London: Hurst & Blackett).

1879   *Glenmavis*: a novel, by Agnes Smith (3 vols., London: Hurst & Blackett).

1880   *The Brides of Ardmore*: a novel, by Agnes Smith (London: Smith Elder).

1884   *Glimpses of Greek Life and Scenery*, by Agnes Smith (London: Hurst & Blackett).

1884   *The Monuments of Athens*, by P.G. Kastromenos, translated by Agnes Smith (London: Edward Stanford).

(1885   Greek edition of *Glimpses of Greek Life & Scenery*, translated by I. Perbanoglos. Leipzig.)

1886   *The Alcestis of Euripedes*, translated by Margaret Dunlop Gibson (London: Williams & Norgate).

1887   *Through Cyprus*, by Agnes Smith (London: Hurst & Blackett).

1892   *Life of the Rev. Samuel Savage Lewis*, by Agnes Smith Lewis (Cambridge: Macmillan & Bowes).

1893   (pamphlet) *Two Unpublished Letters* by Agnes Smith Lewis (Cambridge, privately printed).
        These dealt with the discovery of the palimpsest. They were addressed to *The Times*, but evidently were not printed by the Editor.

1893   *How the Codex was Found*, by Margaret Dunlop Gibson (Cambridge: Macmillan & Bowes).

1894   *The Four Gospels in Syriac, transcribed from the Sinaitic Palimpsest*, by R.L. Bensly, J. Rendel Harris and F.C. Burkitt, with an Introduction by Agnes Smith Lewis.

1894   *The Four Gospels translated from the Sinai Palimpsest*, by Agnes Smith Lewis (London: Macmillan & Co.).

1894   *A Catalogue of the Syriac manuscripts in the Convent of St Catherine on Mount Sinai*, compiled by Agnes Smith Lewis (London: C.J. Clay for the Cambridge University Press).

This volume listed 276 manuscripts. It was No. 1 in a new series to be called *Studia Sinaitica*.

1894 *A Catalogue of the Arabic manuscripts in the Convent of St Catherine on Mount Sinai*, compiled by Margaret Dunlop Gibson (London: C.J. Clay for the Cambridge University Press).
This volume listed 628 manuscripts, and was *Studia Sinaitica 2*.

1894 *The Arabic Version of Romans, Corinthians, Galatians and part of Ephesians*, from a ninth-century manuscript in St Catherine's Convent, Mount Sinai, edited by Margaret Dunlop Gibson. (London: C.J. Clay for the Cambridge University Press.) *Studia Sinaitica 3*.

1896 *Some Pages of the Four Gospels re-translated from the Sinaitic Palimpsest, with a translation of the whole text*, by Agnes Smith Lewis. (London: C.J. Clay for the Cambridge University Press.)

1896 *Apocrypha Sinaitica (Studia Sinaitica 5)*
    i. *Anaphora Pilati*: three recensions, in Syriac and Arabic, edited & translated by Margaret Dunlop Gibson.
    ii. *The Recognition of Clement*: two recensions
    iii. *The Martyrdom of Clement*
    iv. *The Preaching of Peter* ('A lively example of how medieval monks managed to slake the universal human thirst for fiction')
    v. *The Martyrdom of James son of Alphaeus*
    vi. *The Preaching of Simon son of Cleophas*
    vii. *The Preaching of Simon son of Cleophas* (in Arabic) (London: C.J. Clay for the Cambridge University Press)

1897 *A Palestinian Syriac Lectionary*, containing lessons from the Pentateuch, Job, Proverbs, Acts and Epistles, edited by Agnes Smith Lewis with critical notes by Prof. Eberhard Nestlé D.D. and a glossary by Margaret Dunlop Gibson. (London: C.J. Clay for the Cambridge University Press.)
This volume was *Studia Sinaitica 6*.

1898 *In the Shadow of Sinai*: a story of travel and research from 1895 to 1897, by Agnes Smith Lewis (Cambridge: Macmillan & Bowes).

1898 *The Story of Ahikar* from the Syriac, Arabic, Armenian, Ethiopic, Greek and Slavonic Versions, by F.C. Coneybeare, J. Rendel Harris, and Agnes Smith Lewis (London: C.J. Clay for Cambridge University Press).

1898 *The Cid Ballads and other poems and translations from Spanish and German*, by the late James Young Gibson, edited by Margaret Dunlop Gibson, with a memoir of Gibson by Agnes Smith Lewis. (London: Kegan Paul.)

1899 *An Arabic Version of the Acts of the Apostles and the Seven Catholic Epistles* from an 8/9th century manuscript in the Convent of St Catherine on Mount Sinai: with a treatise on the Triune nature of God, with translation, from the same Codex. Edited by Margaret Dunlop Gibson (London: C.J. Clay for the Cambridge University Press).

This volume was *Studia Sinaitica* 7.

1899 *The Palestinian Syriac [Melchite] Lectionary of the Gospels* re-edited from two Sinai MSS. and from Père de Lagarde's edition of the Evangelium Hierosolymitum by Agnes Smith Lewis and Margaret Dunlop Gibson (London: Kegan Paul Trench & Trubner.)

1900 *Select Narratives of Holy Women* from the Syro-Antiochene or Sinaitic Palimpsest as written above the Old Syriac Gospels by John the Stylite of Beth-Mari-Qanum in A.D.778. *Syriac text.* Edited by Agnes Smith Lewis (London: C.J. Clay for Cambridge University Press).

This volume was *Studia Sinaitica 9.* The 'holy women' whose stories are related are Eugenia, Mary-Marinus, Euphrosyne, Onesima, Drusis, Barbara, Mary (slave of Tertullian), Irene, Euphemia, Sophia, Cyprian and Justa.

1900 *Select Narratives of Holy Women etc:* English translation by Agnes Smith Lewis (London: C.J. Clay for Cambridge University Press). This volume was *Studia Sinaitica 10.*

1901 *Apocrypha Arabica*, edited and translated by Margaret Dunlop Gibson.
   i.   Kitel al Magall, of the Book of the Rolls.
   ii. The Story of Aphikia
   iii. Cyprian and Justa (in Arabic)
   iv. Cyprian and Justa (in Greek)
   (London: C.J. Clay for Cambridge University Press)
   This volume was *Studia Sinaitica 8.*

1902 *Apocrypha Syriaca*: *The Protevengelium Jacobi and Transitus Mariae*, with texts from the Septuagint, The Koran, the Peshitta, and from a Syriac hymn in a Syro-Antiochene palimpsest of the 5th and other centuries: edited and translated by Agnes Smith Lewis (C.J. Clay for Cambridge University Press).

This volume formed *Studia Sinaitica 11.*

1903 *The Didascalia Apostolorum in Syriac*, edited from a Mesopotamian manuscript, with variant readings and collations from other manuscripts, by Margaret Dunlop Gibson. (London: C.J. Clay for Cambridge University Press.)

With this volume, the twins began a new series: *Horae Semiticae*, of which it is I.

1903 *The Didascalia Apostolorum in English*, translated from the Syriac by Margaret Dunlop Gibson (London: C.J. Clay for Cambridge University Press).

This volume was *Horae Semiticae II.*

1904 *Acta Mythologica Apostolorum*, transcribed from an Arabic manuscript in the Convent of Deyr-es-Suviani (St Mary Deipara), Egypt, and from manuscripts in the Convent of St Catherine on Mount Sinai; with two legends from a Vatican manuscript by Prof. Ignazio Guidi and an appendix of Syriac palimpsest fragments of the Acts of Judas Thomas from Cod. Sin. Syr. 30. Edited by Agnes Smith

Lewis. (London: C.J. Clay for Cambridge University Press).
This volume was *Horae Semiticae III.*

1904　*Acta Mythologica Apostolorum*, translated from the above by Agnes
Smith Lewis (London: C.J. Clay for Cambridge University Press).
This volume was *Horae Semiticae IV.*

1907　*Forty-one facsimiles of dated Christian Arabic manuscripts*, with text and
English translation by Agnes Smith Lewis and Margaret Dunlop
Gibson; with introductory observations on Arabic calligraphy by
Rev. David S. Margoliouth Litt.D., Laudian Professor of Arabic in
the University of Oxford.
This volume formed *Studia Sinaitica 12.*

1910　*The Old Syriac Gospels, or Evangelion da-Mepharreshe:* being the text
of the Sinaitic or Syro-Antiochene Palimpsest, including the latest
additions and emendations, with the variants of the Curetonian
text, corroborations from many other manuscripts, and a list of
quotations from ancient authors: with four facsimiles. Edited by
Agnes Smith Lewis (London: Williams and Norgate).
Note the change of publisher. Perhaps Cambridge Press felt it
would hardly be fitting for them to issue an edition which
challenged, and was (as it were) in direct competition with, the
University's own Professor Burkitt's volume. See Chapter viii,
page 186 above.

1911　*The Commentaries of Ishodad of Merv, Bishop of Hadatha (c. 850 A.D.)*
in Syriac and English: edited by Margaret Dunlop Gibson, with an
introduction by J. Rendel Harris. *Volume i* – translation.
This volume was *Horae Semiticae V.*

1911　*Ibid, volume ii: Matthew and Mark in Syriac*, edited by Margaret
Dunlop Gibson.
This volume was *Horae Semiticae VI.*

1911　*Ibid, volume iii: Luke and John in Syriac*, edited by Margaret Dunlop
Gibson.
This volume was *Horae Semiticae VII.*
(The above three volumes – London: Cambridge University Press.)

1911　*Codex Climaci Rescriptus:* fragments of 6th cent. Palestinian Syriac
texts of the Gospels, Acts of the Apostles, St Paul's Epistles: also
fragments of an early Palestinian lectionary of the Old Testament:
edited by Agnes Smith Lewis (London: C.J. Clay for the
Cambridge University Press.)
This volume was *Horae Semiticae VIII.*

1911　*An Inscription recording the restoration of a mosque at Hangchow in
China, A.D.1452*, in Arabic and Persian; by Agnes Smith Lewis
(C.J. Clay for Cambridge University Press).

1912　*The Forty Martyrs of the Sinai Desert*, and *The Story of Eulogios*, from
a Palestinian Syriac and Arabic Palimpsest: edited by Agnes Smith
Lewis.
This volume formed *Horae Semiticae IX.*

1913　*Light on the Four Gospels from the Sinai Palimpsest*, by Agnes Smith

Lewis (London: Williams and Norgate).

1913 *The Commentaries of Ishodad of Merv: The Acts of the Apostles and the Catholic Fathers*: edited by Margaret Dunlop Gibson (London: C.J. Clay for the Cambridge University Press).
This volume formed *Horae Semiticae X*.

1913 *The Story of Ahikar*: enlarged and corrected edition

1914 *Leaves from Three Ancient Qurans*, edited by Agnes Smith Lewis and Dr Alphonse Mingana (London: C.J. Clay for Cambridge University Press).

1916 *The Commentaries of Ishodad of Merv: the Epistles of St Paul*, edited by Margaret Dunlop Gibson (London: C.J. Clay for Cambridge University Press).
This volume formed *Horae Semiticae XI*.

1917 *Margaret Atheling and other poems* by Agnes Smith Lewis (London: Williams and Norgate).

PRINCIPAL WORKS CONSULTED

A.S. Lewis, *Life of Samuel Savage Lewis*, (Cambridge: Macmillan & Bowes, 1892).

A.S. Lewis, 'Memoir of James Young Gibson' in J.Y. Gibson, *The Cid Ballads* (London: Kegan Paul, 1898).

A. Guthrie, *Robertson of Irvine* (Ardrossan: Arthur Guthrie, 1889).

J.P.T. Bury, *History of the College of Corpus Christi & the Virgin Mary 1822–1952* (Cambridge: University Press, 1952).

A. Halliday Douglas, *Westminster College, Cambridge: an account of the opening of the College, with a history of the College from its foundation in 1884* (London: Presbyterian Publications Committee, 1900).

W.A.L. Elmslie, *Westminster College 1899–1949* (London: Presbyterian Publications Committee, 1949).

P. Carnegie Simpson, *Recollections* (London: Nisbet, 1943).

H.T. Francis, *In memoriam R.L. Bensly* (Cambridge: University Press, 1893).

Stephen Gwynn, *The Life of Mary Kingsley* (London: Macmillan, 1912).

Olwyn Campbell, *Mary Kingsley – a Victorian in the Jungle* (London: Methuen, 1957).

W. Robertson Nicoll, *Ian Maclaren – the life of the Revd. John Watson* (London: Hodder & Stoughton, 1908).

Mary Paley Marshall, *What I Remember* (Cambridge: University Press, 1947).

Agnes D. Bensly, *Our Journey to Sinai – a Visit to the Convent of St Caterina* (London: R.T.S., 1896).

D.S. Margoliouth & G. Woledge, 'Memoir of Alphonse Mingana' in Vol. III of the *Catalogue of the Mingana Collection* (Cambridge: W. Heffer, 1939).

J. Rendel Harris, *The Apology of Aristides on behalf of the Christians* (Cambridge: University Press, 1891).

J. Rendel Harris, *The Story of Ahikar* (Cambridge: University Press, 1898).

G. Milligan, *The New Testament and its Transmission* (London: Hodder & Stoughton, 1932).

W. Robertson Smith, *The Religion of the Semites* (London: 1894).

W. Robertson Smith, *Kinship and Marriage in Early Arabia* (London: 1907).

A.P. Stanley, *Sinai and Palestine* (London: John Murray, 1864).

C.S. Jarvis, *Yesterday and Today in Sinai* (Edinburgh: Wm. Blackwood, 1933).

J. Galey, G.H. Forsyth and K. Weitzman, *Sinai and the Monastery of St*

Catherine (London: Chatto & Windus, 1980).

Paul Lenoir, *Le Fayoum, le Sinai et Petra* (Paris: H. Plon, 1872).

Mahfouz Labib, *Pèlerins et Voyageurs au Mont Sinai* (Cairo: L'Institut Francais d'archeologie Orientale, 1961).

Murad Kamil, *Catalogue of all Manuscripts in the Monastery of St Catherine on Mount Sinai* (Wiesbaden: Otto Harrassowitz, 1970).

A.S. Atiya, *The Arabic Manuscripts of Mount Sinai* (Baltimore: Johns Hopkins Press, 1955).

J.H. Charlesworth, *The New Discoveries in St Catherine's Monastery: a preliminary report* (American Schools of Oriental Research, 1979).